For Fatha & Mither
    Who have always done
everything to encourage
such projects as this.
        With affection
            — John

Oct. 1, 1956

THE
VICTORIAN
POETS

THE
VICTORIAN
POETS

A Guide to Research

By Paull Franklin Baum, Jerome H. Buckley,
William C. DeVane, Frederic E. Faverty,
Clyde K. Hyder, Howard Mumford Jones,
John Pick, Lionel Stevenson,
and A. McKinley Terhune

Edited by Frederic E. Faverty

HARVARD UNIVERSITY PRESS, Cambridge, 1956

Preface

THE PURPOSE and general nature of this book are explained in the opening chapter. Like its predecessor, *The Romantic Poets: A Review of Research*, it had its origin in the deliberations of the Modern Language Association of America. Four years ago the Victorian Group of this organization decided that a review of bibliography, scholarship, and criticism in the field was desirable, and that it should be addressed to all serious students of Victorian poetry, within or without the institutions of higher learning. As the bibliographies on the period and on individual authors multiply, most of them listing items without comment, there would seem to be ample warrant for a work such as ours — an assembling and critical evaluation of selected materials.

In our reviews we have tried not to adopt an argumentative, controversial tone, and we have striven for readability. We hope we have avoided the impressionistic essay on the one hand and mere annotated bibliography on the other. Absolute uniformity in the selection and presentation of material was in our opinion neither possible nor desirable. The emphasis as a rule is on recent work, loosely that of the last two or three decades. This limitation is necessary for Hopkins on whom all research is recent, and particularly justifiable for Arnold and Browning on whom respectively the *Commentary* (1940) and the *Handbook* (1935, revised edition 1955) are available. On the Pre-Raphaelites, however, no such helpful guidebooks exist. Further, the history of scholarship and criticism on the Pre-Raphaelites presents unusual problems. For this chapter, therefore, an entirely different pattern was required, not only in the limitation of time, but in the general manner of presentation. Variations in procedure in other chapters are dictated partly by the amount, partly by the nature of the materials.

FREDERIC E. FAVERTY
Editor

ACKNOWLEDGMENTS

Thanks are due to the following publishers for permission to quote from copyrighted material:

Appleton-Century-Crofts, Inc., for quotations from *A Literary History of England* (1948), by Kemp Malone, Albert C. Baugh, Tucker Brooke, George Sherburn, and Samuel C. Chew;

Geoffrey Cumberlege, Oxford University Press, for quotations from *Poems of Gerard Manley Hopkins* (1918), edited by Robert Bridges, and from *The Idea of Coventry Patmore* (1921), by Osbert Burdett;

Macmillan & Company, Ltd., and St. Martin's Press, Inc., for quotations from *The Pre-Raphaelites and the Pre-Raphaelite Brotherhood*, by Holman Hunt (2nd edition, 2 vols., 1914), revised from the author's notes by M. E. Holman-Hunt.

CONTENTS

THE
VICTORIAN
POETS

ABBREVIATIONS IN REFERENCES

AL   *American Literature*
CE   *College English*
CBEL *Cambridge Bibliography of English Literature*
ELH   *Journal of English Literary History*
ES   *Englische Studien*
JEGP *Journal of English and Germanic Philology*
MP   *Modern Philology*
MLN   *Modern Language Notes*
MLQ   *Modern Language Quarterly*
MLR   *Modern Language Review*
NC   *Nineteenth Century and After*
N & Q *Notes and Queries*
PMLA *Publications of the Modern Language Association of
           America*
PQ   *Philological Quarterly*
QJS   *Quarterly Journal of Speech*
QR   *Quarterly Review*
RES   *Review of English Studies*
RLC   *Revue de littérature comparée*
SAQ   *South Atlantic Quarterly*
SeR   *Sewanee Review*
SP   *Studies in Philology*
SRL   *Saturday Review of Literature*
TLS   *Times Literary Supplement*
TQ   *University of Toronto Quarterly*

Note: names of periodicals are given in full upon their first appearance.

1 ß∾

General Materials

Jerome H. Buckley

IF SIR HERBERT READ is right in assuming that Coventry Patmore alone among considerable Victorian poets repays further study since "the rest have been fully estimated and their influence, if not exhausted, is predictable," the present guide to research can have no very active reason for being. If, on the contrary, a patient survey discloses few definitive "estimates," even by critics as perceptive as Sir Herbert, this volume may serve as a stimulus to a more thorough investigation and a deeper understanding. That the need for fresh appraisal remains should not, of course, be taken as evidence of the past inadequacy of Victorian scholarship and criticism. For a living literature yields new meanings to every new properly qualified reader; and it is the function of the scholar-critic not to pass final judgment on an exhausted influence but rather to quicken our insight into a literary life beyond time which can still compel our continuing regard. We may remark, then, at the outset that, though the contributors who follow have not come indiscriminately to praise Victorian poetry, neither have they come to bury it; for each, whatever his individual preferences or standards of judgment, is convinced of the abiding vitality of his subject.

The Victorians, to be sure, in a sense "estimated" themselves — insofar as they learned sooner or later to distinguish some eight or ten major figures among the scores of con-

temporary verse-makers. And, though we may feel sometimes that they admired the wrong poems — or the right ones
for the wrong reasons, or at least for reasons other than ours,
— their selection of such poets has not since been seriously
challenged. Long before the end of the period, discerning
readers could recognize the preëminence of Tennyson,
Browning, Arnold, Rossetti, and Swinburne, the real if lesser
significance of Clough and FitzGerald, the quality of Meredith. Nor was Hopkins, though still for the most part unpublished, entirely ignored; in the nineties, when preparing his
compendious anthology of nineteenth-century poetry, A. H.
Miles paused to call special attention to the virtually unknown Jesuit, eight of whose poems, submitted by Robert
Bridges, were being given "publicity for the first time."

Yet the larger "estimate" of Victorian poetry as a whole is
by no means fixed or final, and the general agreement that
Tennyson and Browning, for instance, were major poets in
their own age is no indication that their precise place in the
long history of English verse has been at all accurately determined. The inevitable reaction of the Edwardians and the
Georgians against the authority of Victorian culture left few
reputations secure. By the early twenties, when in fact a good
deal of disinterested research was in progress, the label "Victorian" carried an almost universal connotation of disparagement. So sweeping was the repudiation that reviewers, oddly
enough, pointed to Lytton Strachey, who was setting the pattern for much debunking less sophisticated than his own, as
a revivalist bent upon redirecting public attention to the
quaint, the incredible Victorians. By the same token Harold
Nicolson's study of Tennyson, which summarily dismissed
the poet's most ambitious work, seemed the closest possible
approach to a defense of the fallen idol. Since the twenties,
however, an increasingly large number of critics and artists,
quite un-Victorian in their orientation, have discovered,
often to their surprise or shock, some solid achievement in the
contemned poetry. T. S. Eliot has explained the importance
of *In Memoriam*. W. H. Auden has edited Tennyson and
compared him, perhaps not very cogently, to Baudelaire.

Cleanth Brooks, despite an ingrained hostility to the Victorian mode, finds Tennyson, who was "not always successful in avoiding the ambiguous and paradoxical," stumbling into unwonted rightness with the strangely ambiguous "Tears, Idle Tears." F. R. Leavis, who deplores the intellectual failure of the Victorians, concedes that Arnold's best work, presumably in verse as well as in prose, "comes from an intelligence that, even if not trained to some kinds of rigour, has its own discipline." And Dame Edith Sitwell, who insists that Arnold is admired only by "the people who dislike poetry," sees in Tennyson and especially in Swinburne "a flawless certainty of touch, . . . an impeccable virtuosity." Meanwhile, as the reaction of the post-Victorians has ebbed, other scholar-critics, suspicious of broad indictments and no longer intimidated by the label "Victorian," have been able to estimate the Victorians in a somewhat more dispassionate perspective. As long ago as 1929, Professor Garrod was dismayed to detect an incipient return to the Victorian poetry from which he had been repelled, in his own late-Victorian youth, by the fact that "dull men had over-praised [it], and they had done so because they believed in it." "Today," he complained, "very clever ones are beginning to over-praise it again; but whether because they believe in it or because they are clever, I am too dull to discover." Though the over-praise has not been unduly conspicuous in recent years, we should be by now at a safe remove from the more facile Edwardian and Georgian prejudices. Indeed, the way may at last be clear for an informed and sympathetic reappraisal of Victorian verse, for new estimates by the new Elizabethans and their American contemporaries.

I. *Bibliographies*

An extensive closed bibliography of Victorian poetry will be found in the third volume of F. W. Bateson's monumental *Cambridge Bibliography of English Literature*, which carries separate entries for over two hundred and fifty Victorian poets, great and small, and assembles a formidable array of background materials. First published in 1940, the original work lists few books appearing after 1937; but a supplementary volume (1955), edited by George Watson, now carries the account down through 1953. Though indispensable as a guide to the minor verse of the period, which is nowhere else so fully tabulated, the *CBEL* is nevertheless, like most bibliographies, incomplete and sometimes misleading or even mistaken. Moreover, it is somewhat cumbersome in arrangement, ordered as it is chronologically by headings rather than alphabetically; and, despite its selectivity, it may well by its very abundance confuse the student unfamiliar with the standard works of scholarship and criticism, for by its design it is kept from passing judgment on the relative value of the titles it lists. Likewise "uncritical" is the compilation by T. G. Ehrsam, R. H. Deily, and R. M. Smith, *Bibliographies of Twelve Victorian Authors* (1936), which, citing masters' essays and doctoral dissertations as well as books and periodicals, claims — unfortunately with too much assurance — to be "complete up to July, 1934." Yet the book has a range and solidity which our recognition of some minor errors should not lead us to overlook. The twelve authors include all of the more important Victorian poets except Browning, Meredith, and Hopkins; and the listing for each of the twelve is certainly ample enough to guide almost any initial research.

More helpful in classifying items of special value to the scholar are some of the "open" or continuing bibliographies. The *Annual Bibliography of English Language and Literature*, compiled since 1920 by the Modern Humanities Research Association, lists not only the new works of scholarship but also the scholarly reviews which appraise their worth. The chapter called "The Nineteenth Century and After" in *The Year's Work in English Studies*, issued annually since 1919 by the English Association of London, is a highly selective and eminently readable critical review of the most significant new books and articles. The "Victorian Bibliography" which has appeared each May since 1933 in *Modern Philology* is both inclusive and descriptive; it catalogues many unexpected items bearing on the economic, political, religious, social, intellectual, and aesthetic life of the Victorians, cites key reviews of the principal monographs, and comments succinctly on the argument or importance of some of the general and specific studies. In 1945 the first thirteen issues of this most serviceable compilation were presented in book form, with a convenient cumulative index, as *Bibliographies of Studies in Victorian Literature, . . . 1932–1944*. Less complete than the "Victorian Bibliography" but also useful is the "American Bibliography," prepared annually for a special number of *PMLA*. Taken together, these three yearly lists should furnish as close a check on current publication as we could wish. What none supplies, of course, is a record of the scholarly problems at the moment under investigation. Since 1948, however, *PMLA* has attempted as fully as possible to answer the need by a supplement to its bibliography, known as *Research in Progress*, a continuation of *Work in Progress* initiated ten years earlier by the Modern Humanities Research Association but shortly thereafter discontinued.

In addition to the strictly bibliographical aids, two handbooks may be mentioned as perhaps helpful to the student of Victorian poetry. *The Victorians and After*, by Bonamy Dobrée and Edith Batho, first published in 1939, offers a rapid and somewhat jaundiced survey of the verse, suggestive though sketchy bibliographies of the more important poets, and an interesting note on the parodies and nonsense books. *English Literature of the Victorian Period* (1949), by J. D. Cooke and Lionel Stevenson, presents with a good deal less animus a factual review of the general background, a sensible commentary on the various genres, brief biographies of the major and minor writers, and lists of carefully selected secondary sources. Like the bibliographies, both handbooks should serve as reminders that Victorian poetry, however uneven its fortunes, has quickened no end of discussion and in the process has somehow survived both its admirers and its detractors.

II. *Anthologies*

Most of the many anthologies of Victorian verse that appeared during the period itself have, as we might expect, been superseded by collections which enjoy the obvious advantage of a longer perspective. R. H. Stoddart's *Late English Poets*, for example, prepared as it was in 1865, the year of *Atalanta in Calydon*, seems, in view of subsequent literary history, perceptive enough in recognizing the merit of Swinburne but at the same time singularly inept in bracketing his great "promise" with that of Robert Buchanan. A. H. Miles's *Poets and Poetry of the Century*, however, remains of value for the very range of its selection. Published in ten volumes between 1891 and 1897, and later (1905–1907) rearranged in twelve, it offers us biographical headnotes by well-accredited scholars on innumerable minor writers and assembles hundreds of pieces — lyrics, ballads, hymns, odes, parodies, nonsense jingles — now scarcely accessible in any other form.

Of the later anthologies designed for general reading, Sir Arthur Quiller-Couch's *Oxford Book of Victorian Verse*, which appeared forty years ago, is still perhaps the most attractive, tasteful, and comprehensive. Though "Q's" selection somewhat distorts the achievement of the major writers (Browning, for instance, is presented as primarily a lyric poet), the anthology affords a most satisfactory impression of the serious minor poetry. If it seems to slight the humorous and satiric verse, it may be supplemented by another Oxford volume, the admirable *Century of Parody and Imitation* (1913), edited with lively endnotes by Walter Jerrold and R. M. Leonard, a pleasant testimony that all was not grave in Victorian culture. "Tennyson to Yeats," the fifth and last volume of *Poets of the English Language* (1950), compiled by W. H. Auden and Norman Pearson, is chiefly remarkable as a witness to the fine discrimination of its editors who are intent upon avoiding a merely conventional selection. Much more personal and proportionately less representative of Victorian verse, though certainly no less engaging, is Dame Edith Sitwell's "critical anthology," *The Pleasures of Poetry*, "Third Series: The Victorian Age" (1932). Here we find but eight poets arranged in what appears to be an order of preference: FitzGerald, Swinburne, Rossetti, Morris, Tennyson, Poe (!), Christina Rossetti, and Browning (who is represented by one poem). These at their best, writes Dame Edith, are makers of a pure poetry, creators of a "sheltered world," untroubled by human emotion and full of "the lovely light and colour of the rose," each with a genius for the poetic medium sadly lacking in modern literature.

In serviceability to the student, however, none of the "trade" anthologies compares with any one of three college texts in wide use throughout the United States: George B. Woods' *Poetry of the Victorian Period*, first published in 1930, revised in 1955 in collaboration with J. H. Buckley; *Victorian and Later English Poets* (1934), edited by James Stephens, Edwin L. Beck, and Royall H. Snow; and E. K. Brown's *Victorian Poetry* (1942). Each of these carries a full complement of explanatory notes, bibliographical suggestions, and other scholarly aids. Each aims at a balanced representation of the verse itself rather than at novelty of selection. And each strives, by printing a number of the key longer poems complete, to indicate the success or failure of the major writers in handling large as well as small structural units. Of the three, the Woods and Buckley, which draws on over fifty poets, gives the broadest cross-section of Victorian poetry as a whole, including the humorous, satiric, political, and devotional verse. The Stephens, Beck, and Snow, covering some thirty authors, is designed to offer, in addition to the poetry, some prose — usually in the form of personal letters — by each of the leading poets. Though it benefits from sprightly and informative headnotes, this volume suffers the initial handicap of a most eccentric prefatory essay by James Stephens. The Brown anthology, on the other hand, which is limited to fourteen principal poets, owes its peculiar value to the editor's distinguished critical introduction. All three texts in various ways bear the authority of a disciplined scholarship.

III. *Background Studies*

While Dame Edith admires Victorian poetry as aesthetically "pure," and less aesthetic critics condemn it as morbidly "escapist," most scholars have seen it in close relation to the needs and problems of nineteenth-century society and have accordingly insisted upon a knowledge of the milieu of the poets as essential to a sound evaluation of their work. An ordered survey of the vast literature devoted to an elucidation of the Victorian background would scarcely be possible within the limits of this review of research, nor indeed directly relevant to our present purposes. We might, however, mention in passing a few of the general political and social histories of the period likely to prove most revealing: G. M. Trevelyan's *British History in the Nineteenth Century* (1922); E. L. Woodward's *The Age of Reform, 1815–1870* (1938); R. C. K. Ensor's *England, 1870–1914* (1936); *The Age of the Chartists, 1832–1854* (1930) by J. L. and Barbara Hammond; and *Early Victorian England, 1830–1865* (1934), edited by G. M. Young. And before examining works concerned more specifically with the literature, we should consider the importance of many useful monographs bearing on the intellectual and spiritual life of the age, such as A. W. Benn's tremendous *History of English Rationalism in the Nineteenth-century* (1916); L. E. Elliott-Binns's able and objective *Religion in the Victorian Era* (1936); Alan W. Brown's detailed study, *The Metaphysical Society, Victorian Minds in Crisis* (1947); and D. C. Somervell's workmanlike though hurried survey, *English Thought in the Nineteenth Century* (1929). If the student requires a simpler introduction to the complexities of the culture from which the poetry arose, he may turn to a volume called *Ideas and Beliefs of the Victorians* (1949), edited by Harman Grisewood, which is the record of a remarkable series of BBC broadcasts by G. M. Trevelyan, Harold Laski, Bertrand Russell, Julian Huxley, Lord David Cecil, Basil Willey, and others, and seeks in brief compass to appraise Victorian attitudes towards progress, freedom, faith, science, education, and democracy. And if he wishes integrated interpretation, he may turn to the far from simple yet infinitely rewarding *Victorian England: Portrait of an Age* (1936) by G. M. Young: a brilliant composite study, urbane, ironic, understanding, the nearest approach we have to a synthetic biography of the whole period in all its diversity, confusion, and strength.

The importance of the social and intellectual background seems abundantly clear to the eleven literary historians who contribute to *The Reinterpretation of Victorian Literature* (1950), edited by Joseph E. Baker. While the accent throughout the essays falls on the prose-writers rather than the poets, the symposium as a whole is concerned less with genres than with general trends, neglected areas of research, and new techniques of investigation. Emery Neff in particular argues convincingly for an analysis of the main currents of social thought, both English and Continental, that conditioned the vision and the performance of Victorian authors. Howard Mumford Jones suggests that a comic spirit, too often discounted by recent commentators, helped preserve a Victorian sanity and balance amid the peril of unprecedented change. C. F. Harrold, who writes of the Oxford Movement, and F. L. Mulhauser, who discusses the influence of Edmund Burke, warn against a too-facile reading of the true impulses behind the Victorian regard for a religious and political tradition and the parallel distrust of an ascendant "liberalism." Karl Litzenberg, assailing the myth that Victorian literature suffered from radical insularity of tone and substance, effectively demonstrates the still largely unanswered need for comparative studies which will relate the poetry and prose to a cosmopolitan context of philosophic ideas and aesthetic forms. And Professor Baker in the concluding essay, "Our New Hellenic Renaissance," insists that the basic affinities between Victorian and Greek culture, hitherto for the most part ignored, deserve our closest scrutiny.

Though much, then, remains to be done in relating Victorian literature to its setting in space and time, more than a little has already been accomplished. A number of studies, old and new, rest in various ways on an awareness of the background, a sense that art arises from — and in turn helps shape — a manifold civilization. In his characteristically paradoxical *Victorian Age in Literature* (1913), G. K. Chesterton long ago postulated his notion of "the Victorian compromise," a concept which has since been subject to the widest misinterpretation. To Chesterton the "compromise" was not a common agreement that hypocrisy was the best policy, that sex was unmentionable, or that sentiment could conceal a want of emotion. It meant simply, on the social level, the uneasy alliance between middle-class progress and aristocratic stability and, on the spiritual, the effort to harmonize the demands of the new materialism and the values of the old faith. Whether or not the conflicts of Victorian literature can be adequately described in terms of such dichotomies, there is in both the prose and poetry evidence enough of a sincere ethical and intellectual questioning to indicate that the artist at least could accept no ready and ignoble "compromise" of principle. H. V. Routh's *Towards the Twentieth Century: Essays in the Spiritual History of the Nineteenth* (1937), an able analysis of Victorian malaise, examines a dozen major authors in the light of their quest for certainty and concludes that each, however estimable his personal victories, failed to make the requisite adjustment between the life of the spirit and the claims of modern culture. Though the pattern of his argument becomes at times rigid and even arbitrary, Professor Routh's insights are consistently stimulating, and his knowledge of nineteenth-century intellectual history is profound and acute. By comparison, the view of "Victorianism" taken by Clarence R. Decker in *The Victorian Conscience* (1952) seems stereotyped and superficial. Surveying the Victorian reception of foreign writers, especially the hostility of the popular reviews to the French naturalists, Mr. Decker assumes another sort of "compromise" to which Victorian writers apparently subscribed, a conspiracy of silence to protect a moral squeamishness. But hardly at all does he touch upon the real issues of "conscience," the deeper sources of an opposition to literary naturalism, the serious sanctions behind an ethical theory of art and a spiritual theory of man.

In *Nineteenth Century Studies* (1949), Basil Willey seeks to interpret the Victorian moral and religious background without recourse to formula or generalization. His lucid analysis of specific works by nine considerable prose-writers, from Coleridge to Matthew Arnold, discloses, as we might expect, a marked fluctuation of beliefs rather than a uniformity of faith. If his conclusions are scarcely startling, his criticism nonetheless gives us many a sympathetic insight into the dilemmas of the Christian at a time when new philosophies were calling all in doubt. Drawing on some of the same materials, though for rather different purpose, *The Victorian Temper* (1951) by J. H. Buckley attempts to present the background in terms of a literary sensibility shifting in the variable climate of ethical and intellectual opinion from the exuberant thirties through the "Decadent" nineties. In particular it strives to trace the complex relations of the artist, especially the poet, to his public and to appraise the doctrine of the "moral aesthetic" which allowed the writer no retreat from social responsibility.

Several more restricted literary studies describe the actual media through which the Victorian poets found their public, the standards of taste they were expected to meet, and the levels of audience they were able to reach. Harrold G. Merriam's *Edward Moxon, Publisher of Poets* (1939), for example, gives us not only a vivid portrait of one remarkable publisher but also a broad insight into general publishing conditions in early Victorian England. John W. Dodds' *The Age of Paradox* (1952), a kaleidoscopic review of the 1840's, furnishes a good deal of incidental information on the reception accorded poetry during that boisterous decade. Though sometimes inaccurate and often unscholarly, Amy Cruse's *The Victorians and their Reading* (1935), which includes a chapter on readers of verse, is a useful and most entertaining guide to the literary appetites of the period. Finally we might cite as distinctly valuable to the student of poetry the monographs devoted to the major periodicals: Miriam M. H. Thrall's *Rebellious Fraser's* (1934), George L. Nesbitt's *Benthamite Reviewing* (1934) on the *West-*

minster, Edwin M. Everett's *The Party of Humanity* (1939)
on the *Fortnightly*, Leslie Marchand's *The Athenaeum*
(1941), Merle M. Bevington's *The Saturday Review* (1941),
and Francis Mineka's *The Dissidence of Dissent* (1944) on
the *Monthly Repository*; and we might at least mention the
great rambling *History of The Times* (by various new men of
The Times, who characteristically choose to remain anonymous), especially the second volume, *The Tradition Established* (1939), which concerns the editorship (1841–1877) of
the dynamic J. T. Delane. Such studies help re-create the
various worlds of the reviewers whose values, prejudices, and
enthusiasms shaped the first reputations of the poets and sometimes determined the course of their subsequent development.

IV. *General Histories of Victorian Poetry*

Most studies of the Victorian literary background draw
more or less extensively on Victorian verse, and all comprehensive histories of English literature give it a position of
some importance. Yet there have been relatively few books
concerned exclusively with the general themes and techniques of the poetry itself. In his *Ten Victorian Poets* (1940),
F. L. Lucas offers what his title promises, ten provocative and
discerning revaluations, but conveys no sense of a Victorian
style serving as a common denominator for the diverse effort
of his subjects. Though his estimates are often unsympathetic, his method of separate analyses differs little from that
of a late Victorian critic like Hugh Walker, whose *Greater
Victorian Poets* (1895) approached Tennyson, Browning, and
Arnold with understanding and a high reverence for their
individual talents. It may be that the complexity of Victorian culture in all its changefulness and eclecticism renders
difficult any sound generalization about the verse as a whole.
But it should not be impossible to isolate certain recurrent
patterns, motifs, or ways with words that lend the poetry a
kind of multiple unity in diversity.

E. C. Stedman, at any rate, the earliest to prepare a substantial critique without special bias, was less reluctant than some later critics to reach general conclusions. First published twenty-six years before Victoria's death, his *Victorian Poets* (1875) is already apocalyptic in tone; it assumes that the Victorian era is virtually at an end and suggests that a new poetry, if there is to be one, must move in new directions. The Victorian poets, as Stedman sees them, have been highly self-conscious, distrustful of emotion, modern men living in an "age of prose" that has had no place for heroic sentiment. They "have flourished in an equatorial region of common-sense and demonstrable knowledge," and some of them have been beguiled by "Science, the modern Circe, from their voyage to the Hesperides" and transformed "into voiceless devotees." But the best, finding in art relief from an unaesthetic time, have achieved a formal excellence much to be admired, "a peculiar condensation in imagery and thought." They have been, in short, great technicians, masters of expression; indeed, "never was the technique of poetry so well understood as since the time of Keats and the rise of Tennyson and his school." But by 1875 the virtuosity of Swinburne seems to have carried expression to its ultimate extreme, to the point of exhaustion. The vogue of idyllic and reflective verse, which has dominated the age, has apparently been exploited to the full, and the hope for poetry lies only in a return to dramatic themes.

Though Stedman failed to predict with much accuracy the shape of verse to come, his criticism, Arnoldian as it is in tone, relates Victorian poetry to the context of an analytic age and emphasizes a problem too often neglected by the scholar: the problem of style, which in some form or other has faced all poets since the time of the Romantics. Writing at the end of the period, George Saintsbury was one of the few prepared to extend the argument and to make the emphasis somewhat more specific. A wide-ranging chapter on the poets in his *History of Nineteenth-Century Literature* (1896) suggests that the Victorians excelled "in shorter pieces, more or less lyrical but not precisely lyrics," pieces in which they explored the distinct appeal of the polished phrase and the euphonic cadence. So far did they develop an "elaborate and ornate language" that a later generation, if it were to find an accent of its own, would have to abandon the grand style altogether and to seek other poetic effects.

Saintsbury's attention to form may have led him to a neglect of the themes and attitudes we have come to consider characteristically "Victorian." Yet the distinguishing marks of the poetry itself, the essential differences between Victorian verse and our own, are perhaps stylistic rather than thematic; and our ultimate estimate, I think, depends largely on our acceptance or rejection of the poetic idiom. At any rate, the older studies which attempt a general survey of the content of the poetry, regardless of its form, are of little value to the modern reader seeking the basis of a critical understanding. Arnold Smith's *Main Tendencies of Victorian Poetry* (1907), for instance, identifying "tendencies" with moods, finds optimism, hope, doubt, pessimism, or yearning in each of the several major poets and concludes that the emotion of Victorian poetry was infinitely varied. Arthur Waugh's "Some Movements in Victorian Poetry," a long essay in his *Reticence in Literature* (1915), explains, not very helpfully, that "the history of Victorian poetry is the history of all art; the same eternal impulses underlie it. On the one side the spirit of beauty, on the other the spirit of humanity; on the one side Aesthetics, on the other Ethics." Yet the Victorians, says Waugh, unlike the Elizabethans, are metaphysical in aspiration: "In Elizabeth's time the concern of poetry was the life of man and his relation to his fellows; in the Victorian period it was the soul of man and his relation to his Creator." But the concern, we are told, was scarcely a joyful one; in the world of the poets, "youth and the spring morning are alike over and done with." And the source of weary disenchantment is not so much the failure of belief as the "democratizing spirit" threatening all modern culture.

Recognizing the claims of form as well as of content, John Drinkwater's *Victorian Poetry* (1924) represents a more successful and quite unpretentious attempt to approach the verse on its own terms. Part I of the essay, concerning the "manner" of the poetry, considers the problem of poetic diction, the desire of the Victorian poet to avoid the cliché, the impossibility of his repeating many of the earlier simplicities of language, and the tendency, especially in Tennyson, to actualize, to elaborate the simple statement with precise particular detail. Part II, devoted to the "material," comments sensibly on changing fashions in ideas and deplores the folly of dismissing the Victorians simply because some of their beliefs are no longer current. Much of the verse, Drinkwater concedes, is in a sense occasional poetry (insofar as it draws at will on any occasion within the age), and as such its themes may appear local or accidental. Yet it remains, he insists, to the credit of the Victorians that, whatever their errors of selection, they widened enormously the thematic range of English poetry, that "the actual subjects chosen . . . for poetic treatment far exceeded in number the subjects that had been so chosen in any age before." Unfortunately a detailed analysis of the subjects themselves lies beyond the scope of any general introduction.

V. *The Romantic Tradition*

If the general studies of Victorian poetry are on the whole vaguer and more tentative than need be, the monographs seeking to establish particular lines of continuity from the Romantics to the Victorians and so to place the verse in a literary context are quite specific and even at times unduly self-assured. In many respects the most exemplary of such books is Douglas Bush's *Mythology and the Romantic Tradition in English Poetry* (1937), a definitive yet always vivid examination of the classical themes and genres in Victorian as well as Romantic verse. Without forcing a thesis, Professor Bush argues from reams of specific evidence that, though the true myth-making faculty died with Keats and Shelley, the Victorians retained or developed a capacity to adapt old myths meaningfully to modern needs. And in the process of the demonstration he illuminates the whole problem of Romantic and Victorian Hellenism and casts brilliant critical sidelights on the general course of nineteenth-century poetry.

Studies touching on the similarities or differences between the Romantic and the Victorian sensibility depend frequently, as we might expect, on the particular concept of Romanticism held by the critic, or at least on the special aspect of the Romantic movement he has chosen to emphasize. To Mario Praz in *The Romantic Agony* (1930, 1952), the essential unity of nineteenth-century European verse lies in the persistence of that morbid eroticism which finds its typical expression in the voluminous literature of the *femme fatale* and the Byronic anti-hero. But though his insights may deepen our understanding of a part of Swinburne or Oscar Wilde, the thesis that Signor Praz labors with solemn erudition has little direct relevance to most of the major poets or to the great bulk of Victorian English poetry. C. M. Bowra in *The Romantic Imagination* (1949) sees Tennyson and the Victorians generally as "unromantic" in what he regards as their distrust of the imaginative vision, their this-worldly and anti-mystical attitudes towards experience, and their devotion to "realism and didacticism." Yet he believes that something of the Romantic vision remained in Swinburne and the Rossettis, who held to a modified and narrowed faith in "an unseen order behind visible things," an order to be known only through the intuitive imagination. John Heath-Stubbs, on the other hand, a member of the literary group self-styled "the New Romantics," considers the Pre-Raphaelites quite uninteresting and Swinburne altogether repulsive, empty, and presumably "unromantic." In *The Darkling Plain* (1950), attempting to trace "the later fortunes of . . . the Romantic tradition in English poetry," he damns the Victorians in general for a "lack of integration, of harmony between the conscious and unconscious aspects of the personality," and praises the lonely exceptions, the rebels against a schizophrenic convention, men like Beddoes, Hawker, Patmore, Blunt, Thomson, and Doughty. It is well to be reminded of such poets, who have indeed been too often ignored; and Mr. Heath-Stubbs sheds new light on their value. But to regard such writers, who remain after all figures of secondary importance, as the true heirs of the Romantic tradition is greatly to circumscribe the influence of Romanticism in the Victorian period and to isolate the greater Victorian poets from the poetic conventions closest to them.

That the Victorians, however, did owe a considerable debt to their immediate predecessors is apparent from several competent studies in the Victorian reputation or impact of the major Romantics. Samuel C. Chew's *Byron in England* (1926), though primarily concerned with the poet's vogue rather than his influence, makes it clear that the Victorians most moved by Byronic poetry frequently strove for Byronic effect. James V. Logan's *Wordsworthian Criticism, a Guide and Bibliography* (1947) carefully reviews a widespread critical interest in Wordsworth throughout the Victorian period, while Robert E. Lovelace's "Wordsworth and the Early Victorians," an unpublished University of Wisconsin dissertation (1951), analyzes in detail the Wordsworthian elements in the major Victorian poets before 1860. And George H. Ford's *Keats and the Victorians* (1944) ably combines a brief history of Keats' ever-widening fame and a close examination of his influence on Tennyson, Arnold, Rossetti, and Swinburne. Though I know of no comparable monographs on Coleridge and Shelley in their relation to the Victorian poets, evidence of a real indebtedness to both, especially to Shelley, should not be difficult to amass.

Books describing the various groups or coteries of the Victorian period frequently suggest that the new poetic schools were actuated by some revived "Romantic" ideal or impulse. *The Victorian Romantics* (1929), T. Earle Welby's curiously impressionistic yet often revealing account of Rossetti and his circle, assumes a Romantic character behind the alleged Pre-Raphaelite rejection of contemporary issues and conventions, but ignores in the art those elements of "realism" which may well derive from the spirit and method of mid-nineteenth-century science. Louise Rosenblatt's *L'Idée de l'art pour l'art dans la littérature anglaise pendant la période victorienne* (1931) carefully traces the Aesthetic Movement back to Keats and other Romantic sources, yet pays little heed to the Victorian intellectual conflicts that helped give rise to English aestheticism. *The Last Romantics* (1949) by Graham Hough, concerned with the Aesthetes and others who prepared the way for Yeats, sensitively assesses the quality of the emotion or sensibility of a few Victorians romantically sharing "a common passion for the life of the imagination" as opposed to the materialism of their age. And Albert J. Farmer's useful appraisal of the English *fin de siècle, Le Mouvement esthétique et 'décadent' en Angleterre* (1931), argues — very much as does Holbrook Jackson's *The Eighteen Nineties* (1914) — that the "decadence" was really a period of "Romantic" vitality and liberation, a new Romantic movement dedicated to the overthrow of "Victorianism."

Centered as they are on more or less Romantic strains, such critiques naturally do not seek to define in any detail the elements that lent Victorian poetry, whatever its debt to the past, a distinct character of its own. In a somewhat similar vein, *The Victorian Temper*, mentioned above among the general studies, recognizes a continued or rather attenuated Romanticism, especially in the work of the minor Victorians who constituted the Spasmodic School; but it stresses at the same time an "anti-romantic" impulse in the more significant poets, a self-conscious drive towards greater objectivity, which led to a repudiation and sometimes a burlesque of Romantic sentiment. George Kitchin, in his standard *Survey of Parody and Burlesque in English* (1931), describes the early Victorian period as "the great age of burlesque" and contends that "the various outbreaks of satire in this age are successive efforts to keep romantic art sane." Victorian poetry is not, of course, predominantly satiric, but it typically shares with satire a latent distrust of personal revelation, a regard for general moral and social "sanity," and, more often than most critics have acknowledged, a concern with carefully calculated technique. In an effort to estimate its essential quality, we may turn to analyses of its characteristic form and content.

VI. *The Content of Victorian Poetry*

Unlike the Romantics who for the most part were able to fashion highly personal concepts of God and nature, the Victorians, whether orthodox or agnostic, were forced into a direct consideration of the framework of traditional religion as it suffered ever-increasing intellectual attack throughout the nineteenth century. If it was not invariably their first concern, man's status as a moral being, a spiritual entity, postulated by the old theology but called into doubt by new philosophies, certainly supplied a central theme in much of their most representative work; and their religious assertions, compromises, and denials seemed of prime importance to troubled readers who looked to poetry for guidance and interpretation. We have accordingly a good many appraisals of the spiritual content of the verse, most of them partisan, quite unscholarly, and long since badly dated, nearly all of them confusing "message" with art.

By an odd arrangement of materials that permits Browning to come last, Vida Scudder's *Life of the Spirit in the Modern English Poets* (1895), though published in the skeptical nineties, concludes that Victorian poetry has moved joyously from Romantic pantheism towards Christianity. W. J. Dawson's *The Makers of English Poetry* (1906) finds the Victorians, to whom over half the book is devoted, chiefly remarkable for their spiritual intent, their "moral power," their inspirational uplift. E. M. Chapman's *English Literature in Account with Religion, 1800–1900* (1910) likewise judges the poetry sympathetically in the light of a liberal Protestantism. A. S. Hoyt in *The Spiritual Message of Modern English Poetry* (1924), with a heavy emphasis on the Victorians, similarly draws on standards more Evangelical than aesthetic and ignores the intrinsic function of the moral values in their poetic context. Limiting himself to a single theme, Leslie D. Weatherhead in *The Afterworld of the Poets — the Contribution of Victorian Poets to the Development of the Idea of Immortality* (1929), aware that a Victorian heterodoxy may be a modern liberal orthodoxy, achieves some objective un-

derstanding of the religious conflicts of the period but remains much too literal in his reading of the poems as if they
were direct transcripts of the creed of the poets. From a very
different point of view, Sister Mary Madeleva in a longish
and often penetrating essay called "The Religious Poetry of
the Nineteenth Century," included in her *Chaucer's Nuns*
(1925), insists that the Victorians, apart from the Rossettis
and a few devotional lyrists, were in no real sense religious
poets. Yet the fact remains that, whatever epithet we apply to
them, Tennyson, the Brownings, Arnold, Clough, Meredith,
and even Swinburne did write poems which, traditional
or not, Christian or otherwise, may be regarded as essentially
religious in final effect. Despite the attention accorded the
"spirituality" of the poets, we need therefore closer studies of
the religious and ethical assumptions of the verse itself, of
the images and symbols of faith which enrich its substance.
A suggestive though rather scattered essay in such criticism is
Leone Vivante's *English Poetry and its Contribution to the
Knowledge of a Creative Principle* (1950), an examination of
selected passages from seventeen poets, seven of them specifically Victorian (Mrs. Browning, Tennyson, Emily Brontë,
Meredith, Swinburne, Wilde, Francis Thompson). Viewing
poetry as a mode of truth, Signor Vivante finds the poems
and poets he analyzes each partaking in some degree of the
"self-obliviousness" of the intuitive imagination, each reach-
ing at high moments an essential creative "freedom," and so
laying bare something of "the 'spirit' of life, the very life of
life, its innermost soul." Though it is not his express purpose to do so, he thus reminds us that the Victorian concern
with spiritual values and forces sometimes transcends the
Victorian age and so remains even to us of immediate and
timeless interest.

Discussion of the poetic use of ideas emanating from the
new science, the source of much of the religious doubt, has
been less voluminous, yet in general more scholarly and systematic. In his *Scientific Thought in Poetry* (1931), Ralph B.
Crum describes ably but too hastily the struggle, experienced
by all Victorians interested in science, between a naturalistic

and a spiritual — or, as he calls it, "mystical" — view of the world. The poets, Mr. Crum argues, were reluctant to accept a thoroughgoing Darwinism insofar as it seemed to deprive the evolutionary process of purpose and design. In *Darwin among the Poets* (1932), Lionel Stevenson presents a short survey of evolutionary theories (not necessarily Darwinian) in Victorian verse and then turns to a more specific analysis of four or five major poets. As a whole, his exposition is lucid and convincing, yet arbitrary in emphasis; Tennyson, I think, receives unduly oversimplified and rather hostile interpretation, while Meredith and Hardy are accorded more than generous recognition; Browning, whose interest lay in moral aspiration, "spiritual evolution," rather than in the scientific impact of Darwinism, is granted a full chapter, whereas Swinburne, whose response to Darwin was vigorous, is virtually ignored. Though stronger perhaps on the Romantics than on the Victorians, Joseph Warren Beach in *The Concept of Nature in Nineteenth-Century English Poetry* (1936) develops a powerful theme with impressive authority. Concerned with both philosophy and science, he demonstrates and explains the steady decline of a transcendental view of nature from the time of Wordsworth, until with Hardy at the end of the Victorian period "no trace of teleology" remained, "nature" had lost its solemn connotations, and "for the emotional effect formerly associated with nature, the poet must turn elsewhere." Douglas Bush notes the changed attitude in the stimulating fifth chapter, "Evolution and the Victorian Poets," of his *Science and English Poetry, 1590–1950* (1950) and comments tellingly that Tennyson's lingering trust in an order of nature is no less reasonable than Hardy's apparently "scientific" pessimism, which is itself but "the subjective vision of the poet, a personal assertion of the unprovable." Such an observation properly recalls us to the poetry and rebukes a too-frequent inclination to prejudge its intrinsic worth in the light or dark of our own sentimental reactions to science.

Though most of the background studies (see III, above) assume on the part of the poets a general interest in social and political issues as well as in the conflicts, real or apparent, between science and religion, I know of no specific analysis of the extent to which political beliefs or current social values affected the actual quality of Victorian verse as a whole. There have been, of course, separate accounts of the individual poets — estimates of Tennyson's conservatism, Browning's self-avowed "liberalism," Kipling's jingoism, Elizabeth Barrett's view of woman's rights, Swinburne's revolt from domesticity, and Patmore's respect for the well-ordered home. But we need a more precise knowledge of the relations between the poetry generally and the politics and social conventions of the age, and of the actual role played by the various concepts of democracy, urban living, marriage, and the family in shaping the verse.

That the Victorian poet, to his credit or discredit, did feel a peculiar social responsibility has seemed evident to readers almost from the beginning, though little effort has been made to define the sanctions of his obligation. As long ago as 1870, Alfred Austin in a peevish review of contemporary verse strove to correlate "the feminine, timorous, narrow, domesticated temper of the times, and . . . the feminine, narrow, domesticated, timorous Poetry of the Period." Recently E. D. H. Johnson, with far greater insight and patience, has examined the problem of the poet's social orientation, though not of his social values, in *The Alien Vision of Victorian Poetry: Sources of the Poetic Imagination in Tennyson, Browning, and Arnold* (1952). Each of these poets, according to Professor Johnson, possessed unique gifts of intuition and sensibility, an inner awareness of the demands of art; yet each was somehow driven to compromise with outer forces in the alien unaesthetic world of Victorian society; and each at last sacrificed his status as a pure poet to become a man of letters. So approached, the great Victorians appear temperamentally opposed to the "basic ideology" of an age which "assumed automatic conformity with its dictates"; they seem "lonely and unassimilated figures" able to assert their true emotion only through devious stratagem, whereby their work, always on the surface "blandly complacent," at its deepest may move in dark troubled undercurrents of unconventional and indeed anti-social meaning. Despite a certain carelessness of detail, Professor Johnson presents a fresh and provocative reading of many poems staled by familiarity. Yet his central thesis is open to serious question; for it presupposes a non-existent homogeneity in the social order, the codes of which it fails to explain; it overemphasizes the indirection and ambiguity of the poems themselves; and it ignores the fact that poets have always assailed the materialisms of their time and that overt or concealed attacks on social convention need not imply any radical maladjustment to the cultural milieu. His argument therefore seems to me less tenable than that of Vivian de Sola Pinto who works from a quite contrary premise. Concerned with the divorce of the twentieth-century poet from an inimical society, Professor Pinto, in his *Crisis in English Poetry* (1951), contends that the major Victorians, the last heirs to the great legacies of a Christian and humanistic culture, could still bridge the inner and the outer worlds, could still find shared values and symbols and so achieve social communication. Like Chaucer and Spenser and Milton, Tennyson and Browning "could be 'realistic' in their poetry because the world around them, in spite of many shortcomings, was not hostile to poetry, and they could be meditative and introspective because their inner life was enriched by a great and living poetic tradition." Though such a judgment requires no less supporting evidence than Professor Johnson's view of Victorian society, it permits a more direct appraisal of the verse; it postulates a broad cultural continuity rather than a single basic social "ideology"; and it invites a sympathetic analysis of the conventions which helped determine both the form and the content of the poetry and which the poets frequently accepted without apparent constraint.

VII. *The Form of Victorian Poetry*

"The real case against mid-Victorian poetry, other than Tennyson's," writes F. W. Bateson in *English Poetry and the English Language* (1934), "is not that it rests upon a mistaken basis of theory but that it is badly written." Tennyson, Mr.

Bateson concedes, did do all he could with words, but his time, confusing "a language of the heart and a language of the head," was against any real precision combined with profundity. The other poets, satisfied with vague connotation where precise denotation was required, rested, we are told, in the conviction that the content of their verse, not the style, was all-important; for "the subject was the red herring of Victorian criticism." Whether or not poetic form has become at times the red herring of modern criticism, many modern readers echo the charge that Victorian poetry is formally deficient and ineffective. In a shapeless essay in his *Criticism and the Nineteenth Century* (1951), Geoffrey Tillotson explains that the poets, interested above all in change and development, had little respect for the concept of perfection and most of their work accordingly appears as but unshaped thinking in process, with "the quality of things purposefully on the move." More explicitly E. M. W. Tillyard in *Poetry Direct and Oblique* (1934) has argued that the nineteenth century, with too little regard for a sound rhetorical convention, discarded the poetry of statement in order to practice the obliquities of symbolism and so broke "the general social nexus of versifying." Critics like Cleanth Brooks, however, find Victorian poetry not too oblique but too direct, insufficiently paradoxical and ambiguous, lacking in metaphoric complexity. In an able chapter contributed to Hardin Craig's *History of English Literature* (1950), Joseph Warren Beach rejects much of this attack as unsatisfactory, yet argues that "by and large, most nineteenth-century poets made what Brooks calls the 'frontal approach' to their subject. They undertook to convey their sense directly with a verbal notation common to all discourse in prose and verse," and they therefore achieved "a dispersed and fluent rather than a close-knit texture." Contradictory as they are, each of these judgments surely has at least partial basis in fact, but none extends far beyond a personal prejudice or impression; none fully acknowledges the variety of forms and styles within Victorian poetry or indicates an objective means of assessing the multiple evidence the poets have left behind.

If a defense of the manner and method of the verse is possible at all, it must counter the generalized and rather imprecise hostility with specific analyses and elucidations. Lionel Stevenson in a stimulating article, "The Pertinacious Victorian Poets" (*University of Toronto Quarterly*, 1952), has recently indicated the need for a much closer attention to the aesthetic values of the poetry and, working from a few definite examples, has himself attempted to show that the best poets were neither incomplete philosophers nor pretentious moralizers but essentially serious craftsmen whose "creative imagination embodied itself in significant symbols which were shaped through a mingling of personal emotion and traditional themes." It is no longer enough to declare, as did H. J. C. Grierson in his *Lyrical Poetry of the Nineteenth Century* (1929) — without giving us detailed description of the art and artifice — that Tennyson and Browning were "very great and cunning artists"; nor is it now possible to announce that "the century of the Metaphysical lyric was the nineteenth," unless one is prepared to challenge current concepts of what constitutes the Metaphysical idiom. In the general revival of interest in Victorian literature, problems of poetic form and imagery have received little dispassionate scrutiny, and the major poetic genres as such have been all but ignored. We have, for example, no full-scale modern study of the monologue to extend the argument of M. W. MacCallum's suggestive but necessarily sketchy essay, "The Dramatic Monologue in the Victorian Period" (*Proceedings of the British Academy*, 1924–25), though Ina Beth Sessions' article "The Dramatic Monologue" (*PMLA*, 1947), by classifying some of Browning's poems, indicates one possible technical approach to such a study. And we might learn a good deal about Victorian poetry from fresh scholarly estimates of the Victorian verse novel, the narrative poem, the elegy, or the ballad.

One relatively recent monograph, however, merits special notice as an indication of one direction which future technical analysis might profitably take. This is Josephine Miles's *Pathetic Fallacy in the Nineteenth Century, a Study of a Changing Relation between Object and Emotion* (1942), which painstakingly explores a single poetic device, as used by the Romantics and the Victorians, in order to discover something objective about the evolution of English poetry by approaching language itself. Contrary perhaps to our expectations, Professor Miles reveals a marked decline in the frequency of pathetic fallacy, beginning with Tennyson and the early Victorians; a fresh though limited use thereof; and a clear tendency to closer direct perception of nature, "a plainly developing literal vision." The Victorians, we are told, learned to state emotion by indirection, by reference to the associations of objects, and so achieved a poetry of the senses, of shapes and colors, without immediate relation to subjective feeling. Thus Ruskin, who coined the term, furthered rather than initiated the disrepute into which the pathetic fallacy fell, for "the turning point was reached practically by Tennyson before it was reached critically by Ruskin." Though Professor Miles draws heavily upon statistical counts to support her thesis, her interpretation of the data is sometimes questionable; yet her basic conclusions seem soundly grounded as well as highly original. By confining herself to the one device, she reveals much of the larger movement of thought and emotion that actuated its vogue.

At the risk of promoting the "intentional fallacy," which modern critics have found even less acceptable than the pathetic, we must, I believe, consider the "intentions" of the poets, their aesthetic principles and purposes in writing, if we are to reach any reasonable estimate of their successes or failures, or indeed if we are to understand the proportions and tensions of their work. Despite the fact, however, that we have had several competent monographs on the major aestheticians, including Henry Ladd's brilliant but difficult critique of Ruskin, *The Victorian Morality of Art* (1932), our knowledge of Victorian aesthetics remains on the whole quite inadequate. The recent general study by Alba H. Warren, Jr., *English Poetic Theory (1825–1865)* (1950), therefore, though it makes no pretense at startling discovery, serves as a welcome and useful review of a large body of relevant materials. After a broad survey of early Victorian criticism, Professor

Warren limits himself to a close analysis — by paraphrase and commentary — of nine representative essays. Behind each of these he sees the dominant influence either of Wordsworth's theory of imitation, which he describes as "Aristotelian," or of Coleridge's concern with expression and subjective idealism, which he calls "Baconian." The tenets of the critics were, he shows, frequently contradictory and inconsistent; to some art was clearly less than "reality"; to others it was in essence a revelation of the highest truth; a few saw science as the provider of new facts and new modes of scrutiny, others derided it as a complete denial of spirit; many demanded individuality of style, but nearly all feared personal eccentricity of statement. Yet there were also certain common critical assumptions and recurrent emphases. The theorists as a group believed the poet responsible not only to his own vision but to the world of men and things about him; they rejected didacticism, but stressed the social value, the "morality," of art and its capacity to teach by indirection; they were accordingly less interested in formalistic matters than in psychological and moral values, in the communication of ideas and emotions; they regarded poetry, in short, as important to "the economy of the good life." Insofar as the poets presumably shared this conviction, Professor Warren rightly assumes that an acquaintance with the theory should assist us towards a more satisfactory assessment of the verse; but he chooses merely to present the doctrine rather than to trace its literary consequences. Thus since other scholars have largely ignored the problem, the precise relation between the Victorian aesthetic and the practice of the Victorian poets remains for the most part unexplored, if not entirely unsuspected.

* * * * *

Whatever else it may have accomplished, our survey of the research devoted to the general themes and problems of Victorian poetry should by now have indicated that though much has been taken — or rather given — by scholars and critics, much abides for elucidation and appraisal. In the chapters that follow we shall see how the more significant poets have fared individually under twentieth-century critical analysis. But at the outset it should hardly be necessary to remark that we are in a position to know more of their careers and personalities than we know of any earlier literary group; for the Victorians were virtually the first children of a self-conscious modern world eager to document and publicize its activities, and as such they have left behind countless books of reminiscence, as well as official lives and authorized memoirs, reams of correspondence to, from, and about their literary masters, records of table talk and public interviews, portraits and photographs and caricatures, picture-books of the poets' homes and haunts, full and often fulsome obituaries. Yet the essential character of all but a few of the poets eludes us; we know scarcely any of them as we know, or think we know, each of the great Romantics. We need therefore fresh biographies, assimilating the many sources at our disposal, lives which will show us the poets at work as poets rather than merely supply amusement through chronicles of eccentricities different from our own. For our primary concern as students of literature must rest with the poetic sensibility and the poetry itself and not with the adjuncts of literary history. We must not, of course, be unduly intimidated by the expressed desire of the major poets to detach their private lives wholly from their verse; but we may respect their sense of the autonomy of art, their will to make their performance the ultimate gauge of their value. And we may be helped towards the proper realization that their work was indeed the essence of their real selves, if we take as representative of their attitude the statement of a fellow-Victorian, who was also in his way something of the artist. "I have now mentioned all the books which I have published," wrote Charles Darwin at the close of his brief autobiography, "and these have been the milestones of my life, so that little remains to be said."

Alfred Lord Tennyson

Paull Franklin Baum

I. *Bibliography*

A BIBLIOGRAPHY OF THE WRITINGS OF
ALFRED LORD TENNYSON, by Thomas J. Wise (two
volumes, privately printed in 1908), with annotations, reproductions of manuscripts, a section on pirated issues, and a
section (incomplete) listing whole volumes of biography and
criticism to date, is the fullest Tennyson bibliography. It
should be supplemented by Wise's catalogue of The Ashley
Library, volume VII (1925), and by a few items in the later
volumes VIII, IX, and X. It should also be corrected by reference to John Carter and Graham Pollard's *An Enquiry into
the Nature of Certain Nineteenth Century Pamphlets* (1934),
and by Wilfred Partington's *Thomas J. Wise in the Original
Cloth* (1946); in which nine of Wise's Tennyson titles are
condemned as forgeries and five more as suspect, besides the
false title page for *Idylls of the Hearth*, 1864. For H. Buxton
Forman's authorship of "The Building of the Idylls" in
Literary Anecdotes of the Nineteenth Century (edited by W.
Robertson Nicoll and Thomas J. Wise, 1895–1896), see *Between the Lines* (1945) by Forman, with an introductory essay
and notes by Fannie Ratchford. *Tennysoniana: Notes Bibliographical and Critical* (by R. H. Shepherd; published
anonymously), appeared in 1866, and was followed by a revised and enlarged edition in 1879, which contains a chapter
of parallel passages from *In Memoriam* and Shakespeare's

Sonnets, and a chapter on Tennyson portraits. Shepherd's *The Bibliography of Tennyson . . . from 1827 to 1894* (1896), also published anonymously, contains a chronological list with various annotations still of value, and a scheme, never carried out, for the Complete Works in fifteen volumes.[1]

For Tennyson iconography, one should see Shepherd's chapter mentioned above; Theodore Watts (-Dunton) in the *Magazine of Art* (1893); and especially Julia M. Cameron, *Alfred Lord Tennyson and His Friends* (1893). Millais' portrait of the poet is described in *Burlington Magazine* (15 June 1908); the Lincoln monument by G. F. Watts, in *Athenæum* (29 July 1905); the centennial exhibition at the Fine Art Society's gallery in *Athenæum* (24 July 1909). The *Times Literary Supplement* (30 June, 21 July 1950) discusses photographs; and further references are in *Twelve Victorian Authors* (page 340).

For parodies of Tennyson, one should refer to Jelle Postma's *Tennyson as Seen by his Parodists*, an Amsterdam dissertation (1926).

Morton Luce's *Handbook to the Works* (1895, and frequently reprinted) is a systematic commentary, title by title, on the poems as they occur in the one-volume edition; and his little book in the Temple Primer series (1901) is still worth reading. *A Tennyson Primer*, by W. Macneile Dixon (1896; third edition, 1908, as *A Primer to Tennyson*), covers the same ground but more discursively and with less detail; it contains a list of reviews, incomplete of course.

---

[1] A footnote is the place for a few specimens of the ephemera: *Gems from Tennyson* (1866); *Tennyson Gems* (1889); Charles E. Cooledge, *The Sunny Side of Bereavement as Illustrated in Tennyson's "In Memoriam"* (1890); Alfred Ainger, *Tennyson for the Young* (1891); "Art and Architecture in Tennyson's Poetry" (*American Architect and Building News*, 5 November 1892); *Immortelles in Loving Memory of England's Poet-Laureate* (1893); Elbridge S. Brooks, *Out-of-Doors with Tennyson* (1900); Molly K. Bellew, *Tales from Tennyson* (Six to Sixteen Series, 1902); another with the same title, by G. C. Allen (1900); Alfred P. Sinnett, *Tennyson an Occultist, as His Writings Prove* (1920); Sister Ross Bihn, "Spiritual Message of Tennyson's 'Idylls of the King' to the Youth of Today," Notre Dame Master's essay (1927).

A Concordance "to the Entire Works," by D. G. Bright-well, appeared in 1869. (The concordance by S. Langley, 1870, listed in *CBEL*, is apparently an error.) The complete Concordance is by A. E. Baker (1914); followed by one to *The Devil and the Lady* (1931). Baker also has a Tennyson Dictionary (1916).

II. *Editions*

The standard edition is that published by Macmillan, in one volume (1892 and thereafter): *The Works of Tennyson, with Notes by the Author. Edited with Memoir by Hallam, Lord Tennyson.* This is virtually the same as the Eversley Edition in nine volumes (London 1907–1908; New York 1908, six volumes) with separate title pages and with fuller notes. These editions, however, are not complete. They must be supplemented by *Poems by Two Brothers* (1827; reprinted with additions in 1893); by *Suppressed Poems 1830–1862*, edited by J. C. Thomson (1903, 1910); by *The Devil and the Lady* (1930) edited by C. B. L. Tennyson, the poet's grand-son; and by the same editor's *Unpublished Early Poems* (1932), which first appeared in *Nineteenth Century and After* (March, April, May, and June 1931). (There is a reprint of *Poems, 1842*, in *Famous Editions of English Poets*, edited by J. O. Beaty and J. W. Bowyer, 1931). The Cambridge Poets edition, edited by W. J. Rolfe, 1898, does not contain Tenny-son's last, posthumous volume, but has many of the poems not reprinted by Tennyson in the standard editions, together with useful notes and a partial collation of variant readings. It should be noted that this, and most other editions, do not group the poems according to their original publication, though they often seem to do so; but a convenient table show-ing the contents of Tennyson's successive publications through 1868 will be found in the Oxford Standard Authors edition, edited by T. H. Warren (1913); a new edition, *Poetical Works, Including the Plays,* has recently appeared (1954).

The *Selections*, made under Tennyson's eye and published by Moxon, 1865, should be mentioned; an interesting set of author's corrected proofs of this volume came up for sale in 1942. Annotated "school" editions are legion and of very uneven value; one of the best is that by Henry Van Dyke and D. L. Chambers (Athenæum Press series, 1903); those by Rolfe in this country and by F. J. Rowe in England are well worth consulting. Among the most recent Selections, which testify to the poet's continued popularity, are those by F. L. Lucas (1932), T. S. Eliot (1936), B. Ifor Evans (1936), W. C. DeVane (1940), S. C. Chew (1941), W. H. Auden (1946), F. L. Lucas (*Poetry and Prose . . . with Criticisms*, 1947), Sir John Squire (1947), Douglas Bush (1951), and in the Penguin books (1953); and every year brings one or more reprints. *The Early Poems of Alfred Lord Tennyson* (through 1842), edited by J. C. Collins (1900, 1901) with a critical introduction, contains both explanatory notes and collations and also an appendix of Suppressed Poems, distinguishing those never reprinted by Tennyson and those which appeared later in authorized editions. In 1902 Collins edited similarly *In Memoriam, The Princess, and Maud*. There is a well-annotated edition of the 1842 *Poems*, by A. M. D. Hughes (1914). The *Commentary on Tennyson's In Memoriam* (without text) by A. C. Bradley (1901; third edition revised 1930) should be mentioned here; it contains references to earlier commentaries. Editions from the collector's point of view are discussed by William H. Arnold in "My Tennysons" (*Scribner's Magazine*, May 1922).

The Tennyson manuscripts are fairly scattered; some are still in the possession of the family, some at Trinity College, Cambridge, at the British Museum, and elsewhere. The large and important collection, which formerly belonged to Sir Charles Tennyson, is now in the Houghton Library, at Harvard, and is available for research. A full variorum edition of all the poems, with the various readings of the manuscripts and the successive editions, would be very instructive, but is unlikely now for obvious reasons, among them the fact that many manuscripts are not available to students and that the poet himself deplored any public use of them. Some glimpses of them, however, throwing light on Tennyson's methods of composition, can be obtained from "Tennyson Papers," II, III, IV, by Sir Charles Tennyson in *Cornhill Magazine*, for April, May, and June 1936 (the first of these "Papers," March, is about Dr. Tennyson, the poet's father). Richard Jones, in *The Growth of the Idylls of the King* (1895), collected the variants for "Enid" and "Nimuë," the first two *Idylls*, as they appear in the 1857 and 1859 prints and in proof-sheets at the South Kensington Museum and in later editions; and also variants in the other *Idylls* as they were first published and as in the final text. These are by no means complete, but they are accompanied by critical observations on some of the changes, especially those which reveal Tennyson's altered plans as the *Idylls* grew. Edgar F. Shannon, Jr., has an article on "The Proofs of Gareth & Lynette in the Widener Collection," in *Papers of the Bibliographical Society of America* (1947). Now that the Heath Manuscript (Commonplace Book) has been acquired by the Fitzwilliam Museum and made available to students, there have been three studies of Tennyson interest based on it (besides the use made of it by Joyce Green, in *PMLA*, 1951): on "Sir Galahad" (*Philological Quarterly*, 1949); on "Hail, Briton!" and "Tithon" (*PMLA*, 1949); and on *In Memoriam*, LXXXV (*Modern Language Notes*, 1950); all are by Mary J. Donahue Ellmann.

A few of Tennyson's letters have been printed here and there; four of them recently by Mrs. Ellmann in *MLN* (1950). A collection is now under way by Edgar F. Shannon, Jr.

III. *Biography*

There are two more or less official biographies: *Alfred Lord Tennyson: A Memoir*, By His Son (two volumes 1897; later in one volume), and *Alfred Tennyson*, by the poet's grandson, Sir Charles Tennyson (1949). The former was preceded by "Materials for a Biography of A. T." in four volumes (printed but not published; only a few copies are known), which contains a good deal, both letters and diaries, omitted from the *Memoir*. The *Memoir* itself is unsatisfactory not only because of its filial piety — the author admitted that there might be too much "sonshine" in it — but also because its treatment of documents is often unscholarly. It is nevertheless indispensable and invaluable. With the *Memoir* is associated a volume called *Tennyson and His Friends* (1911) prepared by the second Lord Tennyson, consisting of reminiscences, tributes, and miscellaneous articles (some reprints and some specially written) by various friends, nearly all of biographical interest; along with poems by Tennyson to or about his friends. Sir Charles' biography is in the form of annals (sixty-five chapters and an Epilogue) and is thus more narrative than critical, though it has numerous critical observations in passing. It gives a full background of family history and is especially valuable for the poet's early years. Sir Charles has the advantage of access to much unused material and of his knowledge of family tradition, and though naturally his attitude is "favorable," he writes with great freshness and sincerity. As one of the reviewers put it, the book "is unlikely to be superseded, though it will no doubt be supplemented, by future work upon the same theme."

Besides these two family biographies, there are numerous lesser ones, sketches, and studies, which began to appear during the poet's lifetime — much as he deprecated them and feared their effect after his death. After 1897 they all depend largely on the *Memoir*, but the following should be mentioned: H. D. Rawnsley, *Memories of the Tennysons* (1900); Andrew Lang, in Modern English Writers series (1901); Sir Alfred Lyall, in English Men of Letters series (1902); Agnes G. Weld, *Glimpses of Tennyson* (1903); A. C. Benson (1904). Most of these mingle biography and criticism, so that it is difficult to classify them. It is perhaps sufficient to say that they contain little of biographical value except where they are based on personal knowledge.

There are also many reminiscences and glimpses published in periodicals, by (among others) Lewis Carroll, Sidney Colvin, Moncure Conway, Walter Crane, Edmund Gosse, M. A. DeW. Howe, William Knight, W. G. McCabe, W. F. Rawnsley, J. A. Symonds, Bayard Taylor, Wilfrid Ward, T.

Watts-Dunton. These may be traced in the bibliographies (except that by McCabe, which has been listed as a book but appeared in *Century Magazine* for March 1902). Particular attention should be drawn to James Knowles' "A Personal Reminiscence," in *Nineteenth Century* (January 1893). Moreover, much of biographical value may be found fragmentarily in numerous volumes of Victorian memoirs and correspondence, e.g., by Aubrey de Vere (and note the recent book on de Vere, 1953, by S. M. Paraclita Reilly), Froude, Sir Henry Taylor, FitzGerald, Woolner, and the Duke of Argyll; also in *Edward Moxon, Publisher of Poets* (1939) by Harold G. Merriam. Biographical material also appears in *Literary Anecdotes of the Nineteenth Century*. When the best of all this material has been collected and sifted and the letters have been published, it will be possible for someone to write an impartial critical biography to supplement the two official ones.

Tennyson: A Modern Portrait (1923), by Hugh I'Anson Fausset, is biography of Strachey extraction and is now largely of historical interest. Superior to it in every way, but not unlike it in many aspects is (Sir) Harold Nicolson's *Tennyson: Aspects of His Life, Character and Poetry* (1923). Both of these books, and the contemporary reviews of them, were at the storm-center of the "reaction," for they are more critical than biographical; but Nicolson's book has been very influential, partly because it stood as the only *book* about the poet during the quarter-century before publication of *Tennyson Sixty Years After* (1948), by Paull F. Baum, which is itself mainly critical.

Baum's first chapter contains an account of the "Bard's" exalted reputation at the time of his death, and the second chapter, a biographical outline, adds from contemporary reminiscences some fresh details for the still obscure decade of 1830–1840. But what merit the book has lies in the close analyses (which have been called unsympathetic) of some of the major poems, especially "Ulysses," *In Memoriam, Maud,* the *Idylls,* and "Lucretius." Baum's general estimate is somewhat below the now received standard; while appreciating

the extraordinary richness and felicity of language, he emphasizes the want of what Rossetti called "fundamental brainwork."

IV. *Critical Studies*

In general, the work done on Tennyson falls into two quite
disproportionate parts. The amount of scholarship, in the
technical sense of the recovery and correlating of facts, is not
large, but the amount of criticism, of greatly varying quality,
is quite considerable. And there is a certain quantity of something in between which might be called scholarly criticism or
interpretation, but which cannot always be clearly distinguished from either. In the following pages some attention
will be given to this last; but most of the involute history of
Tennysonian *criticism*, that criticism which is always "devi-
ating into the delicate impertinences of egotism," will be excluded as lying in a different part of the forest. What has been
admitted, however, is enough to show how much of both appreciation and depreciation revolves around a few centers,
and how repetitive it all is in spite of the variations in style
and the shifting points of view.

There is a thoroughgoing analysis of Tennyson's language
in *Tennysons Sprache und Stil* by Roman Dyboski (*Wiener
Beiträge*, 1907). This follows the old standard categories
of grammar and rhetoric and provides "a systematically arranged collection of examples of syntactic, stylistic, and lexi-
cographical peculiarities" set over against the customary
forms of modern English poetical usage. The headings are,
among others, brevity and fulness, intensity, *Anschaulichkeit*,
ornament, prefixes and compounds, archaisms, Miltonisms,
etc. At the end is an index of favorite words — which does not
correspond with one's general impression and may be compared with the frequencies shown in the Concordance. *The
Formation of Tennyson's Style*, by J. F. A. Pyre (1921, written
ten years earlier) has for subtitle "A Study, primarily of the
Versification of the Early Poems," i.e., to 1850. The metrical
parts are less interesting than the incidental critical observa-

tions and the Appendix on Tennyson's early diction. Somewhat surprisingly, there has never been a formal analysis of Tennyson's prosody, though of course there are many comments on it throughout the general criticism. Such a study would be of great interest to specialists, especially if made by some one whose theories are generally acceptable.

Another study, of a sort much needed, is Bernard Groom's *On the Diction of Tennyson, Browning and Arnold* (SPE Tract, 1939); for with the universal praise of Tennyson's craftsmanship there is still little, except here and there, of precise analysis, "yet a scrutiny of his language leads to an ever-deepening admiration of his resource and dexterity." Groom draws attention to the general uniformity of Tennyson's diction, his use of a specially heightened style (some of it "vaguely 'old,' " or confessedly artificial and recherché, even obscure, but seldom eccentric or reckless like Browning's), even in poems on contemporary life, and his many exquisite felicities. "I doubt whether full justice has been done to the skill with which Tennyson reconciles the traditions of poetry with the new terms which were current in his lifetime among the Victorian clerisy."

Thomas R. Lounsbury's *The Life and Times of Tennyson* [from 1809 to 1850] (1915) has enjoyed considerable repute, partly because of the author's distinction in other fields. It was written under severe handicaps and was unfinished at Lounsbury's death; nevertheless it is leisurely in manner and diffuse in style. Its old-fashioned title is misleading, for it is not a biography, and the "Times" (which is its real contribution) is chiefly a survey of the state of reviewing and criticism during the first half of the century. Lounsbury was a complete Victorian, and as Wilbur L. Cross, author of the Introduction, says, he "set himself squarely against the wave of cheap depreciation which at times threatened to overwhelm Tennyson." Since the book was unfinished and that portion written only imperfectly revised, criticism of its errors is somewhat unfair; but it was accepted for a time as sound, and correction became necessary. For one such, see Katherine Burton's "Hallam's Review of Tennyson" (*MLN*

1930), which Lounsbury had misdated. His incautious judgment on the influence of the early reviewers led to no little discussion.

Lounsbury, and Nicolson after him (1923), without too much preparation expressed the opinion that Tennyson's revisions of many of the 1830 and 1833 poems for his 1842 volumes, and the omission of certain others, were independent of the reviewers' strictures. This was first challenged by W. D. Paden in a short article, "Tennyson and the Reviewers (1829–1835)" (*Kansas Humanistic Studies,* 1940) — though a better title would have been "Some of the Reviewers." In "Tennyson and the Reviewers 1830–1842" (*PMLA,* 1943), Edgar F. Shannon, Jr., took issue with Lounsbury and Nicolson, and in "Tennyson's Development during the 'Ten Years' Silence' (1832–1842)" (*PMLA,* 1951), Joyce Green took issue with Shannon. (The first part of Miss Green's article has valuable notes on the dating of the early poems, and also some interesting views on them, e.g. on "The Lady of Shalott" as the expression of an aesthetic principle.) Both Shannon and Miss Green argue closely from ample statistics, with due regard to their interpretation, and both recognize the imponderable element: how far the revision might be due to the poet's maturation during the ten years, regardless of the reviews and of the opinions of his friends; and the question is further complicated by Tennyson's known hypersensitivity to the "mosquitoes." It seems likely to remain a case not proven, but it has again been thoroughly reviewed by Shannon in his book, *Tennyson and the Reviewers; A Study of His Literary Reputation and of the Influence of the Critics upon His Poetry, 1827–1851* (1952). Shannon is continuing the study down to 1892; the latest portion to appear concerns the reception of *Maud* (*PMLA,* 1953). Although his investigation began with a survey of contemporary reviews, the more important contribution of the book is its record of the critics' influence on Tennyson's development: their insistence on a message, and his obliging acceptance of the responsibility to teach as well as to delight. Shannon's conclusion that Tennyson yielded to their demands "not with a shallow desire for popularity and financial success but because he allowed himself to become convinced that the qualities for which they called were necessary to great poetry" is skillfully worded, but leaves the question still open: whether Tennyson did violence to his gifts in *allowing* himself so to become convinced. This only shows once more how difficult it is to write about Tennyson without hedging or seeming to hedge.

A parallel to Shannon's book is J. O. Eidson's *Tennyson in America, His Reputation and Influence from 1827 to 1858* (1943). In the land of Longfellow, the Laureate's reputation followed its own curve. Before 1842 only a few, the Boston literati, had read him, but those few were enthusiastic. Young Lowell, who afterwards turned against him, paid him the compliment of imitation. Soon after the first copies of the 1842 volumes reached this country, an American edition was out in Boston. Emerson was not impressed, but in 1848 on meeting Tennyson "was contented with him, at once." Poe was lyrical in praise, and nearly everyone admired. The ordinary reviewers muddled through as usual and only a small number of them took their cue from the adverse British criticism. *The Princess* was a success also, but with *In Memoriam* America fell behind Britain both in appreciation and in sales. Many complained of its obscurity and monotony and even questioned Tennyson's sincerity and orthodoxy; but eventually the majority was won over. On *Maud* they were again divided. Whitman reviewed *Leaves of Grass* and *Maud* side by side, to the advantage of the former; others compared it unfavorably with *Hiawatha*. But, as in England, all seemed to like "The Brook." Finally, as in England again, *Idylls of the King* restored Tennyson to permanent favor — until the reaction set in, signs of which Bayard Taylor noted as early as 1877. Like Shannon, Eidson is continuing his study down to 1892. At the 1952 meeting of the South Atlantic Modern Language Association, he read a paper on "The Reception of Tennyson's Plays in America": they hastened the reaction.[2]

---

[2] On Tennyson's plays, *The Dramas of Alfred Lord Tennyson* (1926), by Cornelia G. H. Japikse, is the work of an amateur, without technical or

Under the odd title of *Tennyson in Egypt; a Study of the Imagery in His Earlier Work* (1942), W. D. Paden, using a frankly psychoanalytic method, reviewed Tennyson's early reading at Somersby and the themes in Alfred's share of *Poems by Two Brothers*, together with a few later poems. The last chapter, "The Warrior of God," is the most important portion of this very substantial monograph. Tennyson's tale "Mungo the American," written at the age of thirteen–fourteen, "showing, how he found a sword, afterwards how it came to the possession of the right owner" (the inspiration of which is obviously Malory) is, says Paden, "the only very early work in which 'aggression' leads to joyful triumph rather than remorse and disaster." Paden then reviews some eighteenth-century mythological speculations, notably the Helio-Arkite theory of the story of the Ark; traces a parallel between Faber's *The Origin of Pagan Idolatry* (1816) and both the setting of "Morte d'Arthur" and Tennyson's earliest sketch for his treatment of the Arthurian matter (though there is no external evidence that he had read Faber); and ends with a complex of relations between Arthur, Hallam, and Dr. Tennyson (who had died in 1831). "In brief, it may be suggested that the 'Morte d'Arthur' seems to mark the transition between Tennyson's retarded adolescence and the beginning of his emotional maturity." There is much more, carrying on through *The Princess* to *Maud*, which will repay those who can follow the psychoanalytical exegesis. What began as an examination of the sources and imagery of Tennyson's earliest verses culminates in a study of his psychic development during adolescence. Besides this, there is a wealth of careful scholarship in the Notes, which are more extensive than the main part of the monograph.

That Tennyson's verse is full of echoes and parallels, both accidental and conscious, would go without saying; but the uninitiate will be surprised at the extent, the richness, and the assimilative skill of the examples mustered by J. C. Collins in *Illustrations of Tennyson* (1891, 1902; first in *Cornhill*

---

critical merit. Its most useful page is that containing an incomplete description of the vellum-bound manuscripts of the plays.

Magazine, 1880, 1881). The first part (twenty-three pages) contains not only parallels and borrowings from Virgil, but a study of devices and mannerisms common to the two poets (including such rarities as pseudo-anamnesis); but Collins is careful to avoid the implication that Tennyson is Virgil's equal. The remainder of the book runs through all of Tennyson in order, citing numerous authors, from Achilles Tatius and Addison to Xenophon and Young of *Night Thoughts*. Some additional notes will be found in *Alfred Tennyson: Poet, Philosopher, Idealist* by J. Cuming Walters (1893). Not everyone will accept all of these similarities as valid. It may be significant that Collins finds more in the early poems (to 1855) than in the later ones — discounting the *Idylls* and Malory, where the borrowing is of a different sort. He is not interested in charges of plagiarism often made against Tennyson, but only in treating Tennyson as "other classical poets" are treated and in showing "how indissolubly linked is the poetry of England with the poetry of the Greek, the Latin, and the Italian classics." Virgil is obvious.

W. P. Mustard's *Classical Echoes in Tennyson* (1904) is mostly a collection of parallel passages, conveniently arranged by author, from Homer on down. T. Herbert Warren (*Essays of Poets and Poetry*, 1909; first in *Quarterly Review*, 1901) toys with a long, Plutarchian parallel between Virgil and Tennyson, with numerous misstatements (about Tennyson, at least), and though of course similarities are there, the machinery becomes tiresome. The same volume has a paper, written with even more strain, on "Tennyson and Dante," showing that they both were accomplished poets and that Tennyson has borrowed a few touches from the *Divine Comedy;* but it is brightened by the repetition of Tennyson's triumphal understatement about his "Ulysses": "Yes, there's an echo of Dante in it." More on "Dante and Tennyson" will be found in an article by Francis St. J. Thackeray in *Temple Bar* (1894). In "Tennyson's Use of the Bible" (*Hesperia*, 1917), Edna M. Robinson has distinguished six periods — Simplicity, Combination, Allegorizing, Satire and Pessimism, Dramatic (with an excursus on Shakespeare), and Disuse — or six different ways in which Tennyson handled biblical stories and biblical language. These periods may seem arbitrary, but the collection of parallels and allusions is certainly very large. For the rest, one should turn to the long chapter in Douglas Bush's *Mythology and the Romantic Tradition in English Poetry* (1937), which contains not only a full treatment of Tennyson and the classics, poems on Greek and Roman subjects and other related poems, with a great wealth of learning in the footnotes, but also some admirable and admiring criticism of Tennyson in general, yet with pungent phrasing. Inasmuch as Bush has covered his ground so thoroughly, it is not necessary to include here the numerous special studies on Tennyson's classical subjects; they may be traced by means of Bush's footnotes. Some of the same material, together with a brief appreciation, appeared in *TQ* (1935) under the suggestive title, "The Personal Note in Tennyson's Classical Poems," by the same author. "Tennyson and the Classical Poets" by Elizabeth Meldrum, in *Contemporary Review* (1949), is brief but contains interesting suggestions apropos of "Œnone" and "A Dream of Fair Women," and incidentally complains that "Frater, ave atque vale" in the Catullus poem cannot be read with the Latin scansion.

Some brief studies, mainly on sources, may be brought together here. Richard Jones' *The Growth of the Idylls* (1895), was the first to point out that the first-written *Idyll*, "Merlin and Vivien," is dependent not on Malory but on Lady Guest's *Mabinogion*; and Gordon Haight, in "Tennyson's Merlin" (*Studies in Philology*, 1947), was the first to include the Notes to Southey's edition of Malory as a partial source. "Tennyson and Wales," by Herbert G. Wright (*Essays and Studies by Members of the English Association*, 14, 1929), contains a short account of the poet's visits to Wales and his knowledge of Welsh, and a lengthy comparison of the two Geraint *Idylls* with the *Mabinogion*. See also Otto L. Jiriczek, "Die neunte Woge" (*Beiblatt zur Anglia*, 1926). L. S. Potwin identified the mysterious source of "The Lady of Shalott" (*MLN*, 1902). In "Sources of *In Memoriam* in Tennyson's Early Poems"

(*MLN*, 1916), John R. Moore drew attention to the group of three irregular sonnets called "Love," in the 1830 volume but never reprinted by the poet, and claimed that the first nineteen lines (composed of course before Hallam's death) "express the central conceptions of *In Memoriam* with remarkable fidelity to its spirit and phraseology."

Hoxie N. Fairchild suggested that the germ of "The Palace of Art" was a passage from Shelley's "Queen Mab" (*TLS*, 11 January 1947), and also noted the parallel between the "wild bells" of *In Memoriam* and "wild bells" in Bailey's *Festus* (*MLN*, 1949). John Sparrow noted some striking parallels with Tennyson in Thomson's shorter poems in "Tennyson and Thomson's Shorter Poems" (*London Mercury*, 1930). W. D. Templeman, in *Booker Memorial Studies* (1950), presented in full the parallels, both in general outline and in verbal detail, between "Locksley Hall" and the Teufelsdröck and Blumine story taken from the unfinished *Wotton Reinfried;* and argued for Carlyle's influence as the source of the poem, or as he put it, Tennyson's "translation" of *Sartor Resartus*, Book II. David A. Robertson, Jr., suggested that Tennyson's mountain maid was the Jungfrau (see *American Alpine Journal*, 1950). There are two notes on Tennyson's Persian sources by J. D. Yohannan and W. D. Paden in *MLN* ("Tennyson and Persian Poetry," 1942, 1945). Paden also, in "Mt. 1352: Jacques de Vitry, the Menso Philosophica, Hödeken, and Tennyson" (*Journal of American Folklore*, 1945), traced the history of the tale which Tennyson used for *The Devil and the Lady* and found the probable immediate source in the *Quarterly Review* for January 1820.

E. Vettermann's "Die Balen-Dichtungen und ihre Quellen" (*Beihefte zur Zeitschrift für romanische Philologie*, 60, 1918) is a monograph of 311 pages, of which a dozen are given to Tennyson: he departed so far from Malory in treatment and relation to the Arthurian material that his *Idyll* has really nothing to do with the Balen story. On Tennyson and Froude, apropos of "The Revenge," see a series of letters in *TLS*: 15, 22 October 1931; 17, 31 December 1931; and 21 January 1932. In "Alfred Tennyson as a Celticist" (*Modern*

Philology, 1921), T. P. Cross showed "that Tennyson made an honest effort to ground his *Idylls* on the most reputable authorities of his day." E. A. Mooney, Jr., has a "Note on Astronomy in Tennyson's *The Princess*" in *MLN* (1949); and it may be mentioned in passing that G. M. Young in his "Age of Tennyson" lecture caught out the poet in a factual error about the moonrise at the end of *In Memoriam*.

On the biographical side, Edgar F. Shannon, Jr. in "The Coachman's Part in the Publication of *Poems by Two Brothers*" (*MLN*, 1949), disproved the old tradition that the publication of *Poems by Two Brothers* was suggested by Dr. Tennyson's coachman. T. H. Vail Motter ("When Did Tennyson Meet Hallam?" *MLN*, 1942) showed that Tennyson first met Hallam in April 1829. In "Tennyson the Psychologist" (*South Atlantic Quarterly*, 1944; reprinted in *Sex, Symbolism and Psychology in Literature*, 1948), Roy P. Basler has shown how in *Maud* Tennyson "pioneered the uncharted frontiers of psychological phenomena," with emphasis on Tennyson's having so early foreshadowed the findings of Freud and Jung. He also praises Dr. R. J. Mann's *Tennyson's "Maud" Vindicated* (1856) as "one of the most significant critical essays of the century." In "Tennyson's Merlin" (*SP*, 1947), Gordon Haight identifies the source of Tennyson's notion that the name Nimuë (changed to Vivien in the *Idylls*) meant *gleam*, "gleam" being used in his autobiographical poem, "Merlin and the Gleam," for "the higher poetic imagination"; suggests that the meter of the poem was of Welsh origin; that the Wizard was Sir Walter Scott; that the Young Mariner was a local sailor who assisted at Tennyson's crossing to Freshwater at the time of his serious illness in 1888; and confirms, by recognizing the pun in "the croak of a Raven," the identification of Croker as the *Quarterly* reviewer of 1833 (see Haight's footnote there; and see also "Croker and Tennyson Again," *Notes and Queries*, 26 July, 15 November 1947). But T. O. Mabbott, in "Tennyson's Merlin" (*N & Q*, 10 January 1948) has suggested an allusion to the raven on Danish pennies.

The gift of prophecy, not only in the Old Testament sense

but also in a more practical sense, has been claimed for Tennyson, and there are scattered passages which seem to bear this out. His later work contains some dark forebodings for England and the world; in 1886 he predicted the growth of China into a great power; and when earlier in "Locksley Hall" (1842) he "dipt into the future," he foresaw the sky filled "with commerce . . . dropping down with costly bales" and also "airy navies" from which "rain'd a ghastly dew." Clark Emery in "The Background of Tennyson's 'Airy Navies' " (*Isis*, 1944), taking off from DeVane's note (1940) that the poet was thinking only of balloons, accumulated a great mass of historical evidence to prove that "Tennyson had in mind some kind of aircraft." This, Emery says, "may be taken as certain"; he concluded, however, that the idea that it was "something after the fashion of twentieth-century aircraft" is less certain, but the possibility cannot be denied. That the airy navies were only sailing ships he regards as not worth considering. Apropos of "Tennyson's 'Balloon Stanzas' " deleted in 1842 from the first version of "A Dream of Fair Women," Edgar F. Shannon, Jr. (*PQ*, 1952) points out the "evident source" of Tennyson's interest in balloons, and adds that "the conclusion seems unavoidable that when he wrote the prophetic lines in 'Locksley Hall,' future development of the balloon was uppermost in his mind."

Tennyson's political views are generally left to speak for themselves in the "jingo" poems. There is, however, a good chapter (V) in Stephen Gwynn's *Tennyson: A Critical Study* (1899), and an Erlangen dissertation, *Die politischen Anschauungen Tennysons* (1930) by Ernst Blos (n.v.). "Tennyson used his poetic gift," says Gwynn, "and the hold which it gave him on the feelings of his countrymen, not merely with a high sense of his moral mission, but with a singularly wide political forecast." *Tennyson and the Victorian Political Milieu* (a New York University dissertation, 1938) by W. A. Hunton, is, to judge from the published abridgement, a thorough and competent study. It does not take a high view of the poet's politics; but in his conservatism, his indifference for the most part to the Continental struggles for liberty, and his imperialism, Tennyson "spoke for the politically dominant class in Victorian England."

Thus Tennyson was interpreting his age. But there still has been no systematic assaying, fair and objective, of the precise ways and degrees in which Tennyson echoed, followed, anticipated, or helped to form, the principal ideas (what Matthew Arnold called "the main movement of mind") in England during his long life. Such a thoroughgoing analysis might make dull reading, but it ought to be made.

On one point, however, a good deal has been done, and that is Tennyson and Science. Sidgwick regarded him "as preeminently the Poet of Science." Sir Oliver Lodge contributed to the *Friends* volume a paper on his attitude to science. Sir Norman Lockyer, the astronomer, said that Tennyson knew as much about the stars as he himself and in *Tennyson as a Student and Poet of Nature* (1910) described him as "a poet who, beyond all others who have ever lived, combined the gift of expression with an unceasing interest in the causes of things and in the working out of Nature's laws." This claim is substantiated by a series of classified quotations under such headings as Cosmogony, Evolution of Stellar Systems, Evolution of the Earth and Man, Stars, Sun, etc., etc. Nowhere else can one get such impressive evidence of Tennyson's minute knowledge and "grasp" of scientific facts and principles.[3]

At the center of this subject is Evolution. It is misleading to say, as some have done, that the poets "forestalled" or "anticipated" Darwin. Notions of an evolutionary theory go back to Empedocles and Aristotle; they were passed on with accumulated evidence down through the eighteenth century; in various forms they were in the air through the early nineteenth century (witness the popularity of [Chambers'] *Vestiges*, 1844 et seq.); but it remained for Darwin in 1859 to give

[3] There are also many general appreciations of Tennyson's poetic treatment of nature; in addition see, for birds and trees, "Nature in Tennyson," two articles by Morton Luce in the *British Review* (1915); *The Birds of Tennyson* by Watkin J. Y. S. Watkins; Vernon Rendall, *Wild Flowers in Literature* (1934), with numerous references to Tennyson in the index; and for astronomy, C. T. Whitwell, in *Journal and Transactions of the Leeds Astronomical Society* (1906).

these notions fairly precise scientific formulation and "proof." This is of course a matter for the historians of science to deal with. Historians of poetry need only recognize the growing evolutionary views as they appear in verse down to 1859 and note the poets' use of them. The second chapter of Lionel Stevenson's *Darwin among the Poets* (1932) gives a general account of Tennyson and the theory, where something of Tennyson's reading is recorded and the manifold appearances of evolution are traced critically through his poems. William R. Rutland enthusiastically covers the same ground as Stevenson in "Tennyson and the Theory of Evolution" (*Essays and Studies by Members of the English Association*, 26, 1941) which the *Times Literary Supplement* hailed with headlines: "Tennyson as Thinker. Fullest Honours as a Great Poet." Many uncertainties were cleared away by a very solid article by George R. Potter, "Tennyson and the Biological Theory of Mutability in Species" (*PQ*, 1937). Potter calls it a rough sketch, but it goes beyond anything yet attempted to make sense of the loose statements then and still current. In the latter part of his article, Potter again traces chronologically the allusions to evolutionary theory in Tennyson, testing them for signs of particular aspects of the theory in astronomy, geology, and biology as they were commonly known, with special notice of the prodigality of nature and the struggle for existence, and particularly for evidence of any belief in mutability. As to this latter, Potter's answer is one of extreme doubt: though Tennyson must have known about mutation from the *Vestiges*, that he took the final step to an acceptance of mutability before Darwin, "there is no certain evidence."

In "The Natural Theology of *In Memoriam*" (*Review of English Studies*, 1947) Graham Hough explains that Tennyson's purpose is "to make an emotionally satisfying synthesis of current scientific and religious thought," but concludes that his "thoroughgoing subjectivism rather bypasses than meets the difficulties raised by science." (One recalls John Burroughs' blunt remark that science "enlarged his vocabulary without strengthening his faith.") The chapter on Tennyson in Ralph B. Crum's *Scientific Thought in Poetry* (1931) is worth a glance; for the general subject see Douglas Bush, *Science and English Poetry* (1950) and Bonamy Dobrée's review article, "Science and Poetry in England" in *Sewanee Review* (1953). F. W. H. Myers' essay, "Tennyson as Prophet" (*NC*, 1889; reprinted in *Science and a Future Life*, 1893) is largely concerned with pushing the attack on materialistic philosophy and using the poet as the prophet "of a Spiritual Universe" in that "service which humanity will always need." The best work on Tennyson's religion, once a favorite topic, is still C. F. G. Masterman's *Tennyson as a Religious Teacher* (1900). His mysticism has been frequently touched on (see, for example, P. H. Osmond, *The Mystical Poets of the English Church,* S. P. C. K., 1919) but deserves further study.

Under the title taken from W. H. Auden's Introduction (1946), "The Stupidest English Poet," Paul Turner in *English Studies* (1949) endeavored to answer the charges of Nicolson and Fausset so far as they concern "the most important department of Tennyson's thought, his speculative theology." His method is somewhat roundabout, but the ironic conclusion, "that evaluations of Tennyson's thought by twentieth-century critics have sometimes been based upon the assumptions of nineteenth-century science," is not without point.

There is a small literature on *In Memoriam* and on *Maud*, which can be readily traced in the bibliographies; but a special place may be found here for more extended discussion of articles dealing with the *Idylls of the King*, from which, as has been said, Tennyson hoped so much and has gained so little from posterity. Two books for general background are *The Arthurian Epic,* by S. H. Gurteen (1895) and *Tennyson's Idylls of the King and Arthurian Story from the XVIth Century,* by M. W. MacCallum (1894); but neither of these is to be trusted for the complex matter of Arthur as it is now understood by scholars. *The Arthurian Legend* (1938; an Aberdeen dissertation) by Margaret J. C. Reid contains much later bibliography, but its comments are without value. For general appreciation, *Studies in the Idylls* by Henry Elsdale (1878), where the allegory was first elaborated, should be read; and also *The Meaning of the Idylls of the King* (1904, based on earlier articles in *The Catholic World*) by Condé B. Pallen, to whom Tennyson wrote: "You see further into their meaning than most of my commentators have done." F. S. Boas in " 'Idylls of the King' in 1921," a lecture before the Royal Society of Literature (1922, reprinted in *From Richardson to Pinero,* 1937) complained of the "prevalent depreciation of [Tennyson's] most ambitious and, for long, most popular work"; but the critics, he said, have missed its most vulnerable point, the allegorical element ("an illegitimate transvaluation") which "leads to some insoluble entanglements." He had high praise for the other qualities, however, and saw the whole as representing Tennyson's own *Weltanschauung*: "that there is a spiritual principle in the universe, incessantly struggling with the material elements, liable to temporary defeat, but in essence unconquerable and immortal." C. H. Herford, commenting on this, gave as his opinion that the poet's theme of Soul *vs.* Sense was a misleading antithesis: "It was not in these ascetic terms that Dante, the master of all allegorists, . . . interpreted life or created poetry." For an energetic defense one should see F. E. L. Priestley's article, "Tennyson's *Idylls*" (*TQ*, 1949). They "represent one of Tennyson's most earnest and important efforts to deal with major problems of his time." They "do in fact form a pattern"; they are "primarily allegorical" and so illustrate a philosophy which permeates all his poetry, "the strong faith in the eternal world of spirit . . . reinforced by continual warnings of the dangers of materialism." Support for this judgment can certainly be found in the poem, but a little kindly forcing may be required to show what the poet by his "piecemeal composition" did not altogether make clear. In "Tennyson's 'Allegory in the Distance' " (*PMLA*, 1953), S. C. Burchell, taking Jowett's phrase applied to the Merlin and Vivien *Idyll*, defended the whole *Idylls* as "a medley of pure and symbolic narrative" rather than "a true moral allegory," and as such "a revelation, a diagnosis and a lament" for the complexity and decadence of modern life, something indeed like "The Waste Land."

Rather interpretative than factual are the following articles. In "Tennyson's 'Palace of Art' — An Interpretation" (*SP*, 1936), A. C. Howell first reviews the various explanations of the poem, those supplied by the poet himself and those offered by others, together with some account of this "curse of Tennyson's poetry," allegory; these are followed by Howell's own interpretation — worked out with great fullness as one of the "lesser meanings" (Tennyson's phrase), but as so developed appearing larger — namely, that the Palace is Trinity College, Cambridge, "the cloistered life, the life of the scholar, surrounded with art and knowledge, but ignorant of the active life of the common world," and the whole poem represents obliquely Tennyson's disappointment at being forced to leave without a degree and his protest against the College's "deadening influence upon the development of the artist, the genius."

The thirty-five pages on Tennyson in E. D. H. Johnson's *The Alien Vision* may be summarized here. The germ of Tennyson's "divided will" shows itself in the earliest poems and its growth can be traced throughout. Thus the Lady of Shalott in "the manner of her dying symbolizes the extinction of the vitalizing imagination within her." "Tithonus" is likewise "almost certainly a symbolic representation of Tennyson's aesthetic philosophy," his "growing disposition to disguise his private thoughts under extrinsic layers of meaning." This same "extra dimension" is to be found in the domestic idylls and in "Lucretius." Johnson is less successful in showing this disharmony in *In Memoriam* and the *Idylls of the King*: "the final impression left by the [*Idylls*] is one of tragic incompatibility between the life of the imagination and the ways of the world," and in this way Tennyson could speak directly to his age and at the same time give "full expression to his own deepest intuitions." After 1870 the urgency to preserve his own artistic integrity becomes greater and greater in the transcendental poems, as well as "his recognition of the subterfuges that were necessary in order to get Victorian society to listen to his message." All of which neither "can be proven, Nor yet disproven," but it has the merit of generosity and is in its way Victorian. It satisfies our sense of seeing more deeply into the poet's mind than we could hope to do by ourselves. It might be called *extra*pretation.

A recent run of articles on the little lyric "Tears, Idle Tears" illustrates a similar sort of extradimensional criticism. Cleanth Brooks began this with "The Motivation of Tennyson's Weeper" in *The Well Wrought Urn* (1947), emphasizing ambiguity and paradox. F. W. Bateson, in "Romantic Schizophrenia" (*English Poetry: A Critical Introduction,* 1950) maintained that the days that are no more "belong to a public past" and if there are special personal associations also, it is still impossible "to give the poem both senses at once"; hence a "psychic division" in Tennyson's poetry. Graham Hough, in *The Hopkins Review* (1951), starting from Brooks, maintained that "Tears" is a pagan poem; the tears spring from the sin of despair, something daemonic; hence it reveals "a sense of dereliction — arising perhaps from who knows what childish experience." Leo Spitzer, replying to Hough in the same *Review* (1952) elevated "some divine despair" to a god called Life-in-Death, a personification of the *lacrimae rerum,* who is one of the protagonists of the lyric, the poet being the other; hence a dual unity (horizontal and vertical) exists throughout the little poem. Spitzer adds a learned account of other poets who have handled the same theme. Lastly, Frederick L. Gwynn in *PMLA* (1952) compares the two versions of "Tithonus" — the "Tithon" of 1833–34 (cf. *PMLA,* 1949) and the published poem, 1860 — with "Tears, Idle Tears": there are words and phrases common to the three; Tithonus himself might almost be the weeper of "Tears" and certainly "Death in Life" fits him better than it seems to fit the lyric. Most of this would have surprised Tennyson.

"Tennyson, Browning, and a Romantic Fallacy," by Lionel Stevenson (*TQ,* 1944), describes the early influence of Shelley on Tennyson, and Tennyson's revolt against Shelley's isolationist humanitarianism (the "fallacy"), when he turned, as in "The Palace of Art," from the aloof cult of beauty to a more quotidian concept of the poet's function. The same writer, in "The 'high-born maiden' Symbol in Tennyson" (*PMLA*, 1948), traces this Shelleyan figure: from the two "Mariana" poems, "The Lady of Shalott" (in which there is a "definite allegory" of the poet's resolve "to face the painful experiences of real life"), and "The Palace of Art"; through "Lady Clara Vere de Vere" and Amy in "Locksley Hall," and *The Princess* ("a whole institution-full of high-born maidens"); to Elaine in the *Idylls*, as Tennyson "gained emotional stability" and "gradually transformed [her] into a matter-of-fact literary stock-character." This figure Stevenson connects with Jung's "archetypal image of the *anima*."

Two somewhat similar studies are Elizabeth Waterston's "Symbolism in Tennyson's Minor Poems" (*TQ*, 1951) and E. D. H. Johnson's "The Lily and the Rose; Symbolic Meaning in Tennyson's *Maud*" (*PMLA*, 1949). There are Freudian undertones in the former. "Distressed by the atomism of his age, he sought societal symbols, rejecting images whose impact was guaranteed only by his private experience. Hence his life-long experiments with classical myth . . . and with folk-lore. . . ." His most frequent symbols are "landscape, particularly when several levels sharply different can be seen; dark houses or halls, with unusual lighting; rivers, usually with cataracts; mist rising; stars, particularly 'Hesper'; a family group of man, woman, and daughter; yellow colours, and rose; cheerful bells; rust; song-birds; ships at anchor; jewels," — all used for their "general impact." Many of these are illustrated, both in their direct and oblique applications, with a passing comment on the absence of Christian symbols except in *In Memoriam* and the *Idylls*, though even there the figure of Christ is wanting; and with special attention at the end to "The Ancient Sage."

"Tennyson's Garden of Art: A Study of *The Hesperides*," by G. Robert Stange (*PMLA*, 1952), is still another exploratory study of Tennyson's early symbolism and his growing sense of the poetic function. It appears to be a development of Douglas Bush's few sentences on the poem in *Mythology and the Romantic Tradition*, though Bush is not mentioned. Apropos of a study of "Demeter and Persephone" with its "sad, shadowy drama which is typical of Tennyson's poetry," Stange has some interesting generalizations in "Tennyson's Mythology" (*Journal of English Literary History*, 1954), on the poet's uses of classical myths and his ways of modernizing them by reading into them his personal doubts and conflicts.

In Memoriam: The Way of a Soul (1951), a Yale dissertation by Eleanor B. Mattes, makes two valuable contributions. With the help of fresh evidence, Miss Mattes is able to date the sections more fully than hitherto, and in several short chapters she traces parallels (and presumably sources) between certain sections and Tennyson's reading of Wordsworth, Hallam, Isaac Taylor, Carlyle, Lyell's *Geology*, Herschel's *Natural Philosophy*, and Chambers' *Vestiges*. This is just what needed to be done. It is supplemented by Milton Millhauser in a well-annotated article, "Tennyson's *Princess* and *Vestiges*" (*PMLA*, 1954), with evidence supporting the conclusion that "the *Vestiges* was a precipitant but not a determinant of Tennyson's thought . . . he never fully subscribed to its central doctrine . . . . Instead, he made his peace with it by . . . assimilating it into the broad, undoctrinal Christianity of his middle and later years."

Marjorie Bowden's *Tennyson in France* (1930) also fills a notable lacuna in Tennyson scholarship. (Similar studies are needed for Tennyson in Germany and Tennyson in Italy.) This naturally is a review of French critics and criticism, though the author inserts here and there her own views of the poet. It seems that in France, after Taine expressed himself so vigorously on Tennyson as the great dilettante, others became interested, and gradually he became fairly well known, was introduced into the lycées, was translated and imitated, and was more generally appreciated than, considering his Gallophobic attitude, he deserved. In a word, Tennyson has not been accepted by the French but has been cultivated by many Frenchmen. For instance, Mallarmé admired him and Verlaine contemplated translating *In Memoriam* —

which gave George Moore the opportunity to say that Tennyson just missed being translated by a greater poet than himself.

The story of the reaction against Tennyson's great popularity, which was foreseen in the seventies and eighties and even commented on by the poet himself; which became loudly vocal a dozen years after his death when the Victorian age reached its close; and which became a kind of storm center with the two books of Fausset and Nicolson in 1923, belongs to criticism rather than to scholarship, though some good names enter the scene. The reaction, and now the return, have been due as much to social changes and the usual vagaries of taste as to the aesthetic values of Tennyson's poetry. The more he had portrayed and reflected his age the more obvious it became, or seemed to become, that his great mastery of language was not accompanied by a commensurate power of feeling and ideas; and the feeling and ideas of the nineteenth century had been rejected on other than artistic grounds. The story may be traced through the numerous books, chapters, and articles published from, say, 1900 on, while the critics were seeking a balanced judgment, and especially in the reviews and counter-reviews of Fausset and Nicolson. Only a few intermediate landmarks need be mentioned. J. M. Robertson, in "The Art of Tennyson" (*Essays towards a Critical Method*, 1889) adopted the give-and-take method, but in *Browning and Tennyson: Two Studies* (1903) took a harsher stand. Frederic Harrison in *Tennyson, Ruskin, Mill, and Other Literary Estimates* (1900) and W. P. Ker in the Leslie Stephen lecture for 1909 tried to look both ways. The British Academy (*Proceedings*, 4, 1909) recognized the centenary of Tennyson's birth with a lecture by Professor Henry Jones: Tennyson's fame, he said, "is for the moment westering. But . . . it is the earth that turns," not the sun. A. C. Bradley, in an English Association lecture (1914; reprinted in *A Miscellany*, 1929) vigorously attacked "The Reaction against Tennyson." Oliver Elton, who in "Tennyson: An Inaugural Lecture" (1901; reprinted in *Modern Studies*, 1907) had handled the poet rather severely, came over to the side of the faithful in his *Survey* (1920; the chapter revised and published separately, with that on Arnold, in 1924).

Nicolson's *Tennyson* (1923) was written, he said, "frankly, to induce some people to approach Tennyson with an unbiassed mind"; but it impressed others as largely a series of *obiter dicta* and a "devastating" exposure of the Tennysonian weaknesses. The two views which have given most offense are: "For me, the essential Tennyson is a morbid and unhappy mystic"; and "For the secret of Tennyson is to be sought . . . in the conflict . . . between the remarkable depth and originality of his poetic temperament and the shallowness and timidity of his practical intelligence." He defends Tennyson as having fallen on a period of bad taste in 1832–1842, and adds: "We must admit that even if, to us, his thought seems rather shallow and insincere, it was hailed by millions of his countrymen as penetrating, audacious, and profound." In the following year Alfred Noyes, in a Lowell lecture (printed in *Some Aspects of Modern Poetry*, 1924, and separately in 1932) attacked the reaction with almost militant fervor. On the same side, but more judicious, is the chapter on Tennyson by Lascelles Abercrombie in *Revaluations* (1931). In 1942, the semicentenary of the poet's death and the centenary of the 1842 *Poems*, the *Times Literary Supplement*, stating editorially that "the years of disparagement have ended," paid tribute to Tennyson's prophecies of the present disasters; and in the same issue (10 October) printed a special article, "A Great National Poet . . . Tennyson's Mystic Imperialism." But the disparagement was not altogether silent. Nicolson, in *The Spectator* (9 October, 1942) maintained his earlier views, with less emphatic phrasing; but in *The Poetry Review* (1942) withdrew the charge of insincerity and urged the younger generation to concentrate on the "amount of pure poetry which has nothing to do either with his age or with the rather self-conscious attitude which he adopted towards his own poetic mission. . . . I look forward with confidence to a Tennysonian revival."

But the attacks had never seriously threatened Tennyson's position: the critics were merely adjusting themselves to their own contemporary problems. Yet they are interesting, for, as Guinevere said, "The low sun makes the colour." Now the circle has been ironically closed in a brilliant example of modern criticism, part Freudian and part Marxian, by Arthur J. Carr, onetime editor of *Accent*: "Tennyson as a Modern Poet" (*TQ*, 1950). Here many of the old topics are translated into the current language and Tennyson is welcomed back in sympathetic recognition of the parallels between his crises and the predicament of the modern poet, with emphasis on anxiety. The Tennysonian black-blood is seen as erotic aggression, frustration, and the recourse to dream fantasy; the slow disintegration of the Victorian world which Tennyson felt and expressed in his own way is rephrased as "the wealthy attractions of materialistic monism and the dualistic demands of his subjective strife and system of values." Tennyson is hailed as "our true precursor. He shows and hides, as if in embryo, a master theme of Joyce's *Ulysses*. . . . He forecasts Yeats's interest in the private myth. He apprehended in advance of Aldous Huxley the uses of mysticism to castigate materialistic culture. And in *Maud*, at least, he prepared the way for the verse of Eliot's 'Preludes' and 'Prufrock.' " The first two volumes "display Tennyson's rapid and thorough engagement of his characteristic themes and, in particular, his concern with erotic motives to unfold the dialectic of sense and conscience." And in the end, "The price that Tennyson pays for his being a 'representative' poet is great. He suffers our disease and our confusion. He triumphs not as a master but as a victim. . . . As a result, he works out remorselessly the fatal consequences of the romantic tradition . . . and reduces its intellectual ambitions to the accidents of individual perceptions and personal blindness." In a word, Tennyson in becoming modern has not escaped from the bane of his Victorianism. His position on Parnassus is not improved.

There has been, as was noted above, much more criticism of Tennyson — admiring or faultfinding — and critical interpretation, than scholarly work on him. The earlier efforts were naturally to find sources and make comparisons; the later have been, perhaps naturally, to note the personal and social pressures and explore their psychological bearings. Almost always the question has been: what is the poem about? or, why did he write it? But few have even asked the important question, to which considered answers might have spared us many wasted steps: why is it a poem? Considering how much of Tennyson's success, his genius, is due to his workmanship, his art — not merely technique or superficial skills, but the deeper movement of his spirit which convinced him that he was a poet and made him consecrate his life to poetry — it is surprising that we have so little about the aesthetic principles on which he relied to convey his criticism of life. For there was certainly more than the merely didactic, the imposed business of a message, and the desire to satisfy his admirers. He often said that his purpose was to do good and his satisfaction was in having done good to others, yet there remains the question when and how he did it well in his chosen medium. There are observations here and there in his poems on the nature of artistic creation and hints elsewhere about his methods of composition: a study of these would throw new light on his poems as poetry.

3 🦢

Robert Browning

William C. DeVane

THERE HAS BEEN a reluctance on the part of contemporary poets, critics, and scholars to recognize fully the place of Browning in the evolution of modern English and American poetry. They have preferred, like T. S. Eliot, to trace their lineage and award their plaudits to French sources and practices. One is not inclined to deny the profound influence of the Gallic poets and artists upon English and American thinking and performance late in the nineteenth century and early in the twentieth. But there is an element of snobbishness in their preference, or rather, in their relative neglect of Browning's part in the evolution, and the general failure of the critics and scholars to acknowledge that part. A. A. Brockington's *Browning and the Twentieth Century* (1932) does not go far, in spite of its title, to repair this neglect. The native line of development is clearly enough established through Pound to Eliot — through the Mauberly poems to "The Waste Land." The evolution of the dramatic monologue through Browning leads directly to the stream-of-consciousness technique of Joyce. Furthermore, Browning is clearly the forerunner of the modern poet in the matter of diction, as Sir Herbert Read recognized many years ago. He likewise did something to extend the range of possible subject-matter in poetry and of its manner of treatment. One may best see Browning's experiments in this kind in his volume, *Dramatis Personae* (1864), though he had begun such experiments at least two decades earlier.

John Donne, deservedly the idol of the poet and critic in recent years, was first hailed across the centuries for what he truly was by Browning, as J. E. Duncan recognizes in his article, "The Intellectual Kinship of John Donne and Robert Browning" (*SP*, 1953), in which he characterizes the influence of Donne upon the younger poet as general but fundamental. Or as Browning himself put it,

> Better and truer verse none ever wrote . . .
> Than thou, revered and magisterial Donne.

But, as yet, little credit has accrued to the later English poet for his prescience.

The Browning scholar is compelled to ask the reasons for the contemporary reluctance to acknowledge the significance of his poet in the present day. These reasons are several and complex, I think, and not always rational. The first and most obvious, I suppose, is the natural and inevitable failure of sympathy between contiguous or near generations. Browning was read and praised too much by the late Victorians and the Edwardians for the next generations to tolerate him. Psychologically, revolt was necessary to gain independence. Worse still, Browning, in the changing intellectual climate, was praised for the wrong qualities and attributes. The poet's voluminous preoccupation with religious questions was long outdated and wearisome. His reading of life and history, cheerful and optimistic to an offensive degree, seemed incredibly false to generations harried by wars and a vast social unrest. His psychology was that of an inspired amateur, always liable to distortion by his strong and doctrinaire opinions, in a field that has developed professionally since his time. He wrote far too much, and habitually neglected form and beauty. These are some of the objections which the critics and scholars of 1955 raise against Browning, but since Santayana's attack in "The Poetry of Barbarism" at the beginning of the present century, there has been no balanced and full appraisal of Browning's virtues and deficiencies and his effect on modern poetry, and we cannot yet say that his definitive place in the history of English poetry has been authoritatively stated.

As one might expect, the scholars, on the whole, have been more tolerant and appreciative of Browning than the poets and critics. There are signs in the volume and direction of the scholarly studies done upon Browning in the last quarter of a century that he has now receded in point of time sufficiently for us to see him in perspective. The quantity of reputable scholarship upon the poet has begun to increase, and the quality seems to me to be steadily improving. In the comment below it has been my object to appraise the most significant examples of this work.

I. *Bibliographies*

The older bibliographies of Browning, prepared by Thomas J. Wise, must be used with caution since the disclosures of Carter and Pollard in 1934. These are *A Complete Bibliography of the Writings in Prose and Verse of Robert Browning* (1897), and *A Browning Library, A Catalogue of Printed Books, Manuscripts and Autograph Letters by Robert Browning and Elizabeth Barrett Browning* (1929). Late in 1953, the Cornell University Press published (as Vol. 39 of the *Cornell Studies in English*) a complete census of Browning's works, manuscripts, letters, and material about the poet. This volume, entitled *Robert Browning: A Bibliography, 1830–1950,* is a work begun many years ago by the late professors C. S. Northup and L. N. Broughton and completed by Robert Pearsall. It is comprehensive and accurate and will prove invaluable to all Browning scholars. It is to Broughton and to B. F. Stelter that we owe the useful work, *A Concordance to the Poems of Robert Browning,* in two volumes, published in 1924.

II. *Editions*

The most authoritative editions of Browning's poetry are still the Centenary Edition, edited by F. G. Kenyon in ten volumes in 1912, and published as *The Works of Robert*

Browning; and the Florentine Edition, *The Complete Works of Robert Browning*, edited by Charlotte Porter and Helen A. Clarke, published in twelve volumes in 1910. The best single volume is *The Complete Poetical Works of Robert Browning, New Edition with Additional Poems First Published in 1914*, edited by Augustine Birrell (1915). The Cambridge one-volume edition contains a few poems not printed elsewhere, but is not quite complete. Of these works, only the Florentine Edition is profusely annotated, though the Centenary Edition has some valuable introductory comment on many of the poems. Selection and annotation are needed for Browning, and to meet these needs numerous selective volumes have appeared, frequently annotated much more fully and carefully than in editions of the complete works. I need cite here only two such: the late Walter Graham's *The Reader's Browning* (1934) and the present writer's *Shorter Poems of Robert Browning* (1933). Browning's text is well established, but good annotation of the full works is still lacking.

III. *Biographical Studies*

The standard biography of the poet is still W. Hall Griffin and Harry Christopher Minchin's volume, *The Life of Robert Browning, with Notices of his Writings, his Family, and his Friends* (1910). This work was "Revised and Enlarged" by Minchin in 1938 in an effort to repair some of the weakness of the latter half of the biography, and to include some of the more notable results of the research between those years. The changes were not very great, however, and the pagination remains almost identical with the first edition. Mrs. Sutherland Orr's *Life and Letters of Robert Browning* (1891; revised by F. G. Kenyon in 1908) is still valuable for its opinions, because Mrs. Orr was a close friend of Browning's and her personal impressions must be carefully considered. In her work, however, there are numerous inaccuracies, especially in the unrevised edition. The most useful of other, older biographies are Dowden's, Herford's, and more recently H. L. Hovelaque's *La Jeunesse de Robert Browning*, published in Paris in 1932.

It was inevitable that the twentieth century should, sooner or later, apply its own peculiar methods to an evaluation of Browning's personality and career. In *PMLA*, September 1941, Stewart Walker Holmes published a long article entitled "Browning's *Sordello* and Jung: Browning's *Sordello* in the Light of Jung's Theory of Types," in which he undertook to analyze the personality of the poet as it appears in the first three long autobiographical poems, mainly *Sordello*. He found that Browning was the introverted intuitive type, who like Sordello depended upon the woman-symbol — Pauline, Andromeda, Palma, and the "beggar maid" of Venice — and was under the personal necessity of attaining an "unprejudiced objectivity." Such an introverted type often finds matters of communication difficult. Holmes therefore returned to the problem in another article: "Browning: Semantic Stutterer" (*PMLA*, 1945). Here he found Browning in a real dilemma between the necessity to write as a prophet-poet in metaphysical terms and his "verbal impotence." Browning confused the various levels of abstraction, and thought the impression he had was the word. His semantic blockages produced the severe neuralgia from which he suffered. In the process of writing *Sordello* however, Browning discovered his trouble, and went a long way toward developing a homemade psychoanalytic cure for himself, at least temporarily. He learned to accept his limitations as a poet, and to curb his vast humanitarian aspirations. In effect, he shook himself free of Shelley, and began to write short dramatic lyrics and monologues which were neither autobiographical nor long.

The psychoanalysis of Browning was only beginning. In 1952 Mrs. Betty Miller undertook to interpret the personality, character and career of Robert Browning in twentieth-century terms in her volume, *Robert Browning: A Portrait*. Containing a considerable amount of new material, especially upon the poet's earlier years when he closely associated with the Fox-Flower group, the volume is notable primarily for its fresh interpretation of Browning's personality and poetry. The new material is chiefly from hitherto unpublished letters and diaries in the British Museum and the Victoria and Albert Museum, and will also be of interest to scholars concerned with John Stuart Mill. Mrs. Miller's book is a psychological study of the poet's relationship to women, and her interpretation runs directly counter to the traditional notion of Browning's personality. Her thesis is that Browning, having a constant instinct to put himself in the position of a helpless child to its mother, was deeply and almost abjectly dependent upon women older than himself and could only love such women whom, usually by age and sometimes by endowment, he regarded as his superiors. The list of such women is a long and notable one: Browning's mother, Eliza Flower, Fannie Haworth, Elizabeth Barrett, and in later years Julia Wedgwood, Louisa Lady Ashburton, and several others. The prize example is drawn from the Barrett-Browning correspondence before their marriage, in which Browning seems to insist that Elizabeth shall make all decisions, set the tone of their relationship, and direct his opinions. From 1845 when Miss Barrett and Browning first met until her death in 1861, the lady, according to Mrs. Miller, dominates the relationship, and here, I think, Mrs. Miller opens herself to the charge of partisanship. The biography for these years is more Mrs. Browning's than his. Her shadow hovers over the later parts of the book as well.

But this *Portrait* is most stimulating and suggests new interpretations of a number of Browning's poems, some credible and some extravagantly forced. Mrs. Miller pushes her thesis relentlessly, but the book has been widely praised, and with some justice. It has the virtue of looking afresh at the whole relationship of Browning and his wife, and much else in Browning's career, without the rose-colored blinders of romance. It is not, however, the definitive biography of the poet that the popular critics thought it, both in England and in America. Another volume of the same psychological kind, but more concerned with Browning's personality than his poetry, is J. M. Cohen's *Robert Browning* (1952).

Biographical research upon the later part of Browning's life has centered mainly upon the poet's affairs with Louisa Lady Ashburton in 1869–71. This affair was first disclosed with any definiteness, I believe, by me in my study called *Browning's Parleyings, The Autobiography of a Mind* (1927; Chapter Two), though there is an error in date, and Lady Ashburton's name is not mentioned. In his edition of the *Letters of Robert Browning, Collected by Thomas J. Wise* (1933), Dean Thurman L. Hood developed the incident in much greater detail (see his Appendix), making what had appeared as a conjecture in my study an authenticated fact, naming the lady and roughly the date. It has remained for scholars to trace the effect of this affair upon Browning's subsequent career and poetry.

By all odds, the fullest and best illustration of the poet's strong reaction to an act which he regarded as disloyalty to his dead wife may be seen in W. O. Raymond's study called "Browning's Dark Mood: a Study of *Fifine at the Fair.*" This paper first appeared as an article in 1935 and is now included in Raymond's volume, *The Infinite Moment and Other Essays in Robert Browning* (1950), as Chapter Seven. Here we may see Browning in a mood that was to color the rest of his life: fiercely angry at Lady Ashburton and hating himself for his disloyalty. In *Fifine*, the poet is trying to find, with all his subtle casuistry, what kind of case a philanderer might make for himself.

Other scholars have exploited the Ashburton-Browning affair. For example, Kenneth L. Knickerbocker skillfully interpreted the poem, "St. Martin's Summer," in his article, "An Echo from Browning's Second Courtship" (*SP*, 1935). In my *Browning Handbook* (1935) I used the incident in interpreting a number of later poems, such as *Pan and Luna*, the *Prologue to Ferishtah's Fancies*, and of course the *Parleying with Daniel Bartoli*. In Mrs. Miller's *Portrait*, referred to above, she suggestively interprets the poem *Numpholeptos* as a reflection of Browning's mood of resentment in 1876 that the memory of his wife should exercise such tyranny upon his conscience. The Browning-Ashburton affair was an event with very considerable consequences.

Not all of the new biographical research, however, has concerned itself with the love-affairs of the poet. Donald Smalley in 1948 made the notable discovery of Browning's prose article: a long review in 1841 of a new work upon Tasso which, after a few paragraphs, Browning turned into a headlong and injudicious defense of Chatterton. In his book, *Browning's Essay on Chatterton* (1948), Smalley sees the poet laying his blueprint for his "Pattern of Imposture," and setting up a laboratory model in the process of special pleading. Possibly Smalley somewhat overstates his case, but there is no doubt that a characteristic mode of thought was here developed which was to have its effect on all of Browning's analyses of his later villains. In 1938 Sir Vincent Baddeley, K.C.B., performed a service to Browning scholarship by setting right the poet's genealogy in his article, "The Ancestry of Robert Browning, the Poet" (*The Genealogists' Magazine*). Roma A. King, Jr., drawing from the rich resources of the Baylor University Browning collections, published *Robert Browning's Finances from his own Account Book* in 1947. This little volume shows not only the considerable prosperity gleaned by the poet from his investments and from the sale of his own and his wife's books in the last five years of his life, but also his meticulous care in looking after his household accounts. Two informative articles concerning Browning's relationship to his son deserve mention. Gertrude Reese's "Robert Browning and his Son" (*PMLA*, 1946) traces reliably the career of Pen Browning to his death in 1912; Mrs. Betty Miller in "The Child of Casa Guidi" (*Cornhill Magazine,* 1948) explores young Browning's rebellion against his father and England, and his partiality for his mother and Italy.

An event of interest and importance to Browning scholars was the publication in 1953 of *The Diary of Alfred Domett 1872–1885*, edited by E. A. Horsman. Domett, it will be remembered, was Browning's intimate friend in the early forties before he emigrated to New Zealand. Upon his return to

England in 1871, their friendship was renewed. The entries in the *Diary* relating to Browning are fuller, more numerous, and in better context than the portions used by Griffin and Minchin in their *Life of Browning* (1910). The volume adds depth to our knowledge of Browning's later years.

IV. *Reputation*

The matter of Browning's reception by the critics and the public in his own time has concerned a number of scholars in recent years, and one may observe through several papers a tendency to challenge the traditional belief, fostered by the poet himself, that his work was neglected and scorned all through his early and middle years. Maurice Browning Cramer has published three articles dealing with Browning's reputation: "Browning's Friendships and Fame before Marriage (1833–1846)" (*PMLA*, 1940); "What Browning's Literary Reputation Owed to the Pre-Raphaelites, 1847–1856" (ELH, 1941); and "Browning's Reputation at Oxford, 1855–59" (*PMLA*, 1942). The first of these articles does not, in my opinion, alter appreciably the account of the poet's contemporary fame as we see it in T. R. Lounsbury's *The Early Literary Career of Robert Browning* (1911); and Cramer is inclined to confuse Browning's social with his literary success. One has only to look at the record of the poet's sales of his books, and remember that all of his early works, with one exception, were published at the expense of his family. The other two articles by Cramer have more to be said for them, but in each instance the author overstates his case.

Another small group of articles challenges my own statement in my *Browning Handbook* that the publication of *The Ring and the Book* made Browning a national figure. Mrs. Helen P. Pettigrew's "The Early Vogue of *The Ring and the Book*" (*Archiv*, April 1936) amasses a tremendous body of opinions about the poem, from 1868 to the moment of her writing, to show that less and less praise was accorded *The Ring and the Book* after the first volume was published. B. R. McElderry, Jr. published two articles on this point:

"Browning and the Victorian Public in 1868–69" (*Research Studies of the State College of Washington*, 1937); and "Victorian Evaluation of *The Ring and the Book*" in the same periodical (1939). The main point of McElderry's first article is one that has never been in question, namely, that Browning's reputation had been growing steadily in the decade of the sixties, and that the Victorian public and critics were prepared to welcome him warmly when his long poem began to appear in 1868. The second article is a good analysis of the most competent criticism of *The Ring and the Book* — admiration mixed with disappointment — in 1868–69. The poem, I think, called the nation's attention to Browning as a poet to be ranked with Tennyson.

The matter of Browning's fame should not be left without a reference to Louise Greer's comprehensive and reliable account of the poet's reception in this country. Her *Browning and America* was published in 1952.

V. *Letters*

Letters are, of course, frequently the most important sources for an author's biography. In Browning's case there are hundreds of them still unpublished, but no part of his career is without representation in the collections now available in print. Early letters, however, are scarce. Since Dean Thurman L. Hood published his large and thoroughly edited collection, *Letters of Robert Browning, Collected by Thomas J. Wise*, in 1933, several notable additional collections have been made. In 1937 Richard Curle edited a correspondence under the title, *Robert Browning and Julia Wedgwood, A Broken Friendship as Revealed by their Letters*. These are biographically important for the years 1864–68 when Browning was writing *The Ring and the Book*, and especially so for his defense of his own poetic method and subject against Julia Wedgwood's attack. He explains and defends his professional interest in evil. Frequently he comments upon the poetry of his contemporaries, and gives an illuminating account of what he would have done with the Enoch Arden story. He sets at rest, also, any lingering doubts about the date and circumstance of his first sight of the *Sonnets from the Portuguese* and their publication (pp. 99–103). Browning's mild flirtation with Miss Wedgwood, a bluestocking of a distinguished intellectual family, was broken off by the lady herself when it seemed to her that she was becoming emotionally involved. The incident served as a prelude to the affair between Browning and Louisa Lady Ashburton a few years later.

New Letters of Robert Browning, edited by William Clyde DeVane and Kenneth Leslie Knickerbocker (1950), contains approximately four hundred letters from every period of Browning's career. A good many of the letters included in this volume are merely for the record, but there are some significant ones from William C. Macready, the tragedian, having to do with the poet's plays, and from John Forster, the critic. But the most important letters in this volume are written by Browning to Chapman, his publisher between 1849 and 1867, and reveal both the poet's financial difficulties before Kenyon's bequest came to his rescue in 1856, and also the meager sale of his books, notably *Christmas-Eve and Easter-Day* and *Men and Women*.

In 1923 A. J. Armstrong of Baylor University published the *Letters of Robert Browning to Miss Isa Blagden*, a collection most important for the years 1861–72, that is, the period of Browning's return to England after the death of his wife. Through these letters, scholars (notably W. O. Raymond, as we shall see) have been able to trace the history of the genesis and composition of *Dramatis Personae* (1864) and *The Ring and the Book* four years later. They have also proved most fruitful as a record of Browning's moods in these years, his interests and movements, and his reading. Armstrong presented the letters, however, without sufficient editorial apparatus, and with some mistakes in dating. In 1951 this fault was handsomely remedied by Edward C. McAleer, who published the letters, augmented by others to Miss Blagden and excellently edited, under the title *Dearest Isa, Robert Browning's Letters to Isabella Blagden*. It is a great satisfac-

tion to Browning scholars to have this important correspondence in thoroughly usable condition.

Besides these large collections of letters, a few other smaller
groups have appeared in recent years. In 1935 a little volume
was published by The United Feature Syndicate in New
York with the title, *Twenty-two Unpublished Letters of
Elizabeth Barrett Browning and Robert Browning, Addressed
to Henrietta and Arabella Moulton-Barrett*. No editor's name
appears, but there is a Foreword by J. A. S. Altham, a grand-
son of Captain Surtees Cook who married Elizabeth Barrett's
sister, Henrietta. This volume is properly a pendant to
Leonard Huxley's volume of 1929, *Elizabeth Barrett Browning: Letters to her Sister, 1846–1859*. These letters reveal the
intimate married life of the Brownings, especially in the early
years. Two other small groups of letters have been published
by W. H. G. Armytage: "Robert Browning and Mrs. Pattison:
Some Unpublished Browning Letters" (*TQ*, 1951–52); and
"Some New Letters of Robert Browning, 1871–1889" (*MLN*,
1951). In the first group the lady is Mrs. Emily Pattison, later
the wife of Sir Charles Dilke, who was the original of Doro-
thea in George Eliot's *Middlemarch*. The second group is
addressed to the wife and daughter of A. J. Mundella, a
liberal politician and champion of trade unions who was in
Gladstone's second, third and fourth administrations. These
are social letters of no great consequence, but those to Mrs.
Pattison are biographically interesting for Browning's life
in the seventies. There are numerous single letters published
in scattered places, but one in particular deserves mention
for its vivid description of the poet's home in Warwick Cres-
cent, and of the poet himself as he appeared in the eighties.
He is described by Caroline Chase in July, 1883, as short,
well-proportioned, with white hair and penetrating blue eyes,
kindly and full of vitality (W. L. Phelps, "A Conversation
with Browning" in *ELH*, 1944). He came from his writing
desk in his slippers and with no tie. He had evidently recov-
ered from the physical prudery which Mrs. Miller remarks
upon as a prominent characteristic of his in her *Portrait*.

Besides the letters from Browning to his various correspondents, three groups of considerable usefulness to the Browning scholar have been published from the collections at Baylor University. In 1934 A. J. Armstrong assembled a large number of letters written to the poet, and published them with the title, *Intimate Glimpses from Browning's Letter File.* This book frequently enables the scholar to follow the course of a correspondence between Browning and a friend much more satisfactorily than could otherwise be possible, and we learn many intimate details which might be lost if these letters had not been preserved. In 1932 a group of hitherto unpublished letters of W. S. Landor was published in the *Fifth Series of Baylor University's Browning Interests* (pp. 12–64), and Landor's early comments upon and to Browning shed credit on both authors. In 1936 a larger volume was published from the same rich store: *Letters from Owen Meredith (Robert, First Earl of Lytton) to Robert and Elizabeth Barrett Browning,* edited by Aurelia Brooks Harlan and J. Lee Harlan, Jr. These letters from Browning's first ardent disciple allow much insight into the personality of the poet as seen in Florence in the fifties, and it is pleasant and informative to see the author of *Men and Women* instructing Lytton in the poetry of John Donne (pp. 144, 187).

VI. *Studies of Ideas*

There is a solid foundation of works devoted specifically to Browning's philosophy and ideas, such as Henry Jones' *Browning as a Philosophical and Religious Teacher* (1891), which is still authoritative in this area of thought; F. R. G. Duckworth's *Browning, Background and Conflict* (1923), Part II of which is especially valuable; and my early work, *Browning's Parleyings,* which traces the development of the poet's thought in the major fields of his interest. Notice should be taken here of Robert Spindler's exhaustive and able study of Browning's classical poems in his large work, *Robert Browning und die Antike* (1930). Half of this volume is devoted to the Balaustion poems, and the other half to the *Agamemnon,* the shorter poems, and classical allusions throughout Browning's verse. Spindler is especially interested in the English poet's attitude towards Euripides and Aristophanes, and draws the shrewd conclusion that Browning is interested in the non-classical features of the classics. This book is a definitive achievement in its scholarship, though the criticism of Browning's poetry is perhaps too eulogistic.

Much new work of a high caliber has been done recently. F. A. Pottle's small but excellent volume, *Shelley and Browning, A Myth and Some Facts* (1923), cleared the way for a sounder consideration of Browning's relationship to Shelley, and therefore opened the broader question of his debt and reaction to his romantic predecessors in poetry. This is the problem dealt with in Lionel Stevenson's "Tennyson, Browning, and a Romantic Fallacy" (*TQ*, 1943–44). As Tennyson won his freedom from some romantic trends in his early poems, such as "The Lady of Shalott" and "The Palace of Art" (entering perhaps into an equal tyranny), so Browning through *Pauline, Paracelsus,* and *Sordello* freed himself from the vague, vast schemes for human betterment which were characteristic of the romantic Shelley. Browning's departure from his romantic beginnings appears frequently in different forms in a good deal of recent comment, notably in the work of S. W. Holmes referred to above. The last word upon Browning's relationship to the romantic poets, and to Shelley particularly, has not been written; there is, for example, a wish on the part of writers psychologically inclined, as Mrs. Miller is, to read into Browning's Puritanical abandonment of Shelley a profound sense of sin, as if he had betrayed Shelley and his own freedom in his submission to the more orthodox views of his family and his time upon religion and society. E. D. H. Johnson, however, in his volume, *The Alien Vision of Victorian Poetry* (1952), without invoking "the sense of sin," sees the strong individualistic personality of Browning in constant, but veiled, rebellion against the social and moral shackles of orthodox Victorian thought. This book is characterized by its insight and steady judgment throughout, and many new interpretations of Browning's poetry are suggested.

The failure of Browning as a dramatist for the acting stage is now generally admitted, but the reasons for the failure are matters still requiring study. In a comprehensive paper entitled "Robert Browning, Dramatist" (*SP*, 1936), Arthur E. DuBois analyzes the plays into their various types, and sees Browning moving in his sympathy away from the ideal toward the real and the ironic, but never achieving a sufficient distance to attain the healing attribute of laughter. Each play pictures a protagonist caught between an impossible idealization and a disillusioning reality — Strafford and a worthless king, for example. Hence the irony, and therefore the tragedy. Only *A Soul's Tragedy* escapes into prose, comedy, and irony. But in most of his plays Browning stopped indecisively short of the irony and consequent laughter which he attains in such dramatic monologues as *Bishop Blougram's Apology* and *Fra Lippo Lippi*. The reasons for Browning's failure as a dramatist are several: his failure to follow through his ideas to their ultimate social and ethical conclusions; his inability to handle pure drama or melodrama; his failure to improve with experience; and the strong tendency of his age towards hero-worship and a self-centered individualism. But in his conclusion, DuBois has a good word for the bold experimentation of Browning in *Pippa Passes*. His final judgment, however, is that Browning's failure to revivify the stage is the most sensational failure in nineteenth-century drama.

In one of a series of papers on several aspects of Browning's poetry that ought to be collected into a book, H. B. Charlton approaches the matter somewhat differently. His brilliant article, "Browning as Dramatist," was published in the *Bulletin of the John Rylands Library* (1939). Browning's failure as a dramatist, in Charlton's opinion, resulted from the poet's temperamental blindness to the group as an organic unit. As a Nonconformist, Browning saw nothing between God and the individual. But the theatre is a corporate thing, and requires corporate emotions and corporate language. Not recognizing society as an entity, Browning was unfortunate in choosing political themes for several of his plays, and principles as political motives disappear in the presence of single moral giants, preferences, and animosities. There was a unique genius in Browning, closely allied to the genius which produced great drama, but the conventional drama stifled his dramatic gifts. Because he hardly recognized society as a separate being and a force, he inevitably moved to the dramatic monologue. Nevertheless, in Charlton's opinion, if Browning had written nothing after *Pippa Passes*, it would have been said that the world had lost a stupendous dramatist, for the scene between Ottima and Sebald is the finest single scene of drama in the whole of the nineteenth century. However, continues Charlton, that judgment would have been mistaken, for Browning was incapable of including the great world with its multitudinous interests, as a truly great dramatist must have done. The primary cause of his failure was his conviction that man's relation to God is infinitely more important than his relation to his fellow men.

Two shorter articles dealing with Browning and dramatic matters deserve comment here. In his volume, *From Shakespeare to Joyce* (1944; especially Chapter Seventeen), E. E. Stoll deals with the matter of improbability of the action in drama. There are higher things than the probable in a play, and "Improbability, at the outset, is the inescapable price of the supreme situation. . . ." But improbabilities should not come *within* the play. Stoll's illustration of his point is Browning's *In a Balcony*; he finds Constance and Norbert convincing, however, in the love scene. But he finds Browning esoteric, too philosophical and erudite, and the play, relying upon conventions no longer acceptable, not meant for the common man. The ending, besides not being clear as to what actually happened and what motives caused whatever happened, lacks the needed depth of tone.

In a short paper entitled "The Dramatic Monologue" (*PMLA*, 1947), Ina Beth Sessions analyzes this poetic form in its relationship to the lyric on one side and the drama on the other. She sets up seven criteria for perfection in the dramatic monologue: (1) the speaker; (2) the audience; (3) the occasion; (4) interplay between the speaker and his audience;

(5) revelation of character; (6) dramatic action; and (7) action taking place in the poem's present. The paper is clear and useful. A much longer treatment of this genre is B. W. Fuson's *Browning and his English Predecessors in the Dramatic Monolog,* in the State University of Iowa's Humanistic Studies in condensed form in 1942 and again in 1948. This work is a timely reminder that Browning had innumerable predecessors in the use of the dramatic monologue, from classical literature, through Chaucer and Donne among others, to the nineteenth century. Browning was "not pioneer but past master." His "contribution to the genre . . . lay in his transfer of focus from melodrama and exploitation of emotion *per se* to psychological subtlety in a dramatic monolog." (But this comment hardly gives sufficient credit to Browning's real achievements in refining and developing the dramatic monologue.) The first chapter of Fuson's work is especially valuable for its study of the form.

One of the most illuminating chapters in W. O. Raymond's volume *The Infinite Moment* is his eighth, entitled "Browning's Casuists." As we have seen above, Browning vigorously defended his interest in evil when he was attacked upon that score by Julia Wedgwood. To him it was in the first degree necessary for the kind of poet he was to understand the motives that activated men in the conduct of their lives, and evil in its varied guises was obviously a major element in human lives. As Raymond says, Browning's intellectual agnosticism enters as an important element in the casuistical monologues, though it is not a complete explanation of their genesis. We must add his psychological bent, his passion for case-making, his pleasure in the adroit play of the mind, and his love of the odd and bizarre, and above all, perhaps, the ethical necessity he felt to cope with the fact of evil in the world in view of his instinctively optimistic reading of life. From these bases, Raymond analyzes Browning's casuists from *Sordello* to the *Parleyings,* and does it with the acumen and steady judiciousness that we have come to expect of him.

Donald Smalley, as was suggested above, is primarily concerned in his book, *Browning's Essay on Chatterton*, with Browning's "pattern of imposture," and sees in the *Essay* that pattern in the early stages of its formation. He shows in his analysis of the poet's slippery characters that the formula, once arrived at, became rigid, and is of the opinion that Browning largely created what he dissected. This accounts, in part, for the large amount of Browning doctrine and language which is allowed to such personages as Djabal, Blougram, Sludge, Hohenstiel-Schwangau, and Disraeli. All these characters voice the poet's ideas concerning the art of ruling their fellow men, and illustrate Browning's confident willingness to let his villains make the best case for themselves that they can.

In an interesting article, "Browning, the Simple-hearted Casuist" (*TQ*, 1949), Hoxie N. Fairchild develops the thesis that Browning, in spite of his subtlety of thought, its difficulties and ambiguities, sinuous twistings and casuistical rationalizations, could never resist the obligation he felt to satisfy the demands of his healthy and almost boyishly simple heart. Therefore Browning almost always provided a "giveaway," usually at the end of his monologues. The speakers often unmask themselves with excessively naïve alacrity, and the reader is told what to think. This is true, and is an artistic flaw in a number of Browning's poems, but perhaps Fairchild does not give sufficient weight, as an extenuation, to the fact that the innovating poet was employing a form of poetry that was relatively new to his Victorian readers, and also that he had ample and bitter experience with the failure of his dull and obtuse audience to understand his meaning.

One of the best of contemporary writers upon Browning is H. B. Charlton of the University of Manchester. In his essay, "Browning's Ethical Poetry," published in the *Bulletin of the John Rylands Library* (1942–43), the poet's ethical tenets are thoughtfully examined and illustrated. Such topics as natural character and moral choice, Browning's conception of the good man, and the validity of his conception for us are considered. Can we adopt his ethics without subscribing to his metaphysical doctrines? Charlton concludes that Browning at his best does satisfy our understanding, and wins our sympathy. He has through his imaginative apprehension added permanently to our awareness. These gifts of the poet are best seen in the *Dramatic Lyrics, Dramatic Romances, Men and Women, Dramatis Personae,* and are capped by the monologue of the Pope in *The Ring and the Book.* Apprehension is the poet's truth, a combination of imagination and thought. After 1868 Browning's confidence in his religious premises became less, and his inspiration gave way to ratiocination and didacticism. As I have said before, Charlton's studies of Browning ought to be collected into a book and made available to a wider audience than they now reach.

Browning's religious ideas, as we are perhaps oppressively aware, engaged the attention of late Victorian critics to the exclusion of many other aspects of his poetry. Of course, his preoccupation with the subject, especially in his later and ratiocinative days, is responsible for this. The subject, however, continues to interest scholars but in a very different way and with the advantage of perspective. W. O. Raymond in the second chapter of *The Infinite Moment* traces and analyzes the poet's deep concern with the Higher Criticism of the Scriptures. This chapter, called "Browning and Higher Criticism," is the authoritative account of the poet's attempts, from *Christmas-Eve and Easter-Day* onward, to confront the historical biblical scholars of Germany, France, and England with a defense of orthodox Christian belief. In the course of his defense, Browning developed a profound distrust of reason, amounting at last to intellectual agnosticism, and came to regard the Incarnation and the Crucifixion as historical facts incapable of proof or disproof. He fell back upon his faith in the intuitive testimony of his heart to the existence of a loving, self-sacrificing God, working with a redemptive and transfiguring power in human experience. This faith he held to the end of his life. Thus, though holding to orthodox conclusions, he freed himself completely of orthodox dogmas. His position, as one should expect, is an intensely individualistic one.

The primary concern of C. R. Tracy in his article, "Browning's Heresies" (*SP*, 1936), is to show that the poet as a young man was deeply affected by the teachings of William J. Fox, the powerful Unitarian preacher of South Place Chapel and Browning's champion in literary matters for many years. (As early as 1840 Philip Harwood gave a series of lectures on Strauss, the rationalist and biblical critic, at the Chapel and it is probable that Browning attended them.) At any rate, Fox's views upon Calvinism, original sin, predestination, eternal punishment, the Incarnation, and atonement produced a conflict in Browning, reared as he was in a conservative, Nonconformist home, and many of Fox's beliefs became permanent features of Browning's thinking. Tracy follows up his arguments here with a brilliant analysis of Browning's *Caliban upon Setebos* (*SP*, 1938). In this later essay he shows that the poem is not primarily an attack upon anthropomorphism, as is often thought, but rather that an anthropomorphic conception of the Deity is necessary to man at any stage of his development. Caliban conceived of Setebos empirically to explain the hard facts of his everyday experience. The Quiet, the other half of the Deity, is not anthropomorphic, but is an intuitive answer to the deeper needs of Caliban's dawning perception. Caliban's deficiency in theology is that he has not seen the connection between the Quiet and Setebos; but the parallel with Christian theology is intimated, for man needs both the infinite, omnipotent, mysterious God and also God incarnate in Jesus, who knows love, anger, joy, and sorrow as we do.

For a final study of Browning's religious ideas we turn again to H. B. Charlton, whose essay, "Browning as Poet of Religion," published in the *Bulletin of the John Rylands Library* (1942–43), is analytical rather than historical in its method. Charlton insists that we regard Browning as a poet rather than as a philosopher. His creed was simple, and most valid where it is most poetically expressed: the God of Power is revealed as the God of Love by the Incarnation. This is the essential miracle and revelation, for the Incarnation provides the human spirit's access to God, and assures the individual of immortality. In contrast to Raymond and Tracy,

Charlton turns for evidence chiefly to the poems of Browning's *Men and Women*. He sees that in the still and thoughtful years of the poet's life in Italy, Browning arrived at certain conclusions in his attempt to resolve into unity the diversities of man and God, time and eternity, the relative and the absolute, the real and the ideal. The first conclusion was that the central and most important fact of history was the Incarnation of Christ; the second conclusion, also secondary in importance, was that after the Incarnation, the Renaissance was the most important epoch in human history. This second conclusion rose naturally in Browning because of his intense interest in individuality, and the Renaissance was *par excellence* the era in which men found personality. He was thus naturally led to the artist, preferably highly eccentric, for the artist is a priest in the temple of the world. And so too is the lover. Through this happy combination of Art, Love, and Religion, we get *Men and Women*. "The Pope" is unquestionably Browning's clearest argument for his religious position, but in *Men and Women* we apprehend the underlying belief even better, since it comes to us in terms of human love, color, and personality in action.

VII. *References to Individual Poems*

In dealing with the almost overpowering wealth and excellence of research upon Browning's poetry in the last quarter of a century, one is forced to be highly selective. Perhaps here is the best place to mention the new edition of my book, *A Browning Handbook* (1955). The new edition, rewritten in part and brought up to date in its scholarship, attempts to deal with each of Browning's poems in chronological order, in every case giving as far as possible the genesis, sources, and history of the poem, together with the appropriate critical and scholarly works upon it. In the *Handbook* many articles and books which lack of space has excluded from the present commentary are referred to, used, and appraised.

The Ring and the Book, as Raymond asserts, has unquestionably received more attention than any other single poem in Browning's canon. Based upon the solid foundation of A. K. Cook's *Commentary upon Browning's The Ring and the Book* (1920), and Raymond's own work, now collected as Chapters Four, Five, and Six of *The Infinite Moment*, scholarship upon the poem has enjoyed a strong renaissance. Perhaps the most recent comprehensive study of the poem is B. R. McElderry's study, "The Narrative Structure of Browning's *The Ring and the Book*" in *Research Studies of the State College of Washington* (1943). This is an excellent statistical study of the poem, showing its psychological unity, the extraordinary organizing power it exhibits, and the extreme skill and ingenuity of the poet in avoiding repetition and digression. Through McElderry's tables one is able to see the perspective of each speaker upon the same events, as well as Browning's progress towards the central matter of the murder-trial. Paul Cundiff, "The Dating of Browning's Conception of the Plan of *The Ring and the Book*" (*SP*, 1941), shows that though Browning had not begun to write the poem until 1864, the subject was much in his mind in 1862. Cundiff modifies somewhat Raymond's "New Light on the Genesis of *The Ring and the Book*," which is now the fourth chapter of *The Infinite Moment*, but the pioneer work of Raymond still stands as a notable achievement, and as the essential truth. In another article, Cundiff clarifies Browning's title, "The Clarity of Browning's Ring Metaphor" (*PMLA*, 1948). In a brief but significant article, "Fra Celestino's Affidavit and *The Ring and the Book*" (*MLN*, 1943), Paul E. Beichner, C.S.C., points out that under the seal of confession, the affidavit of Fra Celestino in Pompilia's behalf, upon which Browning puts so much faith in his favorable view of her character, is not valid as evidence, since Celestino could have said nothing else, and to remain silent would have been an admission of Pompilia's guilt.

J. E. Shaw's excellent article "The *Donna Angelicata* in *The Ring and the Book*" (*PMLA*, 1926), gave strong impetus to the growing conviction among scholars since Cook's *Commentary* that Browning, for all his attention to the detailed facts in his sources, The Old Yellow Book and The Secondary Source, and his insistence that he had faithfully followed his story, has written a chivalric study of life and character rather than a history of an obscure Roman murder-case involving very ordinary people. This position is reinforced by my paper, "The Virgin and the Dragon," in *The Yale Review* (1947) where I point out that the theme of the rescue of the innocent woman in distress had been used steadily by Browning since *Pauline* in many poems. In *The Ring and the Book* there are at least thirty allusions to the Perseus-Andromeda myth and the cognate legend of St. George's slaying of the dragon. How each speaker deals with the myth serves as a touchstone of his character.

This article, by the way, is related to the modern penchant for imagery and symbolism. J. K. Bonnell's "Touch Images in the Poetry of Robert Browning" (*PMLA*, 1922) is one of the earliest as well as one of the best studies of this kind. In my *Browning's Parleyings*, Chapter Two, I surveyed Browning's use of the moon-symbolism in his references to Mrs. Browning. C. Willard Smith makes an interesting study of the poet's use of the stars in his book *Browning's Star-Imagery* (1941). This study is particularly fruitful in its analyses of "Pompilia" and "The Pope." In the first of these books of the poem the star-image signifies Caponsacchi; in "The Pope" the stars represent an ideal of universal truth. Smith's work is significant of a new trend in Browning scholarship, as well as arresting in itself.

Since the publication of *The Ring and the Book* a large amount of new material concerning the Roman murder-case has come to light. I shall touch only upon recent developments in this area. Series Eleven (1939) and Twelve (1941) of the *Baylor Bulletin* contain documents which Browning could not have known, but which shed a good deal of light upon the actual happenings in Rome in 1698, and indirectly upon Browning's judgment of the case. The most interesting, voluminous, and illuminating store, however, is that described by Beatrice Corrigan in her paper, "New Documents on Browning's Roman Murder Case" (*SP*, 1952). Here we

learn a great deal about Pompilia's birth (she was not illegitimate), her introduction into the Comparini household, and
her marriage; and much else about Pietro and Guido. To end
this section upon a lighter note, F. E. Faverty has discovered
the facts concerning the career of the Abate Paolo subsequent
to Guido's execution and recorded them in "The Absconded
Abbot in *The Ring and the Book*" (*SP*, 1939). Ten years after
his flight, we see Paolo seeking a pension and a bishopric
from King Charles III of Spain, still servile, importunate, and
wily. As Faverty says, he probably became a bishop and lived
to a villainous and prosperous old age.

There are many excellent articles upon others of Browning's poems, but of necessity one must be highly selective,
and they can receive here only the briefest of comments,
though they deserve much more. Two articles upon *Pippa
Passes* must be mentioned. These are F. E. Faverty's " The
Source of the Jules-Phene Episode in *Pippa Passes*" (*SP*,
1941), and J. M. Ariail's "Is *Pippa Passes* a Dramatic Failure?" (*SP*, 1940). The title of the first indicates its nature; the
second is a vigorous defense of Browning's poem. Two other
articles, dealing with *The Flight of the Duchess*, are noteworthy: "New Light on the Brownings," by Edward Snyder
and Frederick Palmer, Jr. (*Quarterly Review*, 1937); and
Fred M. Smith's "Elizabeth Barrett and Browning's *The
Flight of the Duchess*" (*SP*, 1942). Each of these independently
emphasizes the fact that the poem was written while Browning was courting Miss Barrett and was a part of his campaign,
and Snyder and Palmer make a great deal of the criticism
which Elizabeth Barrett gave the poem during its composition. They base their arguments upon an unpublished letter
of Miss Barrett's written in July, 1845. An article which is a
model of its kind of scholarship is Louis S. Friedland's
"Ferrara and *My Last Duchess*" (*SP*, 1936). Friedland con-
clusively proves, I think, that the person from whose character and career Browning's duke is drawn is Alfonso II, Fifth
Duke of Ferrara, and the duchess was Lucrezia de' Medici,
who was fourteen years old at her marriage and died at seventeen under suspicious circumstances, after living with her

husband a little more than a year. The other details fit admirably.

Several poems from *Men and Women* profit by a close attention from scholars. In 1945, J. A. S. McPeek wrote "The Shaping of *Saul*" (*Journal of English and Germanic Philology*), to show how closely Browning follows the structure and development of the incident about David's cure of Saul in Sir Thomas Wyatt's *Seven Penitential Psalms*. Wyatt introduces the redemption theme to the story and anticipates Browning in so doing. I think Browning found in Wyatt the addition he needed to make *Saul* complete after he had exhausted the help which Smart's *Song to David* had given him.

Johnstone Parr's article, "The Site and Ancient City of Browning's *Love among the Ruins*" (*PMLA*, 1953) shows that the poem was written at a time when great excavations were being conducted in Italy, Egypt, Assyria, Greece, and Babylon, and that Browning was certainly familiar with the literature upon the subject. The ancient city may be Nineveh. He seems unaware, however, of a first draft of the poem in the Harvard Library which is headed by the title "A Sicilian Pastoral." For F. E. L. Priestley's keen and closely reasoned paper, "Blougram's Apologetics" (*TQ*, 1946), one can have only a profound admiration. He shows that the victory is entirely Blougram's, as that clever master of debate forces Gigadibs to abandon position after position. Priestley agrees with C. R. Tracy ("Bishop Blougram," *Modern Language Review*, 1939) that Browning's purpose in the poem was not to satirize the Catholic Bishop (Wiseman) but rather to comment upon the problem of faith in a skeptical world.

A good deal of excellent research has been done on a number of Browning's later poems but most of it is included in the major books which I have mentioned above. Two notable exceptions should be mentioned: Martha Hale Shackford's pamphlet, *The Brownings and Leighton* (1942), and Donald Smalley's article, "A Parleying with Aristophanes" (*PMLA*, 1940). These papers shed light upon Browning's classical interests, and emphasize his strong partiality for Euripides.

I cannot leave this survey without expressing the conviction that research upon Browning has improved in quality significantly during the last quarter of a century. I am unhappily conscious of failing to mention here much that is very good. I should also like to speak a word of welcome to a new periodical which has appeared in the last decade: *The Explicator*, whose brief interpretative essays, such as Louise S. Boas' paper on *The Glove* (II, Item 13) and the lively discussions on *A Toccata of Galuppi's, Pictor Ignotus*, and other poems of Browning, add materially to our understanding.

4 ᘰ

Elizabeth Barrett Browning
Edward FitzGerald
Arthur Hugh Clough

A. McKinley Terhune

ELIZABETH BARRETT BROWNING

I. *Bibliography*

DESPITE REVELATIONS of the errant zeal of Thomas J. Wise in "discovering" rare first editions of nineteenth-century writers, his *Bibliography of the Writings in Prose and Verse of Elizabeth Barrett Browning* (1918) remains as a thorough compilation of the major publications of the poetess. The scholar must note, however, that the 1847 "Reading Edition" of *Sonnets* (p. 71) and "The Runaway Slave at Pilgrim's Point," 1849 (p. 84), were condemned by John Carter and Graham Pollard in *An Enquiry into the Nature of Certain Nineteenth Century Pamphlets* (1934). To these, Wilfred Partington added "A Song" (p. 138) printed "from ms.," 1907, citing it among newly identified suspected publications in *Thomas J. Wise in the Original Cloth* (1946).[1] Harry Buxton Forman's "bio-bibliographical note," *Elizabeth Barrett Browning and Her Scarcer Books*, privately printed (1896), was also included in *Literary Anec-*

---

[1] An earlier, though not identical, edition of this work was published in New York in 1939 with the title *Forging Ahead*.

dotes of the Nineteenth Century, edited by W. R. Nicoll and
T. J. Wise (two volumes, 1896). *Twelve Victorian Authors*
provides an extensive general bibliography. A recent Italian
bibliography is Livio Jannattoni's *Elizabeth Barrett Browning, con un Saggio di Bibliografia Italiana* (1953).

Gardner B. Taplin in "Mrs. Browning's Contributions to
Periodicals: Addenda" *(Papers of the Bibliographical Society
of America,* 1950) makes one correction to Wise's list and
adds twelve items. Hewette E. Joyce's "Mrs. Browning's Contributions to American Periodicals" *(MLN,* 1920) had been
anticipated by Wise. A brief but convenient reference list is
included in Dorothy Hewlett's *Elizabeth Barrett Browning*
(1952). Every bibliography of Robert Browning includes
items pertaining to his wife. Reference to the *Baylor University Bulletins* describing that university's Browning collection is essential in any study of Mrs. Browning. *Browning-
iana in Baylor University,* a bibliography by Aurelia Brooks
[Harlan], *Baylor University Bulletin* (1921) devotes three
pages to the poetess. The entries include many articles in
periodicals, although Miss Brooks states that she did not attempt to make the list complete. *Robert Browning: A Bibliography, 1830–1950* by L. N. Broughton, C. S. Northup, and
Robert Pearsall (1953) should also be consulted.

II. *Works and Correspondence*

The standard *Complete Works of Elizabeth Barrett Browning* is that edited by Charlotte Porter and Helen A. Clarke
with notes (six volumes, 1900). The poetical works have
appeared in single volumes in three authoritative editions:
the Globe, edited by F. G. Kenyon (1897); the Cambridge,
edited by H. W. Preston (1900); and the Oxford (1904).
Mrs. Browning's *Poems* (two volumes), first published in
1844, went through five editions in the following twenty
years. In successive editions, the number of poems was increased and those previously published were subjected to
considerable revision. The posthumous *Last Poems* was published in 1862. The following year (1863) *The Greek Chris-*

tian Poets and the English Poets was issued in book form. This essay had been published in *The Athenaeum* in ten installments between February and August, 1842. In 1866 *Elizabeth Barrett Browning's Poetical Works* appeared in five volumes. Although this is described on the title page as the "Seventh Edition" (of *Poems*), it was the first complete edition of her poetry. All these issues were published in London. The first edition of *Poems* was published in 1844 (postdated 1845) in New York with the title *A Drama of Exile: and Other Poems*. In 1914 F. G. Kenyon published *New Poems by Robert Browning and Elizabeth Barrett Browning* (1914) containing six of the latter's poems and "Miss Elizabeth Barrett Barrett's Criticisms of Some of Her Future Husband's Poems (1845)." All the poems and parts of the "Criticism" had been previously published. H. Buxton Forman edited *Elizabeth Barrett Browning: Hitherto Unpublished Poems and Stories* for the Boston Bibliophile Society (two volumes, 1914). Wise points out that the title is misleading, for many of the contents are fragments and the more important pieces had already appeared in print. The volume, however, contains an "inedited autobiography." A noteworthy recent publication is *Sonnets from the Portuguese, Centennial Variorum Edition*, edited with an introduction by Fannie Ratchford, with notes by Deoch Fulton (1950). It includes variant readings, transcribed from the Pierpont Morgan Library, British Museum, and Houghton Library manuscripts.

Many separate collections of Mrs. Browning's correspondence have been published. *The Letters of Elizabeth Barrett Browning to Richard Hengist Horne* was edited by S. R. T. Mayer (two volumes, 1877), and F. G. Kenyon published *The Letters of Elizabeth Barrett Browning* (two volumes, 1897). *The Letters of Robert Browning and Elizabeth Barrett Barrett (1845–1846)* contains two hundred and eighty-seven letters by the poetess (two volumes, 1899). This work has been reprinted a number of times. Wise published *Letters to Robert Browning and Other Correspondents by Elizabeth Barrett Browning* (1916); the "other correspondents" being Isa Blagden, Sarianna Browning, and Sir Uvedale Price. According to Wise, only thirty copies of the book were printed. In 1929 appeared *Elizabeth Barrett Browning: Letters to Her Sister, 1846–1859*, edited by Leonard Huxley. *Twenty-Two Unpublished Letters of Elizabeth Barrett Browning . . . to Henrietta and Arabella Moulton-Barrett* (1935) contains the rest of this correspondence. One letter only was withheld by a member of the family. The preface states that the Huxley edition contained "about one half the text of some 108 letters . . ." William Rose Benét published *From Robert and Elizabeth Browning: a Further Selection of the Barrett-Browning Family Correspondence* (1936). Eighteen new letters and three fragments appeared in *Letters from Elizabeth Barrett to B. R. Haydon (1842–1845)*, edited by Martha Shackford (1939).

Three recent additions have been made to the published correspondence. "Twenty Unpublished Letters of Elizabeth Barrett to Hugh Stuart Boyd" was published by Bennett Weaver in *PMLA* (1950). Through internal evidence, for most of the dates had to be conjectured, the editor assigns the letters to the period 1827–1838. "New Letters from Mrs. Browning to Isa Blagden" by Edward C. McAleer (*PMLA*, 1951) added nine new letters to that correspondence and supplied two passages deleted by Sir Frederick Kenyon in preparing his 1897 edition. Betty Miller's *Elizabeth Barrett to Miss Mitford* (London, 1953; New Haven, 1954) provides a selection of 142 from a total of 381 unpublished letters in the collection at Wellesley College. The letters were written between 1836 and 1846, years which Mrs. Miller appropriately describes as "the most significant and formative in the life of Elizabeth Barrett." The editor was confronted not only by a major problem in selecting letters to be published — " A high proportion," she states in her preface, "was found to vary in length between two and four thousand words a letter" — but also by the equally difficult one of making deletions from those selected. An associated item is "Some Unpublished Papers of Robert and Elizabeth Browning," edited with a commentary by George S. Hellman (*Harpers*, 1916). The article contains letters to the Brownings from Elizabeth's brother, G. G. M. Barrett, Fanny Kemble and others, and a note by Boyd recording Elizabeth's reading with him during 1830.

III. *Biography*

The task of treating adequately in limited space the biographies of Elizabeth Barrett Browning (often combined with the story of her husband's life) confounds the writer. The Kenyon one-volume edition of Mrs. Browning's poetry (1897) contains a brief prefatory note by her husband, written to correct errors in a memoir by John H. Ingram which appeared in 1887 (post-dated, 1888). Earlier biographical essays had been published by Peter Bayne. Lillian Whiting's *The Brownings, Their Life and Art* (1911) touches their art lightly but recounts their daily lives in great detail. Miss Whiting writes of the French and Italian settings in which the Brownings moved and of political events in Italy with a sure hand. The passages from the correspondence in Percy Lubbock's *Elizabeth Barrett Browning in her Letters* (1906) are selected with discrimination and are accompanied by illuminating independent commentary. In *La Vie et l'Œuvre d'Elizabeth Barrett Browning* by Germaine-Marie Merlette (1905), the poetess is enthusiastically recommended to French readers. Anne Thackeray Ritchie in *Records of Tennyson, Ruskin, and Browning* (1892) provides intimate glimpses of the Brownings in England, France, and Italy. "The most celebrated honeymoon of literary history" is reported, in part, by five letters written by Mrs. Anna Jameson in whose company the bride and groom journeyed from Paris to Italy. The letters were published by George K. Boyce under the title "From Paris to Pisa with the Brownings" (*The New Colophon*, 1950).

With 1928 came a flood of Browning biography; the crest was reached in 1929 and 1930. Some of the books which appeared deal with Elizabeth alone; others combine the story of the two Brownings; some are restricted to their love affair and married life; some are fictionalized treatments of their subjects. Three only will receive special comment: Osbert Burdett's *The Brownings* (1928), Jeannette Marks's *The Family of the Barrett* (1938), and Dorothy Hewlett's *Elizabeth Barrett Browning* (1952). Mr. Burdett's book is mentioned, not because he has any new contributions to make, for he does not; but he did succeed in adequately compressing the story of the two lives for the first time within a single volume. Although errors creep into the story, Burdett's psychological insight makes the book noteworthy. He is objective and impartial but never dull. His evaluations of the poetry are pertinent and sound but all too brief and incidental. The book is not documented. Miss Marks's book is the antithesis of Burdett's. She has much to tell us that is new; the fifty-three pages of documentation should satisfy the most exacting scholar. Although the subject is the entire Barrett family, Elizabeth and her father are selected for full examination. The book strives to make clear the motives behind the elder Barrett's attitudes toward his offspring and to correct the popular "ogre" portrait which has become fixed in the public mind. The sections of the book devoted to the poetess are indispensable to an understanding of her; the approach is sympathetic but not sentimental. The effect of Elizabeth's ailments on her personality and her dependence on narcotics are examined. Miss Marks ignores literary criticism — that is not her concern; but attention is given to the emotional and social patterns which produced *Aurora Leigh* and other poems. Criticism of the poetry is lacking in Miss Hewlett's book also, but the work is the first competent full-scale biography of which Mrs. Browning is the sole subject. The substance is drawn chiefly from the correspondence, some of it unpublished; but the new letters add little to what was already known. The book furnishes a good account of Mrs. Browning's many-sided personality and manifold interests in causes. In the main, the biography follows a year-by-year plan and is almost devoid of documentation. Because of features peculiar to each, these three biographies are superior to the majority on the subject, of which Isabel Clarke's adulatory *Elizabeth Barrett Browning* (1929) and Frances Winwar's

(Francesca Vinciguerra) *The Immortal Lovers* (1950) are examples. The approaches in these biographies range from informality to the blatant familiarity of David Loth's *The Brownings, A Victorian Idyll* (1929).

IV. *Criticism*

The contemporary and early criticism of Elizabeth Barrett Browning's poetry presents a bizarre mosaic of adulation and censure. She was generally hailed as England's greatest woman poet, and her strength of intellect was emphasized. One critic described her work as "the poetry of pure reason," while E. P. Whipple in *Essays and Reviews* (1848) objected to her "vast and vague imaginations" and charged that "a number of her poems are absolutely good for nothing." Margaret Fuller found her "singularly deficient in the power of compression" (*Art, Literature, and the Drama*, 1860); but John Ingram, in *Elizabeth Barrett Browning* (1888) stated that "apart from Dante and Shakespeare it would be difficult to meet with so great a condensation of thought . . ." Outspoken both in praise and censure was Edgar Allan Poe who, in "Miss Barrett's 'A Drama of Exile and Other Poems'," maintained that she "has done more, in poetry, than any woman, living or dead . . . Her poetic inspiration is the highest . . . Her sense of art is pure in itself, but has been contaminated by pedantic study of false models . . ." (*The Works of Edgar Allan Poe*, ten volumes, 1895). Peter Bayne, the most diligent of her early critics, published "Mrs. Barrett Browning" in *Essays in Biography and Criticism* (1857). *A Study of Elizabeth Barrett Browning* by Lillian Whiting (1899) is a full-scale critical examination; and L. E. Gates analyzes Mrs. Browning's work as part of the nineteenth-century reaction against Romanticism in "The Return to Conventional Life" (*Studies and Appreciations*, 1900).

Biographical studies of Elizabeth Barrett Browning have flourished at the expense of criticism. Even critiques of individual poems take a biographical bias. This is noted in Vir-

ginia Woolf's essay on "Aurora Leigh" (*Yale Review*, 1931).
Mrs. Woolf describes the poem as both stimulating and
boring, yet "a masterpiece in embryo." For all its imperfec-
tions, "it still breathes" and "Aurora the fictitious seems to be
throwing light on Elizabeth the actual." Mildred Wilsey examines the same poem for biographical elements in "Elizabeth Barrett Browning's Heroine" (*College English*, 1944).
Aurora Leigh has been the subject of many critiques, a recent
essay being that by Martha Shackford in *Studies of Certain
Nineteenth Century Poets* (1946). Browning's "The Flight
of the Duchess" as a reflection of his love affair with Elizabeth Barrett is analyzed by Frederic Palmer and Edward
Snyder in "New Light on the Brownings" (*QR*, 1937) and by
F. M. Smith in "Elizabeth Barrett and Browning's 'The
Flight of the Duchess' " (*SP*, 1942); see also Mr. Smith's ad-
dendum, "More Light on . . . 'The Flight of the Duchess' "
in the same periodical (1942). In "Elizabeth Barrett's Influence on Browning's Poetry" (*PMLA*, 1908), John W. Cunliffe states that "her best work is to be found not in her
own writings, but in his." Professor Cunliffe attributes "the
human sympathy, passionate fire, and lyrical beauty" of
poems in *Christmas-Eve and Easter-Day* (1850) and *Men and
Women* (1855) to Mrs. Browning's influence. These were the
only volumes published by the poet during his married life.

Mrs. Browning's rhymes have been roundly condemned by
critics, both sympathetic and hostile, since her poems first
appeared. F. M. Smith comes to her defense in "Mrs. Browning's Rhymes" (*PMLA*, 1939). He compares her rhymes with
those of Archibald MacLeish, W. H. Auden, and C. Day
Lewis, and asserts that if these poets are praised for " 'extend-
ing the gamut of rhyme . . .' then the opinion of Mrs.
Browning's rhymes should be revised." Mr. Smith maintains
that with Emerson and Emily Dickinson, Mrs. Browning engaged in a "revolt against traditional rhyming." The *Variorum Edition* of *Sonnets from the Portuguese* has already
been referred to (see "Works," above). The book contains an
introductory essay by Miss Ratchford. Rilke's translation of
the sonnets is the subject of "Rilke und Elizabeth Barrett

Browning" by Helmut Rehder (*JEGP*, 1934). According to Rehder, Rilke in his translation tends to convert the concrete and specific ideas of the original into general concepts. Thus:

> . . . meanest creatures
> Who love God, God accepts, while loving so

becomes

> Gott nimmt Geringe an, die sich gebärden
> so wie sie sind.

Rilke, Rehder asserts, was influenced by Mrs. Browning.

A record of the Brownings' Italian residence and the national events of the period, with the effect of both on the works of the poets, is the subject of "The Influence of Italy on the Poetry of the Brownings" by Ethel de Fonblanque in the *Fortnightly Review* (1909). "I honor America in much," Mrs. Browning wrote to Mrs. Jameson; and American readers repaid her esteem with whole-hearted approval of her poetry. The relations of the poetess with her American public are dealt with in *The Brownings and America* by Elizabeth P. Gould (1904) and are also touched upon in passing in *Browning and America* by Louise Greer (1952).

Of all Mrs. Browning's works, *Sonnets from the Portuguese* has best withstood a century of criticism. What balance will finally be struck in the evaluation of her poetry remains an open question. A new, comprehensive study, *Elizabeth Barrett Browning: A Critical Biography* by Gardner B. Taplin, has been accepted for publication in both England and the United States. Mr. Taplin reports that he expects the book will appear in 1956, the centenary of *Aurora Leigh*.

EDWARD FITZGERALD

I. *Bibliography*

Edward FitzGerald poses a dual bibliographical problem. His translation of the *Rubáiyát of Omar Khayyám* has engendered a literature of such formidable bulk that the most complete listing records almost 1,400 items. Ehrsam, Deily, and Smith's *Twelve Victorian Authors* provides scholars with the most comprehensive general bibliography to date. The only comparable list is that compiled by Charles Van Cise Wheeler before he sold his FitzGerald collection in 1919. The bibliography (with collations of all items in the Wheeler collection) was intended for private circulation, but publication was never completed. Copies of this work — three volumes in typescript — are deposited in the Library of Congress and the Newberry Library in Chicago. Until Mr. Stanley Pargellis, Librarian at the Newberry, very recently called that copy to my attention, the Library of Congress copy had been considered unique, as the title page states. The Newberry volumes are a carbon copy which, internal evidence establishes, Mr. Wheeler retained when he gave the original to the Library of Congress. Some, but not all, typographical errors have been corrected.

Complete bibliographies and collations of FitzGerald's works and casual writings (pamphlets and contributions to local periodicals) are found in W. F. Prideaux's *Notes for a Bibliography of Edward FitzGerald* (1901) and in the *Variorum and Definitive Edition of the Poetical and Prose Writings of Edward FitzGerald*, edited by George Bentham (seven volumes, 1902–1903). Prideaux's entries are annotated. He errs in assigning the undated first edition of FitzGerald's translation of *Agamemnon* (actually 1868) to 1865. Bentham implies a comparable date by placing the entry between publications of 1865 and 1868. Through frequent citation, unmerited value has been attributed to a number of brief and casual bibliographies. This is true of one bearing the title, *Edward FitzGerald, 1809–1883*, published by the Brooklyn Public Library (1909) and of that found in Holbrook Jackson's essay, *Edward FitzGerald and Omar Khayyám* (1899). The bibliographical appendix to Thomas Wright's *Life of Edward FitzGerald* is extremely informal and, in part, erroneous. The *CBEL* mistakenly lists *Edward and Pamela Fitzgerald* by G. Campbell (1904); Lord Edward Fitzgerald, the Irish patriot (1763–1798), not the translator, is the subject of the book.

Selective general bibliographies are available in two Fitz-Gerald biographies. A. McKinley Terhune in *The Life of Edward FitzGerald* lists 101 items with occasional annotations. Only four magazine articles are included. A representative list of books and articles up to 1900 may be consulted in *The Life of Edward FitzGerald* by John Glyde.

In part, the bulk of the "Omar Khayyám" and "Rubái-yát" literatures which have developed from FitzGerald's translation is peripheral to our subject. But also they are segments of the FitzGerald problem. Fortunately, the energy of writers in creating these literatures has been matched by the zeal of bibliographers in recording them. Much of this work has been done by non-professionals. One would err little by stating that *all* the literature on the subject up to 1929 has been recorded by Ambrose G. Potter in *A Bibliography of the Rubáiyát of Omar Khayyám* (1929). Mr. Potter lists 1,395 items. A second bibliography on the subject, less comprehensive though no less meritorious, appears in Nathan Haskell Dole's *Rubáiyát of Omar Khayyám, Multi-Variorum Edition* (two volumes, 1896).[2] Most of the entries include extensive commentary. Edward Heron-Allen's *Rubáiyát of Omar Khayyám* (1898) also contains an excellent list of references.

II. *Works and Correspondence*

The standard edition of FitzGerald's works is the *Letters and Literary Remains*, edited by William Aldis Wright (seven volumes, 1902–1903). This is a compilation of five separate publications of works and correspondence produced by Wright between 1889 and 1901 (see Terhune, p. 358) and should be considered the standard reference. Bibliographers persist in citing the original three-volume edition bearing

[2] This same work was issued by other publishers in both Boston and New York in 1898. The bibliography begins at volume II, p. 438, not p. 467, as stated in *Twelve Victorian Authors*.

the same title (1889) as though it were the standard, apparently unaware that it is not complete and was made obsolete by the 1902–1903 publication. Confusion has resulted. Wright's 1889 edition was preceded in 1887 by *Works of Edward FitzGerald* (two volumes) issued by FitzGerald's publisher, Bernard Quaritch. The most complete edition of FitzGerald's works, except for correspondence, is Bentham's *Variorum and Definitive Edition*.

Variations in the contents of these three principal editions should be noted. Wright alone published the correspondence and *The Bird Parliament*, translated from Attar's *Mantic ut-Tair*. Bentham gives the successive versions of FitzGerald's chief works as they evolved through revisions. Wright gives successive versions of *The Rubáiyát* only. Bentham published *Polonius, A Collection of Wise Saws and Modern Instances*; FitzGerald's venture into lexicography, *Sea Words and Phrases*; and the entertaining essay, "Percival Stockdale and Baldock Black Horse." All of these were ignored by Wright. *Polonius* and *Sea Words* were also published by Quaritch. In the margins of his edition Bentham gives the original pagination of FitzGerald's works, and he has noted corrections which the author made in some of his minor writings.

One editor and one biographer have attributed to Fitz-Gerald works of questionable authorship. The former was Charles Ganz, editor of *A FitzGerald Medley* (1933), a book most appropriately titled. With miscellania extracted from FitzGerald's correspondence, Ganz reprinted "Percival Stockdale and Baldock Black Horse" and *Sea Words and Phrases*, with additions to the latter written by FitzGerald in copies of his pamphlets. Ganz published for the first time *Little Nell's Wanderings*, an abstract, for children, of the *Old Curiosity Shop*. The volume requires comment chiefly because it includes the contents of a small book of poems attributed to FitzGerald by Thomas J. Wise. The volume, entitled (in part) *Translations into Verse from Comedies of Molière and Casimir Delavigne . . . to Which Are Added Original Poems . . . School Exercises* [etc.], was published in Paris, bearing the date 1829. *The Ashley Library*: A *Catalogue* states, "The little book . . . now ranks among the rarissima of nineteenth-century poetry." The validity of the ascription to FitzGerald's authorship is highly questionable. Thomas Wright, the biographer, attributed two poems, "The Old Beau" and "The Merchant and His Daughter," and character analyses of a number of FitzGerald's friends to the poet; but FitzGerald's authorship was denied by Aldis Wright in a letter to the *Athenaeum*. The claims of Ganz and Thomas Wright are evaluated and rejected in the Terhune biography.

On the scores of quality and quantity FitzGerald's correspondence merits consideration as part of his works. As a revelation of personality, interests, and activities it merits consideration as biography. All the letters published by Aldis Wright are contained in four volumes of his final edition. These were only a portion of the total; additions have since appeared in smaller collections. Mr. Wright's stated purpose is to permit his letters to tell the story of FitzGerald's life. The result is an admirable selection, and FitzGerald emerges as a likable though rather formal figure. A warmer and more humorous personality is revealed in F. R. Barton's *Some New Letters of Edward FitzGerald to Bernard Barton* (London, 1923; published in New York in 1924 as *Edward FitzGerald and Bernard Barton*). This volume is a delightful introduction to FitzGerald as a letter-writer and as a personality. FitzGerald's experience as the owner of a herring lugger is recorded in *Edward FitzGerald and "Posh"* by James Blyth (1908); his correspondence with his publisher appears in *Letters from Edward FitzGerald to Bernard Quaritch*, C. Quaritch Wrentmore, editor (1926); and a portion of his correspondence with his friend William Bodham Donne was published in *A FitzGerald Friendship*, Catharine B. Johnson and Neilson C. Hannay, editors (1932). Numerous letters are found in the memoirs and biographies of FitzGerald's friends, Tennyson, W. B. Donne, and Edward Byles Cowell, and in *The Letters and Papers of William Makepeace Thackeray*, edited by Gordon Ray (1945–1946). *Letters to*

Frederick Tennyson, Hugh J. Schonfield, editor (1930), sometimes cited with FitzGerald's correspondence, contains not one of his letters. Much of FitzGerald's correspondence is still unpublished. A complete edition is being prepared by A. McKinley Terhune.

III. *Biography*

I have already mentioned Aldis Wright's intention to permit FitzGerald to be his own biographer through his correspondence. However, through the process of selection, Wright became the biographer. He chose to reveal only those portions of FitzGerald's career and character consonant with the editor's concept of a Victorian gentleman of refinement and taste. Admirable as the work is, it fails as biography.

For almost fifty years *The Life of Edward FitzGerald* by Thomas Wright (two volumes, 1904) was accepted as the principal source of FitzGerald biographical data. The published correspondence and works were available to him for reference, but he could not consult the unpublished material in the possession of Aldis Wright. (The two Wrights were unrelated.) To balance this handicap the biographer was able to interview many persons who had known FitzGerald. In his book Mr. Wright found it difficult to omit any Fitz-Gerald association, however remote. The *Life* is discursive. Much of the information was drawn from gossip and hearsay garnered in the vicinity of Woodbridge and in FitzGerald's haunts along the Suffolk coast. To Thomas Wright, therefore, may be traced most of the apocryphal anecdotes and legends with which the reputation of FitzGerald has been burdened. Minor writings erroneously attributed to the translator by Wright have already been mentioned. He is also responsible for assigning the publication of FitzGerald's translation of *Agamemnon* to 1865. Despite shortcomings, the bulk of Wright's volumes enabled him to include a mass of detail which other biographers have been compelled to ignore. The numerous illustrations in the work are helpful in re-creating FitzGerald's physical environment. Wright's errors were given wider circulation by A. C. Benson's *Edward FitzGerald* (1905), written for the *English Men of Letters* series. Benson drew heavily on Thomas Wright for biographical data. He read the correspondence primarily for substance for his criticism. The book contributes nothing of biographical significance.

Two less pretentious biographies are *The Life of Edward FitzGerald* by John Glyde (1900) and *Omar's Interpreter* by Morley Adams (1909). Both are readable portraits, casual in approach, but often inaccurate in detail. A brief and informal but more reliable portrait is found in *Two Suffolk Friends* (1895), written by Francis H. Groome, son of Fitz-Gerald's lifelong friend, Archdeacon Robert H. Groome. The most recent sketch of FitzGerald's life achieves the questionable fame of being the least meritorious. *Into an Old Room* by Peter de Polnay (1949) is an inaccurate, flippant memoir with but one redeeming item: a genealogical chart of the Purcell family (in an appendix) — information neglected by previous biographers. FitzGerald's father was a Purcell, a family related to the FitzGeralds through a number of marriages. On the death of his father-in-law, Mr. Purcell adopted the name of his wife's family.

The Life of Edward FitzGerald, by A. McKinley Terhune (1947), the first authorized biography, is based on a mass of source material not available to any writer since Aldis Wright ended his editorial labors in 1903. The biography combines FitzGerald's life with critical evaluations of his works. Considerable new material is contributed to both subjects. The book is thoroughly documented.

IV. *The Rubáiyát*

As a result of FitzGerald's translation of *The Rubáiyát*, Omar, considered a minor poet in Persia, has won attention "far exceeding that bestowed on all the other poets put together," as one Persian scholar recently stated. Besides interpretation, the critical literature deals chiefly with three problems: the veracity of FitzGerald's translation; the authenticity of Omar's quatrains (a convenient translation for *rubáiyát*); and the relative validity of literal or symbolic interpretation of Omar's imagery. Only the principal essays dealing with these problems can be mentioned.

The veracity of FitzGerald's translation was questioned by Jessie E. Cadell in "The True Omar Khayyám" (*Fraser's Magazine*, 99,[3] 1879). FitzGerald published "a poem on Omar, rather than a translation of his work," she stated. John Payne in *The Quatrains of Omar Kheyyam* (1898) charged Fitz-Gerald with "a sin against literary morality." To expiate FitzGerald's, Payne committed a sin of his own in attempting to make a translation which was uncompromisingly literal — an impossible task. The introduction to Mr. Payne's book, however, is valuable to scholars interested in a study of Omar Khayyám. FitzGerald's adverse critics were answered by Heron-Allen in *Edward FitzGerald's Rubáiyát of Omar Khayyám* (1899).[4] Comparing FitzGerald's quatrains with their Persian originals, Heron-Allen definitely established the proportions of literalness and deviation, revealing that for the most part FitzGerald followed his sources closely. The dispute results, essentially, from that which FitzGerald ignored in his manuscript sources, and from the fact that, as he stated, "many Quatrains are mashed together." His defenders are represented by C. E. Norton, who maintained in a review of FitzGerald's second edition (*North American Review*, 1869) that FitzGerald had remained true to the spirit of the original, a claim which others have questioned. This and contingent problems have been clarified and resolved by Professor A. J. Arberry of the University of Cambridge without detraction from FitzGerald's achievement.

Professor Arberry's *Omar Khayyám* (1952) is a translation of a manuscript dated 1207, about seventy-five years after the poet's death. It is the oldest Omar manuscript yet discovered.

[3] Misnumbered "19" in *Twelve Victorian Authors*.

[4] *The Ruba'iyat of Omar Khayyām* by Heron-Allen (1898) contains a facsimile of the Bodleian manuscript used by FitzGerald and a transcript in modern Persian characters. The quatrains are literally translated and liberally annotated.

The reader at first regrets the alteration of rhythm effected by the use of the *In Memoriam* stanza into which the poem is converted. Nevertheless, Mr. Arberry succeeds where previous scholars have failed. The new translation reveals the *Rubáiyát* to be a penetrating and predominantly caustic analysis of life, lighted with humor and expressed with a subtlety characteristic of Persian poetry. One becomes aware that FitzGerald did not retain the spirit of the original but distilled from his sources an amiable hedonism and refined resignation with, now and again, rebellious protests against God and Fate. Yet FitzGerald lurks in almost every line of the new translation. The old substance is there; the matrix is altered. Mr. Arberry's introduction is invaluable for its examination of most of the Omar and Omar-FitzGerald problems. It discusses briefly but adequately the fluctuations of Omar's reputation and the authenticity of his quatrains. The author concludes that "Omar really was a substantial poet." In contrast, C. H. Rempis maintained that Omar was not a person but an accretion of poems attributed to the name but found in many sources (*Die Vierzeiler 'Omar Chajjams*, Tübingen, 1934, New York, 1935).

Many of Persia's chief lyric poets were Sufis, Mohammedan mystics who held pantheistic views. To disguise their heterodoxy they invested the traditional Persian lyric imagery with symbolic significance. From el Kifti, an Arabic writer of the twelfth century, to Arberry in 1952, most competent scholars have denied Omar's affiliation with Sufism. Despite this, a few scholars and many writers have insisted that Omar was a Sufi, that his poetry should be interpreted as a mystical allegory. The leading proponent of the theory is J. B. Nicolas, a French scholar who published *Les Quatrains de Khèyam* (1867). Nicolas's preface is translated in *The Sufistic Quatrains of Omar Khayyám*, a volume in *Universal Classics Library* (1903). The volume contains a second essay on the subject by Robert Arnot. The theory is also maintained by C. H. A. Bjerregaard in *Sufism: Omar Khayyám and E. FitzGerald* (1915); J. E. Saklatwalla in *Omar Khayyám as a Mystic* (1928); and others.

The scholar can most conveniently approach these problems through Dole's *Multi-Variorum Edition of the Rubáiyát*. The editor compares FitzGerald's five versions with English, French, and German translations. The lengthy introduction analyzes the subjects reviewed succinctly by Arberry. A volume of appendices contains the bibliography and a mass of material that defies listing. The notes to the quatrains in the second volume provide explications for allusions in Fitz-Gerald's poem. Another exposition of the work is found in *The Rubáiyát of Omar Khayyám* by H. M. Batson (1900). Explication is mixed with considerable subjective commentary. An analysis of the poem also appears in the Terhune biography.

FitzGerald's "Monkish Latin" version of the *Rubáiyát*, the form in which he first began to cast the poem, was published as *The Golden Cockerel Rubáiyát* (1938). The Latin has been translated and collated with FitzGerald's English quatrains by Sir E. Denison Ross. The result is of questionable value, considering the large proportion of editorial interpolation required to fill the many *lacunae* left by Fitz-Gerald in his manuscript. Note should be taken of J. R. Tutin's *A Concordance to FitzGerald's Translation of the Rubáiyát of Omar Khayyám* (1900).

V. *General Criticism*

Much criticism has been devoted to FitzGerald. Most of it, however, is general; much is eulogistic; little is objective. It is marked by extremes. "As a translator," says Saintsbury, "he stands almost alone, his peculiar virtue, noticeable alike in his versions from the Spanish and Greek . . ." Of the latter works Benson states, "But the plain truth is . . . that they are not really worth a very critical examination." Fitz-Gerald, like most of the lesser figures of the period, requires fresh analysis and criticism.

Benson's *FitzGerald*, the only extensive critique of Fitz-Gerald's works, is unfortunately one of the most hostile. "Perhaps it is ill to quarrel with a method deliberately adopted," said Benson of the translations from Calderon, Aeschylus, and Sophocles, "but . . ." and he proceeds with his quarrel. From the academic point of view much of Benson's adverse criticism is valid, but FitzGerald translated for those "not Greek." He strove to anticipate the criticism of scholars by explaining in his prefaces both his methods and purposes. These Benson ignored. It is evident that the critic felt little zeal and less sympathy for his subject. The book demonstrates the danger involved in writing criticism "on assignment." For more sympathetic yet balanced appraisals of FitzGerald, one should turn to the all-too-brief essays by Hugh Walker in *The Literature of the Victorian Era* (1921) and Oliver Elton in his *Survey of English Literature, 1780–1880* (four volumes, 1920). Comparable divergent reactions to FitzGerald's treatment of his originals are illustrated by criticisms of his Calderon translations. In his review, John Chorley, a contemporary Spanish scholar, considered it "quite unnecessary to treat as a serious work" so free a translation (*Athenæum*; No. 1350, 1853, p. 1063). On the other hand "Calderón en Inglaterra" in *Ensayos Críticos de Literatura Inglesa Española* by José de Armas (1910) is an analysis of FitzGerald's translation and a spirited defense of his method and achievement. John Addington Symonds, reviewing FitzGerald's translation of *Agamemnon* in *The Academy* (1877), observes that "the Greek student will find many of the most impressive passages suppressed, and some most carefully prepared effects omitted." He also remarks that "the strong sonorous verse has the richness and the elasticity of Marlowe's line; and for the first time . . . the English reader catches . . . a true echo of the pompous Æschylean manner."

Edmund Gosse described the essays in his *Critical Kit-Kats* (1896) as a combination of biography and criticism. FitzGerald was one of his subjects. So far as the translator is concerned, "kit-kats" have been as prolific as rabbits and have produced an incredible progeny. Most of the essays about FitzGerald are portraits composed of skimmings from the correspondence or an amalgam of data culled from biographies and the letters. Their chief contribution has been to circulate as much fiction as fact about FitzGerald's life and work. Some are sprightly and entertaining; some offer sound interpretation; the criticism, when it appears, is usually appreciative. FitzGerald sits for his portrait in Torrey Bradford's *Friends on the Shelf* (1906), and Gamaliel Bradford searches the correspondence for FitzGerald's soul in *Bare Souls* (1924). Even critics of repute seem to fall under the spell of FitzGerald's *dolce far niente* life, as Carlyle termed it, when they write of the translator. George E. Woodberry's essay "Edward FitzGerald" in *Literary Memoirs of the Nineteenth Century* (1921) is simply another portrait. Paul Elmer More in the *Shelburne Essays* (Second Series, 1905) writes on "Kipling and FitzGerald," but his remarks on the latter are injected as something of a footnote to a brilliant analysis of the sources of Kipling's popularity.

Among the superior essays are those by A. Y. Campbell in *The Great Victorians* (H. J. and E. Massingham, editors, 1932), and by May Harris, who identifies FitzGerald as "the last of the Epicureans" in "A Victorian Pagan" (*SeR*, 1926). Francis Gribble's essay, "Edward FitzGerald" (*Fortnightly*, 1909), likens FitzGerald to Sénancour, Amiel, and Lafcadio Hearn. *Ecclesiastes and Omar Khayyám* by J. F. Genung (1901) is one of the comparisons naturally suggested by the Persian's quatrains. "The Philosophy of Omar Khayyám and Its Relation to that of Schopenhauer" by C. D. Broad (*Westminster Review*, 1906), compares Omar "The Realist" with Schopenhauer "The Transcendental Idealist." "Lucretius and Omar" appears in *Post Liminium* by L. P. Johnson (1911). (But Paul Elmer More dismisses the similarity between Omar and Lucretius as a "superficial resemblance.") FitzGerald's place in the stream of rationalism is considered by A. W. Benn in *The History of English Rationalism in the Nineteenth Century* (1906). In *The Rubáiyát*, Benn finds evidence to support the contention that "by the end of the sixties a greatly preponderating weight of English intellect . . . was cast against the religious revival, and was moving . . . on the lines of rationalistic thought."

ARTHUR HUGH CLOUGH

I. *Bibliography*

Though Arthur Hugh Clough has been rather neglected by bibliographers, there is a detailed bibliography of his poetry in the notes to *The Poems of Arthur Hugh Clough,* edited by H. F. Lowry, A. L. P. Norrington, and F. L. Mulhauser (1951). *Twelve Victorian Authors* and *CBEL* provide general bibliographies, and the biography of Clough published in 1938 by Goldie Levy contains a list of publications valuable for association items. This bibliography notes books which contain letters by Clough not included in his *Prose Remains.* "Collections toward a Bibliography of Arthur Hugh Clough" in the *Literary World* (1884) lists only twenty-four items.

II. *Works and Correspondence*

Clough published only two volumes of poetry during his lifetime. In November, 1848, appeared *The Bothie of Toperna-Fuosich* (the place name later being changed to Tober-na-Vuolich). Two months later, in January, 1849, he published, with his friend Thomas Burbidge, *Ambarvalia,* in which twenty-nine poems are by Clough. At the time of his death in 1861 he was corresponding with Charles Eliot Norton about a collection of his poems to be published in America.

Editions of *Poems* by Arthur Hugh Clough were published simultaneously in London and Boston in 1862. The two publications are almost identical, although Lowry, Norrington, and Mulhauser point out that the London volume, edited by the poet's wife, contains shorter poems and portions of *Dipsychus* and *Mari Magno* which do not appear in the American issue. The London edition contains a memoir by F. T. Palgrave; that published in Boston, one by Norton. In 1869 appeared *The Poems and Prose Remains of Arthur Hugh Clough* (two volumes). These volumes, edited by Mrs. Clough, include an unsigned memoir, eight essays, and a considerable number of letters. This edition has been re-printed many times. The letters and essays of the 1869 edition were published as *Prose Remains of Arthur Hugh Clough* (1888). *Poems*, with an introduction by Charles Whibley, was published in 1913. The Lowry, Norrington, Mulhauser *Poems* has provided a definitive edition of Clough's poetry. From manuscript sources the work supplies portions of the poems which had been deleted in previous editions, restores the original readings to passages which other editors had altered, and adds complete poems which were omitted in 1869. The notes in the volume are confined, for the most part, to textual sources and variants. Explication is only incidental.

Mr. Mulhauser reports that the typescript for his *Correspondence of Arthur Hugh Clough* has been completed and will be sent to England for publication before the end of the year. He describes the work as a selection from the Clough manuscripts, including "letters of Carlyle, Emerson, Froude, Shairp . . . and many other Victorian figures, as well as the letters of Clough and his wife."

III. *Biography*

If Clough's wife did not actually write the memoir which prefaces the 1869 edition of his prose and poems, she must, at least, have guided the writer in its composition.[5] Considering this, the sketch is far more dispassionate and objective than one has come to expect from a nineteenth-century family source. Other memoirs, by Palgrave and Norton, it will be recalled, appeared in the 1862 editions of *Poems*. The first full biography, largely critical, was by Samuel Waddington, *Arthur Hugh Clough* (1883). Waddington tends to be eulogistic, but he understood Clough; and his critiques, except for eulogy, do not differ markedly from many which have been written in recent years. *Arthur Hugh Clough* by James I. Osborne (1920) is more a critique than a biography. The author makes no attempt to give a thorough account of

---

[5] It is recorded that John Addington Symonds aided Mrs. Clough in editing the prose remains.

the poet's life but concentrates on an interpretation of his character and the forces which molded it. This he does well. Osborne's appraisals of the poems in their relations to Clough's personality are discerning. However, his casual introduction of names of persons and titles of books without identification is far from helpful. A more recent writer, Goldie Levy, provides a biographical narrative with some criticism in *Arthur Hugh Clough, 1819–1861* (1938). This work, though not penetrating, is the most detailed record of the poet's life which has yet appeared.

The Clough literature is rich in biographical essays written by his contemporaries. Some of the writers had been his companions at Oxford. Among these were Thomas Arnold, younger brother of Matthew, who contributed "Arthur Hugh Clough: a Sketch" to *The Nineteenth Century* (1898); F. T. Palgrave, "Arthur Hugh Clough" (*Fraser's*, 1862); and J. C. Shairp, *Portraits of Friends* (1889). Considerable data is to be found in the biographies, journals, and correspondence of his friends: Shairp, Hutton, Palgrave, A. P. Stanley, William Allingham, Florence Nightingale, Emerson, Lowell, Norton, and others. Of prime importance in a study of Clough are *The Letters of Matthew Arnold to Arthur Hugh Clough*, edited by H. F. Lowry (1932) and *The Emerson-Clough Letters* which Mr. Lowry edited with R. L. Rusk (1934). This edition was restricted to 165 copies. Mr. Lowry's introduction to the former volume includes a sharply-drawn portrait of Clough and an examination of the influences to which he was subjected at Rugby and Oxford. A significant recent biographical study is "Arthur Hugh Clough at Oriel and at University Hall" by G. P. Johari (*PMLA*, 1951). The essay is based on manuscript letters and notes at Oriel, and records and correspondence of Clough and his superiors at University Hall. The paper establishes that Clough resigned his fellowship at Oriel, but that his principalship at University Hall was terminated by action of the Council.

Through the acts of his comparatively short life and the content of his poetry, Clough bequeathed to posterity riddles of personality and motivation which remain unsolved to the present day. From the outset writers have felt a compulsion to "explain" the poet. A mass of evidence but little enlightenment has resulted. The independence of Clough's opinions and actions and the humor of his poems and letters clearly reveal facets of character which, thus far, have eluded satisfactory synthesis.

IV. *Criticism*

Criticism about Clough in recent years has produced a number of searching studies. His work was in need of examination to balance such criticism as that of Stopford Brooke, who found in the poet "no obscurity, no vagueness" and observed that "to a certain degree then, he was above scepticism" (*Four Poets*, 1908). However, much of the earlier criticism is of superior quality. The critique of Walter Bagehot, whose acquaintance with the poet dated from Clough's University Hall days, is objective and discriminating (*Literary Studies*, three volumes, 1879). R. H. Hutton's review of the 1869 volumes is noteworthy as an analysis by another who knew Clough personally (*Literary Essays*, 1892). Henry Sidgwick (*Miscellaneous Essays and Addresses*, 1904) and John Addington Symonds ("Arthur Hugh Clough," *Fortnightly*, 1868) are also objective in their appraisals. Both writers were friends of persons who had known Clough intimately. The Sidgwick essay is especially recommended. A contemporary clergyman, John Dowden, who contributed "Arthur Hugh Clough" to the *Contemporary Review* (1869), is more concerned with religious opinions and personal qualities revealed in the poems than he is with the poetry *per se*.

Although much recent research on Clough has been devoted to individual poems, a number of significant studies have examined inherited judgments of the poet's work. "Was Clough a failure?" is asked over and over again in the literature. The question is answered with an emphatic negative by F. W. Palmer in "Was Clough a Failure?" (*PQ*, 1943). Palmer examines the poetry as "a criticism of life" and, with the help of the letters, deduces Clough's social opinions. He concludes that Clough held "positive moral convictions and positive social attitudes" and expressed them "in his work as in his own life." Humbert Wolfe, in "Arthur Hugh Clough," contributed to *The Eighteen-Sixties* (1932), sees Clough as a poet "who might and should have taken his place among the great English satirists" smothered "not by his own doubts but by the doubts thrust upon him by his friends." Mr. Palmer, in a second article, "The Bearing of Science on the Thought of Arthur Hugh Clough" (*PMLA*, 1944), takes issue with the statement of J. I. Osborne that Clough "had no training in science, and little that was scientific in his habit of mind." The essay makes out a good case for Clough's familiarity with Higher Criticism and with the science of his day. Madeleine Cazamian, who examines the influence of science in the years 1860–1890 in *Le Roman et les Idées en Angleterre* (1923), also considers Clough in relation to contemporary science.

No doubt the greatest riddle to confront Clough during his life was that reflected in his struggle between faith and doubt. Critics have been no less concerned with the problem, and the majority of essays about the poet deal with the matter in varying degrees. Treatment of the subject at intervals since Clough's death may be examined in "The Poetry of Doubt — Arnold and Clough" by John Pickford (*Church Quarterly Review*, 1878); *Faith and Doubt in the Century's Poets* by R. A. Armstrong (1898); *English Literature in Account with Religion* by E. M. Chapman (1910); and *Pessimistische Strömungen im Englischen Geistesleben des 19. Jahrhunderts* by Paul Meissner (*Englische Studien*, 1929). In his essay on the poet, F. L. Lucas observes that Clough "remains the impersonation of an age when religious doubt was not, as now, a rare and mild green-sickness, but a crippling, even a fatal malady" (*Eight Victorian Poets*, 1930; *Ten Victorian Poets*, 1940). A recent examination of the subject is "Arthur Hugh Clough as Dipsychus" by Kingsbury Badger (*Modern Language Quarterly*, 1951). There is no doubt about the form and degree of Clough's skepticism in the mind of A. W. Benn (*English Rationalism*, two volumes, 1906). Divesting the poet of verbiage and equivocation, Benn exposes Clough's position in a brief, clear-cut analysis. For Clough, he states, "not only religious belief but even religious feeling vanishes as a distinct element of life by being absorbed into the enthusiasm for duty and practical philanthropy."

The vitality of professional interest in Clough was attested by the recent exchange of opinion over the relationship between his "Say not the struggle naught availeth" and Arnold's "Dover Beach." In December, 1951, D. A. Robertson offered "the theory that 'Say not' may have been Clough's reply to 'Dover Beach'" (*PMLA*, 1951). The essay elicited two responses that were perhaps written immediately, but, observing a decorous academic pace, were not published until exactly a year after Robertson's essay. Paull Baum in "Clough and Arnold" submitted evidence which, he believed, "seriously weakens the contention that the poem ['Dover Beach'] may have been written before October, 1849, when Clough sent a copy of *his* poem to Allingham" (*MLN*, 1952). F. G. Townsend established the date of the first publication of "Say not" as 1855 by revealing that it appeared in August of that year in *The Crayon*, an American art journal, under the title, "The Struggle" ("Clough's 'The Struggle': The Text, Title, and Date of Publication," *PMLA*, 1952). Six months later H. W. Rudman contended that there was "no need of relating Clough's poem in any way with 'Dover Beach.'" Rudman maintained "that the destruction of Mazzini's Roman Republic occasioned the poem" (*N&Q*, 1953).

The quality of Clough's hexameters has been debated almost as persistently as his struggle for faith. Bagehot and Waddington defended them in the nineteenth century, and in the twentieth Lucas declares "Clough's hexameters to be the only successful specimens of their kind in English," well suited to the half-mocking tone of *The Bothie* and *Amours de Voyage*. C. H. Herford, on the other hand, states that Clough "may perhaps still claim to have written three or four of the finest English hexameters; but it is almost as certain that he has to answer for a hundred or more of the worst" (Introduction to *English Tales in Verse*, 1902).

Clough himself discusses the difficulties of using the form in the "Letters of Parepidemus" in the *Prose Remains*. A. L. P. Norrington recommends the examination of the hexameters found in Sir Humphrey Milford's edition of *The Poems of Clough* (1910). Mr. Norrington provides a brief analysis of his own in the preface to the Lowry, Norrington, Mulhauser volume. Clough's prose is considered by S. T. Williams in *Studies in Victorian Literature* (1923) and by J. M. Beatty in "Arthur Hugh Clough as Revealed in His Prose" (*SAQ*, 1926).

Two noteworthy special studies should be mentioned. In "A Study of Clough's *Mari Magno*" (*PMLA*, 1929), A. M. Turner proposes that the substance for the frame of the poem was derived from the poet's voyage to America in 1852. The poem is also examined "to determine just what elements appear to be derived from Crabbe and what from Chaucer." Noting the charges of impersonality and intellectuality frequently lodged against Clough's early love lyrics, Frederick Mulhauser, in "Clough's 'Love and Reason' " (*MP*, 1945), traces the development of the poem through four revisions. In the first version, concerned with the problem of when to marry, Clough reveals, according to Mulhauser, a "certain sympathy and understanding" in his treatment of the subject. As revision progressed, the poem became "an impersonal analysis of the relation of love and reason."

5

Matthew Arnold

Frederic E. Faverty

I. *Bibliography*

THE LAST TWENTY-FIVE YEARS have not been very productive in bibliographical studies on Arnold. Thomas Burnett Smart's *Bibliography of Matthew Arnold* (1892 and 1904), with its list of the poems in each volume, its record of exclusions and republications, its "synoptical index," and its chronological arrangement of critical material concerning Arnold, has been supplemented but not superseded. The most complete recent bibliography is that found in *Twelve Victorian Authors* by Ehrsam, Deily, and Smith. It is also the easiest to use since it is arranged alphabetically. The annual Victorian bibliography which appears in *Modern Philology* (for the years 1932–1944, brought together in one volume, *Bibliographies of Studies in Victorian Literature* [1945], by the editor, W. D. Templeman) is of course indispensable for all new works since 1932 and for its lists of reviews.

Miss Marion Mainwaring in "Notes toward a Matthew Arnold Bibliography" (*MP*, 1952) corrects and supplements T. H. V. Motter's "A Check List of Matthew Arnold's Letters" (*SP*, 1934) which attempted to coördinate the material to 1933. Miss Mainwaring also gives the fullest record to date of Arnold's Oxford orations and his occasional speeches. In addition to the correspondence included in the principal collections [1] there are hundreds of scattered letters, published and unpublished, that remain to be brought together. In "Matthew Arnold and his Publishers" (*Victorian News Letter*, April 1953), William E. Buckler describes a projected edition of Arnold's letters to his publishers. In the same issue of *Victorian News Letter*, Arthur Kyle Davis, Jr. outlines his "Project for a Check-list of Matthew Arnold's Letters." Three recent articles serve to emphasize the need for a complete edition of the letters. In *RES* (1953), W. H. G. Armytage published "Matthew Arnold and T. H. Huxley: Some New Letters, 1870–80." Included in Diderik Roll-Hansen's "Matthew Arnold and the *Academy*" (*PMLA*, 1953) were five hitherto unpublished letters from Arnold to Dr. Charles Edward Appleton, first editor of the *Academy*. And in *MP* (1955) appeared Robert Liddell Lowe's "Two Arnold Letters," one to Thomas Arnold the Younger, the other to Sidney Colvin.

II. *Editions*

Arnold is fortunate in his recent editors. Along with Boswell he has been adopted by Yale University, and out of the great Yale Collection of manuscripts, papers, and volumes printed by Arnold have come three noteworthy editions and a Commentary. The first of these is H. F. Lowry's edition of *The Letters of Matthew Arnold to Arthur Hugh Clough* (1932). No single work has contributed more to the Arnold revival of the last several decades. It presents a mine of new critical and biographical material. The editor's introductory essays and the notes are invaluable for tracing Arnold's development from 1845 to 1861. *The Poetry of Matthew Arnold: a Commentary* (1940) by C. B. Tinker and H. F. Lowry, and *The Poetical Works of Matthew Arnold* (1950), edited by

---

[1] *Letters of Matthew Arnold: 1848–1888*, collected and arranged by G. W. E. Russell, two volumes (1895), revised for vols. XIII–XV of *The Works of Matthew Arnold* (1904); *Letters of Matthew Arnold to John Churton Collins* (1910); *Unpublished Letters of Matthew Arnold*, Arnold Whitridge, ed. (1923); *The Letters of Matthew Arnold to Arthur Hugh Clough*, H. F. Lowry, ed. (1932).

the same pair, are companion volumes and therefore should be considered together. All future students of Arnold's poetry will be heavily indebted to Messrs. Tinker and Lowry. Drawing upon all available materials, published and unpublished, the co-authors of the *Commentary* have brought together in compact and manageable form the necessary information for an understanding of every poem — sources, influences, biographical details, dates, and the editorial history of each work up to 1890. In view of the sanity and good judgment displayed in the occasional literary evaluations, it is to be regretted that the plan of the book ruled out interpretation. Also to be regretted is the absence of an over-all discussion of Arnold's aesthetics. The companion volume, *The Poetical Works*, supersedes the Oxford editions of 1909 and 1945. For the first time, the complete poetical works are given and are edited by modern standards. The only objection thus far raised to the edition is that it follows Arnold's own order and classification of the poems rather than the more convenient chronological arrangement of the Oxford editions. Fourth and last is the monumental *Note-Books of Matthew Arnold*, edited by H. F. Lowry, Karl Young, and W. H. Dunn (1952). Only literary items are included. All references to his finances and official engagements are omitted. Students who expect the intimate revelations of a journal will be disappointed, for the *Note-Books* record only what Arnold read, and tell us little about his reactions to his reading. The editors have identified most of the thousands of quotations from six literatures. When so much has been given, it is perhaps ungrateful to complain that there is no index for seventy-seven pages of reading lists, and that the editors did not find it "appropriate to attempt any detailed essay on the significance of the note-books or their bearing on Arnold's own work." So much for the poetry and the *Note-Books*.

What of Arnold's prose works? They still await their Tinker and Lowry. That a critical edition is badly needed is demonstrated by E. K. Brown in his *Studies in the Text of Matthew Arnold's Prose Works* (1935). Brown's book is an attempt, and a successful one, "to illuminate Arnold's personality, thought and art by a study of his revisions." The major changes in text, editorial and stylistic, give proof of Arnold's improving architectonic sense, and of his intellectual honesty. Brown's running commentary is invariably suggestive, sensitive in offering the right clues to Arnold's motives in revision. The book is a rich source for further deductions and an excellent example of the method by which purely technical matters can be humanized and be given wider significance.

III. *Biography*

Of all the great Victorians, Arnold has received the least adequate treatment in biography. In fact there is no life of Arnold, certainly none worthy of a place beside Froude's life of Carlyle or Mackail's life of William Morris. The chief biographical contribution of the last twenty-five years is that provided by *The Letters of Matthew Arnold to Arthur Hugh Clough* (1932). Most writers since 1932 have leaned heavily on this volume. Alan Harris in his informative "Matthew Arnold: the 'Unknown Years'" (*Nineteenth Century and After*, 1933), and W. S. Knickerbocker in "Semaphore" (*SeR*, 1933), for example, use the letters in an attempt to reconstruct the relationship with Clough. Much more baffling is the Marguerite episode, on which almost every commentator has exercised his ingenuity. Where the facts are few, the field is open to conjecture. Tinker and Lowry have rummaged among the tombstones of Thun, but the grave retains its secret. The 1848–49 register of the Hotel Bellevue has been destroyed. Thus we are thrown back upon Arnold's letters and the internal evidence of the poems. On the basis of these, a number of critics (for example, W. S. Knickerbocker, "Thunder in the Index," *SeR*, 1939, and A. S. Cairncross, "Arnold's 'Faded Leaves' and 'Switzerland'," *TLS*, 28 March 1935) conclude that Marguerite was not a real person. T. S. Eliot in *The Use of Poetry and the Use of Criticism* (1933) finds her a mere shadow, a "pretext for lamentation." Another group, more numerous — including H. W. Garrod in

Poetry and the Criticism of Life (1931), E. K. Chambers in his Warton lecture on English poetry, *Proceedings of the British Academy* (1932), Iris Sells in "Marguerite" (*MLR*, 1943), and P. F. Baum in "Arnold's Marguerite" (*Booker Memorial Studies*, 1950) — are inclined to believe that the episode is autobiographical. They also are agreed that in renouncing Marguerite, Arnold renounced passion and poetry and emerged into the light of common day. Louis Bonnerot in "La Jeunesse de Matthew Arnold" (*Revue Anglo-Américaine*, 1930) goes even further. He deplores the puritanical attitude of the English critics regarding this very important phase of Arnold's development. In his view, Arnold is haunted for the rest of his life by this memory of his youth. To Marguerite, Bonnerot attributes many significant later developments — the accentuation of the tendency toward elegiac poetry, the theme of isolation so important in Arnold's work, even some of Arnold's philosophical and religious attitudes.

Of the two book-length biographies (Louis Bonnerot, *Matthew Arnold, Poète: Essai de Biographie Psychologique*, 1947, and E. K. Chambers, *Matthew Arnold, A Study*, 1947) that by Chambers is the slighter. Coming from so eminent a scholar, it is a disappointment. It is done evidently with his left hand in the intervals of his severer labors in earlier periods of English literature. For this reason, perhaps, he provides no documentation at all. He is content with a brief, brisk factual account, unimpeded and unrelieved by much in the way of criticism and interpretation. As a factual account, however, it is the best and the fullest that thus far has been made. Bonnerot attempts more, more also that is open to question. He calls his work "an essay in psychological biography." Many of Arnold's contemporaries, neurotic, exotic, and erotic (Carlyle, Ruskin, D. G. Rossetti, etc.), have fallen prey to the psychologists. Even Arnold could not elude them forever. Bonnerot's main thesis is that Arnold suffers from pathological doubt, a disease of the affections. From this spring his various dualities, oscillations, wanderings between worlds. Although Bonnerot fails to convince the reader that

Arnold suffers from a psychoneurosis, the psychological interpretations do suggest new and deeper meanings for many of the poems. The subtle biographical reading of "Tristram and Iseult" is a case in point. Based on a thorough knowledge of all Arnold's works, and the literature upon them, the book, in spite of its extravagant central thesis, is the most impressive attempt yet made to explain Arnold's personality.

As early as 1930, H. M. Walbrook in "The Novel in Matthew Arnold's Poems" (*Bookman*) suggested that the Marguerite episode would provide ideal material for a romantic novel. In *The Buried Self: a Background to the Poems of Matthew Arnold, 1848–1851* (1949) Isobel Macdonald carried out this suggestion. Her fictional treatment of Arnold's relationships with Marguerite and with Lucy Wightman involves "the description of the background against which Arnold lived during these years; the imagining of conversations, and the imagining of incidents." Eleven pages of notes appended to the novel indicate to what extent the incidents described are based on fact.

IV. *General and Introductory Studies*

From the mass of general and introductory material only a few items have been selected for comment. The wealth of such material in the Arnold literature is really a sign of its poverty. After an acquaintanceship of a hundred years, the world, at least the scholarly portion of it, no longer needs to be introduced to Arnold. What it does need is more studies that give thorough consideration to particular aspects of his work. The very excellence of some of the general studies lessens the need at present for more works in this kind. The worst general introduction is probably "Hugh Kingsmill's" *Matthew Arnold* (1928). The best is certainly Lionel Trilling's *Matthew Arnold* (1939; new edition 1949). Somewhere between these extremes lie the modest summary by Harvey and the illuminating critiques by Garrod, Chambers, and Stanley.

As prelude to a consideration of the books by Trilling,

Garrod, and the others, a few words should be said, perhaps, of the verdict of the twenties on Arnold. From this decade there is a considerable body of comment, most of it without benefit of scholarship. The critics adventuring among Arnold's masterpieces try to determine whether he is greater as a poet or as a writer of prose; from what ultimate sources his melancholy springs; and where and how he failed as an artist. None of the commentators speaks with final authority but taken together they do establish a perspective necessary for evaluation of the later book-length studies.

Arnold's turning from poetry to prose is explained very simply, and inadequately, by Sir Arthur Quiller-Couch in *Studies in Literature* (1919). It is "testimony to the perfect development of a life which in due season used poetry and at the due hour cast it away, to proceed to things more practical." In spite of his frequent poetic clumsiness, his overworking of interjections, his use of italic type for emphasis, his occasional bad ear for rhyme, his lack of the bardic, the architectonic gift, Arnold does have a vein of "the most real and rarest poetry." And his sense of natural atmosphere and background deserves high praise. In "The Second-Order Mind" (*The Dial*, 1920) T. S. Eliot mildly regrets Arnold's desertion of poetry for the writing of editorials, but concludes that the temptation was probably irresistible. Sir Walter Raleigh in *Some Authors* (1923) also prefers the poetry, for it "deals only with the great things," the themes which though they are invoked as memories and appealed to as standards in the prose, are distant there "as they are never distant in the poems." Further, the prose takes on a tone of mockery. C. H. Herford in "Matthew Arnold as a Prophet" (*Living Age*, 10 February 1923) is chiefly concerned with Arnold's role as apostle of culture, but the same fundamental characteristics are observed of the poet as of the prophet. It is the "stoic exaltation" that appeals to Herford, "the hidden ground of thought and impassioned resignation," which even more than the radiant form account for the vitality of his poems. On Arnold's melancholy there are two articles: G. R. Elliott, "The Arnoldian Melancholy" (*PMLA*, 1923; repub-

lished in *The Cycle of Modern Poetry*, 1929); and Douglas
Bush, "The Varied Hues of Pessimism" (*Dalhousie Review*,
1929). In Elliott's view Arnold did not himself realize the
profundity of his sorrow, for he ascribed it, as others have, to
contemporary conditions. But Arnold's mood is not "so fully
resolvable into temperamental and temporary conditions"
as are those of other major Victorian poets. Its source lies in
differentiated emotional currents which give a sense of deep
oppositions. Elliott sets up two types of struggle, that "between two conflicting times" and that "between a time and
an eternity," in the latter of which Arnold's melancholy has its
origin. Douglas Bush finds a number of similarities between
Arnold and Hardy. Neither is a spontaneous singer. And
their subject matter being what it is, "neither would be improved by the traditional post-romantic graces of diction and
rhythm." In emotional tone also the two are alike, since both
are inspired by "a kind of melancholy that is more universal
than that of religious disillusionment." It is to Arnold, however, that Bush gives the preference, for unlike Hardy,
Arnold "attaches himself to no set of religious beliefs, but
interprets the deep, broad facts of disillusioned melancholy."
Finally, although Arnold is not a creator of character, he is
more fundamentally humanistic in his view of man. Hardy's
characters seldom have any inner life of reflection, but much
of Arnold's emotional power consists in his appeal to the
inner life of self-discipline and to a serene possession of soul.
In *Studies in Victorian Literature* (1923), S. T. Williams devotes a chapter to "Three Aspects of Arnold's Poetry" — the
mastery of mood-creating detail, the habitual sacrifice of
narrative to philosophical details, and the particular type of
Hellenism. Assuming that a writer's basic thought is often
evident in his early minor poems, Williams chooses "The
Forsaken Merman," "Mycerinus," "The Sick King in Bokhara," and "The Strayed Reveller" to illustrate these characteristics. J. M. Murry's "Matthew Arnold the Poet" in
Discoveries (1924) attributes Arnold's early exhaustion as a
poet to his failure to "strike the source of life within himself." His classicism was the culmination of his romanticism,

for he "sought safety as an artist in a principle outside himself, and alien to his own nature." Murry believes that Arnold's turning to criticism was well advised, since in the critic's function his creative weakness became his strength and his "indecision was transformed into catholicity."

Lionel Trilling's *Matthew Arnold* has been so widely acclaimed as one of the finest examples of recent American scholarship and criticism that it need not be discussed here at any length. It is at once an exposition, a vindication, a criticism, and an interpretation; it is admirable alike for its tone and erudition. As Harold Nicolson says, he gives us "not only Arnold's mind, but also the mind of an age." The book has served as a model for other works of its type, notably the recent *Leslie Stephen* by Noel G. Annan (1952). The chief charge that has been brought against Trilling's book is that it deals less than adequately with Arnold the poet. C. H. Harvey's *Matthew Arnold: A Critic of the Victorian Period* (1931) is in the main an industrious paraphrasing of Arnold's prose works. The tone throughout is one of eulogy. It is a useful but not very important book. With H. W. Garrod's *Poetry and the Criticism of Life* (1931), E. K. Chambers's Warton lecture on Arnold in *Proceedings of the British Academy* (1932), and Carleton Stanley's *Matthew Arnold* (1938), however, we move on a higher level. All three men are perceptive, discriminating critics. They are persuasive spokesmen for Arnold. Stanley, writing after the appearance of the letters to Clough, can speak with more factual authority. Garrod's voice, however, is more commanding, better to listen to. Chambers is much interested in the Marguerite episode, but also discusses Arnold's poetic theory and practice.

In the general revaluations of the thirties and the forties, Arnold the poet receives higher praise than Arnold the writer of prose. Even Garrod admits that the critical writings are going out of fashion. According to Edmund Blunden ("Matthew Arnold," in *The Great Victorians*, edited by H. J. Massingham and H. Massingham, 1932), the prose covers fields that are too technical for the treatment Arnold gave them, fields that have now been taken over by expert treatises and monographs. Louis Kronenberger, in "Re-reading Matthew Arnold" (*SRL*, 15 September, 1934), is more damning — Arnold's social and religious criticism has dwindled to nothing; much of the literary criticism will follow. Only his style will remain. And in the same vein of detraction, T. S. Eliot remarks (*The Use of Poetry and the Use of Criticism*, 1933) that in philosophy and theology Arnold is an undergraduate, in religion a Philistine. For all these views, it should be remarked, authority and precedent can be found among the nineteenth-century critics of Arnold — Frederic Harrison and George Saintsbury, for example. T. S. Eliot's unflattering comments on Arnold's philosophy and religion are echoes of the earlier strictures by F. H. Bradley and J. M. Robertson.

On Arnold's poetry the general verdict is more favorable. But there are reservations. He is too intelligent to be a great poet (Harold Nicolson, "On Re-reading Matthew Arnold," in *Essays by Divers Hands: Being the Transactions of the Royal Society of Literature*, 1948). His poetry is academic in the best sense (T. S. Eliot, *The Use of Poetry and the Use of Criticism*). He is a little bleak, too serious, too melancholy, too much the preacher (F. L. Lucas, *Ten Victorian Poets*, 1940). A number of critics — T. S. Eliot; G. L. Strachey in his "Victorian Critic" in *Characters and Commentaries* (1933); and J. W. Cunliffe, "Mid-Victorian Poets" in *Leaders of the Victorian Revolution* (1934) — object to Arnold's moral prepossessions, and to the definition of poetry as a criticism of life. Garrod's reply to such charges is that Arnold was merely giving sharp expression to what had passed as a truism for centuries. That it is not the business of a great writer to teach virtue is an absurdly modern thesis. We ought to get over the feeling that a moral idea will bite us. With another group of critics (Chambers, Blunden, and Stanley) Arnold's greatest success is in his elegiac poetry, and in bringing to mind the English landscape. It is not mere acceptance and resignation that the poetry reflects, however. There is also the note of courage. And in any case, his philosophy is infinitely preferable to Browning's. At his best he is better than Tennyson.

So runs the chorus in his praise, until the *Times Literary Supplement* could say, "In 1952 Arnold is with the great poets."

V. *Special Studies*

ARNOLD AND FRANCE. In the field of comparative literature there is no more fascinating topic than Matthew Arnold and France. On such a theme we should have a work like C. F. Harrold's *Carlyle and German Thought*, in which sound and thorough scholarship is combined with critical insight and good judgment. Instead we have *Matthew Arnold and France* (1935) by Iris E. Sells, which gives too much, and *The Critic's Alchemy* (1953) by Ruth Z. Temple, which gives too little, significance to Arnold's relationship with France. Iris E. Sells's book, which is mainly concerned with Arnold's debt to Quinet, Sénancour, and George Sand, has met with an unfavorable reception because of her fanciful and sentimental recreation of the Marguerite episode, and her inability in source studies to distinguish between a parallel and an influence. A similar defect is apparent in Joseph W. Angell's study, "Matthew Arnold's Indebtedness to Renan's 'Essais de morale et de critique' " (*Revue de Littérature Comparée*, 1934). Angell too often attributes to a single work and a single author ideas that were generally current and could have been derived from many writers. More temperate and in every way more impressive than Angell's source study is Lewis W. Mott's "Renan and Matthew Arnold" (*MLN*, 1918). But Sidney M. B. Coulling in "Renan's Influence on Arnold's Literary and Social Criticism" (*Florida State University Studies*, V, 1952) contends that Mott and Angell have greatly exaggerated Renan's influence on Arnold's critical writings. Further evidence of this influence on Arnold's literary and social criticism and particularly on the religious writings is supplied, however, by F. E. Faverty in *Matthew Arnold the Ethnologist* (1951).

The harshest verdict to date on Arnold as an apostle of French culture is that delivered by Ruth Z. Temple in "The

Strayed Reveller," "The Second Best," and "The Better Part," the first three chapters of *The Critic's Alchemy: A Study of the Introduction of French Symbolism into England* (1953). She insists that "his service to the cause of his countrymen's appreciation of French literature and especially French poetry was dubious at best." With the masterpieces of French prose his acquaintance was neither wide nor deep nor sympathetic. Echoing Emile Legouis, E. K. Brown, Lionel Trilling, and others, she condemns him as a critic of French poetry for his indifference to the qualities of the language, and his failure to appreciate the music of the alexandrine. His errors in judgment she attributes partly to his lack of information, partly to the bizarre application of his touchstone system. In "Matthew Arnold and Sainte-Beuve" (*PMLA*, 1938), Arnold Whitridge emphasizes the similarities between the two critics: their agreement that French poetry was second-rate, that criticism must be combined with charm; their intellectual conscience, and dislike of pedantry; and their aristocratic preference for subtlety, distinction, and refinement rather than pure genius. Yet, Whitridge says, there is a fundamental difference. Arnold is a moralist for whom literature is a matter of ethics. Sainte-Beuve is more catholic in taste and understands the value of things of the mind for their own sake. On the basis of this chief difference, Miss Temple concludes that "Arnold's criticism has no real resemblance in theory, in spirit, or in practical method to that of his great contemporary." Miss Temple also believes that Arnold's likeness to Renan has been overemphasized. Arnold, she says, lacks epigram, eloquence, elegance, wit, even the power to persuade — all distinguishing traits of Renan. The only French critic with whom he has any real kinship is the dogmatist Edmond Scherer. Not content with robbing Arnold of his claims as an intermediary between France and England, Miss Temple denies him eminence as a critic of any literature, including his own. Three French influences on Arnold — George Sand, Sénancour, and Marguerite — are discussed by Florence Wickelgren in "Matthew Arnold's Literary Relations With France" (*MLR*, 1938). She attempts to reconstruct the visit to George Sand in 1846; and to show what Arnold had in common with Sénancour. The influence of the affair with Marguerite she believes has been overstressed by Iris E. Sells.

ARNOLD AND GERMANY. Although there is sufficient material to justify a monograph on Arnold and Germany, none has yet appeared in English. The subject has been treated, however, in a number of German doctoral dissertations (Margarete Lassen, *Matthew Arnolds Verhältnis zu den Deutschen und zur Deutschen Literatur*, 1923; Johannes Renwanz, *Matthew Arnold und Deutschland*, 1927; Paul Wilhelm Zorn, *Matthew Arnold und seine Beziehung zu Deutschland*, 1924). Of these, Renwanz's *Matthew Arnold und Deutschland* is representative. With what Arnold calls "the steady humdrum habit of the creeping Saxon," Renwanz has extracted from Arnold's published works the leading references to Germany and has arranged them neatly in their proper categories: descriptions of German districts in the verse and correspondence; the use of the German people as examples of Philistinism; the relationship between Arnold's liberal republicanism and his unfavorable view of Prussian monarchy; his praise of W. von Humboldt and the German educational system; his unflattering comments on the German language and his mixed views on German literature; his adoption of Goethe's conception of Spinoza; his references to the Reformation, his indebtedness to the higher critics of the Bible, and, in his attempt to free Christianity from Semitism, his dependence on Schleiermacher, W. von Humboldt, and Bunsen; his scattered comments on German music and the plastic arts. Unfortunately, Renwanz does not often or for very long allow himself any higher function than that of a cataloguer.

J. B. Orrick ("Matthew Arnold and Goethe," *Publications of the Goethe Society*, 1928), however, is no mere thesis-compiler. He subjects the evidences of Arnold's dependence on Goethe to a thorough critical analysis. Arnold's idea of Goethe, he contends, was derived secondhand from Carlyle. And like Carlyle, Arnold transformed and sometimes misinterpreted what he found. Orrick traces Arnold's admiration for Goethe in the numerous allusions, in the incidental criticism of Goethe's works, in the essays that have special reference to him, and in the passages reminiscent of Goethe. On Arnold's estimate of three writers in particular — Byron, Heine, and Spinoza — Goethe's influence is paramount. And in all three cases it is Goethe qualified or misinterpreted. Arnold modifies Goethe's judgment on Byron. Arnold's conception of Heine as Goethe's successor in the work of liberation is not "sufficiently thoroughgoing." And Spinoza's appeal to Goethe was an emotional one, not as Arnold thought a moral and intellectual one. Arnold's judgment of specific works by Goethe is marred by the application of a preconceived standard. Arnold also places too great a restriction on Goethe's love of Greek art and form in using it as a support for his own English classicism. Finally, Arnold is wrong in supposing that Goethe was primarily a thinker. Rather, he was "an artist, a liver of the creative life."

From this critical but nonetheless sympathetic survey Orrick concludes that Arnold learned no habits and methods from Goethe. For Arnold, Goethe was primarily a standard of reference and a perpetual source of inspiration:

The influence of Goethe, though very constant and very great when viewed in detail, was fundamental only where it corresponded with certain preconceived attitudes in Matthew Arnold. It was not, therefore, quite what one would call a primary influence. Matthew Arnold's conception of Goethe, that is to say, did not influence his mode of thought quite as much as his mode of thought influenced his conception of Goethe.

ARNOLD AND AMERICA. Turning to Arnold and America, we again have a topic that deserves but has not yet received a comprehensive treatment. Arnold's relationships with this country are more interesting and certainly more significant than Browning's, yet a book, *Browning and America*, by Louise Greer, has recently appeared, and on Arnold we have thus far only an unpublished doctoral dissertation, by C. H. Leonard: *Arnold in America: a Study of Matthew Arnold's Literary Relations with America and of his Visits to this country in 1883 and 1886* (1932); and scattered articles: William T. Beauchamp, "Plato on the Prairies (Matthew Arnold at Galesburg)" (*Educational Forum*, 1941); Walter E. Bezanson, "Melville's Reading of Arnold's Poetry" (*PMLA*, 1954); John B. Hoben, "Mark Twain's 'A Connecticut Yankee,' a Genetic Study" (*American Literature*, 1946); Harriet R. Holman, "Matthew Arnold's Elocution Lessons" (*New England Quarterly*, 1945); H. M. Jones, "Arnold, Aristocracy, and America" (*American Historical Review*, 1944); E. P. Lawrence, "An Apostle's Progress: Matthew Arnold in America" (*PQ*, 1931); John P. Long, "Matthew Arnold Visits Chicago" (*TQ*, 1954); James Dow McCallum, "The Apostle of Culture Meets America" (*New England Quarterly*, 1929); R. H. Super, "Emerson and Arnold's Poetry" (*PQ*, 1954); W. D. Templeman, "A Note on Arnold's 'Civilization in the United States'" (*MLN*, 1944). On C. H. Leonard's excellent dissertation Trilling has drawn heavily in the last chapter of his *Matthew Arnold*. Most of the articles attempt to discover the causes of Arnold's failure with his American audiences. J. D. McCallum distinguishes between the receptions given Arnold by the literary class — highly favorable; and by the general public — highly unfavorable. Paradoxically, the general public thought him lacking in humor, yet was offended by his witticisms. E. P. Lawrence finds Arnold himself entirely to blame. His inaudibility in New York, his tactless depreciation of Emerson in Boston, his supercilious attitude, priggishness, unconscious rudeness, and lack of a sense of humor made his message unpalatable. A similar comment is made by W. T. Beauchamp on Arnold's appearance in Galesburg, Illinois. His self-absorption, cold formality, affectation, monotonous delivery, and egotism alienated his audience. But the audience in this case was also at fault, for in its sturdy Midwest Philistinism it was incapable of receiving or understanding Arnold's message. To these basic causes H. M. Jones adds Arnold's spiritual kinship with the aristocracy, his instinctive feeling that the majority is always bad and usually wrong. His doctrine of culture, according to Jones, rested on a deep distrust of the people. Furthermore, it was closely bound up with racial snobbery and anti-democratic political action. Harriet Holman shows that Arnold took as a matter of course, and spoke with marked condescension of, the elocution lectures which the Reverend J. W. Churchill offered as a favor. With no sense of public address, none of the instincts of a speaker, Arnold was more heavily indebted to Churchill than he cared to admit for whatever success he achieved on the American lecture platform. In his interesting and informative article, John P. Long for the first time has brought together all the materials on Arnold's visit to Chicago in 1884. His article is based on F. W. Gookin's *The Chicago Literary Club* (1926) and on the files of four Chicago newspapers: the *Daily Inter-Ocean*, the *Tribune*, the *Daily News*, and the *Evening Journal*. Long's most significant contributions are the story of Eugene Field's aversion to Arnold, and "The Matthew Arnold Hoax," a full account of the *Tribune's* altercation with Arnold, or Joseph Medill's "melancholy experience with the apostle of sweetness and light."

According to John B. Hoben, however, Arnold's American visit had in one instance, at least, a good effect. The raging Anglophobia which Arnold inspired in Mark Twain awakened him from a literary lethargy and evoked the spirit which transformed an unpromising sentimental romance into the satirical *A Connecticut Yankee in King Arthur's Court*. R. H. Super explains the purpose and the limits of his article as follows:

I have not been dealing here with influence in the limited sense. I have been suggesting, rather, large areas of correspondence between Emerson and the young Arnold, and intimating how many of Emerson's specific ideas were congenial to him, despite the fundamental difference between a transcendentalist and a rationalist who, while well aware that the human mind was not the ultimate power in the universe, preferred not to explore what lay beyond.

Walter E. Bezanson analyzes all Melville's marginal comments in his copies of *Poems* and *New Poems*. The analysis reveals that Melville was most profoundly impressed by "Empedocles on Etna." In his struggles with the spiritual dilemmas of the nineteenth century he found Arnold a helpful guide.

ARNOLD AND THE CLASSICS. According to Ralph E. C. Houghton in *The Influence of the Classics on the Poetry of Matthew Arnold* (1923), Arnold's classicism "consists in the production of the same kinds of effect upon our minds that the Classics produce." In determining the extent of the classical influence on Arnold, Houghton notes detailed resemblances in style and in spirit.

Arnold's style, Houghton believes, is full of classical reminiscences. In "Sohrab and Rustum" and "Balder Dead" the epic similes and the catalogues of place names show Homeric influence. "Sohrab and Rustum" lacks Homeric "rapidity," but possesses the other qualities Arnold listed as Homeric — "simplicity" and "nobility." The classical device of style — *Epanalepsis* — is detected in "Alaric at Rome" and in "The Scholar Gypsy." Arnold's examples of English hexameters are regarded as unfortunate. His unrhymed lyric poems often imitate the rhythms of the Greek choral odes in a wooden way, without sufficient regard for the genius of English. And finally, Arnold's insistence on design and unity is classical.

On Arnold's spirit the influence of the classics is even more marked. Houghton finds the works permeated with the classical feeling of sanity, sincerity, and reticence. And there is a Roman *gravitas* in Arnold's character and judgments. Although the situation in "Sohrab and Rustum" is Homeric, the treatment is Virgilian. In both "Sohrab and Rustum" and "Balder Dead" the Virgilian elegiac note is strong. Arnold's stoicism obviously derives from the classics. The influence of Sophocles, Houghton says, is general rather than specific; that of Theocritus and Moschus is evident in the pastoral poems. The very titles show that the subjects of many of Arnold's poems are drawn from the classics — a practice defended in the preface of 1853. "Merope" is vitiated because dramas on Greek models do not grip a modern audience. In spite of its imitation of Sophocles, its observance of Aristotle's rule for the tragic hero, and its use of Greek tragic irony, "Merope" fails as drama because Arnold is "not dramatic in the sense that one may call Browning dramatic." In many of his poems Arnold displays a classical instinct for a quiet ending.

With many of Houghton's judgments on individual poems Douglas Bush in *Mythology and the Romantic Tradition in English Poetry* (1937) disagrees. Bush's work is the most significant that has appeared on Arnold and the classics. Most of his predecessors in the field [2] had devoted themselves to the study of sources and to tracing Homeric adaptations and echoes in Arnold. Although Bush in his footnotes does justice to these subjects, he is mainly concerned with other matters. Landor's classical culture, he says, is largely Latin; Arnold's is Greek. Landor is "a man of letters, a pure artist": Arnold is "a prophet and preacher" seeking intellectual and spiritual discipline in the classics. For Arnold classical mythology serves as a refuge, a partial escape from the perplexities and disharmonies of his own era. But it also ministers to his desire for the reign of law in nature and in himself, and to his search for high seriousness in poetry as in life. "It was Arnold's personal tragedy, and the source of his special quality and power, that he could not reconcile his poetry and his philosophy, for both were rooted in his instincts." The early poems — "The Strayed Reveller," "The New Sirens," and "Mycerinus" — illustrate the range and intensity of this conflict. In "Empedocles on Etna" it finds its fullest and most striking development, with Empedocles as Stoic and intellectual contrasted with Callicles who represents a simple dependence on feeling and intuition. Arnold's melancholy,

[2] *Matthew Arnold's Merope: to which is appended the Electra of Sophocles translated by Robert Whitelaw*, ed. J. Churton Collins, 2d ed. (1917); John Bailey, "Ancient Tragedy and Modern Imitations" [*Merope*], *Poets and Poetry* (1911); Frank L. Clark, "On Certain Imitations or Reminiscences of Homer in Matthew Arnold's 'Sohrab and Rustum'" (*Classical Weekly*, 1923–24); Milo G. Derham, "Borrowings and Adaptations from the 'Iliad' and 'Odyssey' in Matthew Arnold's 'Sohrab and Rustum'" (*University of Colorado Studies*, 1909–10); Ruth I. Goldmark, *Studies in the Influence of the Classics on English Literature* (1918); W. P. Mustard, "Homeric Echoes in Matthew Arnold's 'Balder Dead'" (*Studies in Honor of Basil Lanneau Gildersleeve*, 1902); T. S. Omond, "Arnold and Homer" (*Essays and Studies by Members of the English Association*, 1912); John A. Scott, "Matthew Arnold's Interpretation of *Odyssey* iv. 563" (*Classical Journal*, 1920–21).

Bush believes, has three sources: religion, renunciation of romantic passion, and the critical contemplation of the unpoetical era in which he lives. In some of his best lyrical and ethical poems it is the classical symbol that gives distinctness, unity, and noble connotations to the presentation. The classical doctrines expounded in Arnold's prose essays, particularly in the preface of 1853, Bush finds valid today as yesterday. But the classicism of the longer poetic works — "Merope," "Sohrab and Rustum," and "Balder Dead" — he thinks is synthetic and academic. Though "Merope" does reproduce the form of Sophoclean tragedy, and "Sohrab and Rustum" imitates, frequently with artificiality, the Homeric style, both poems fall short of classical models in subject matter: the subject of "Merope" is insignificant, that of "Sohrab and Rustum" is pathetic rather than tragic. It is not in such academic exercises but rather in the poems which are concerned with his various spiritual struggles and his attempts to achieve order that Arnold is most the classical poet.

POLITICAL IDEAS. Twenty years ago J. Dover Wilson called for some competent student of politics to assign Arnold his true place in the role of English political thinkers. The call is still unanswered. In the early thirties it was possible for Leonard Woolf (*After the Deluge*, I, 1931) to condemn Arnold as a reactionary authoritarian, and for R. H. Tawney (in Chapter Two of *Equality*, 1931) to claim him as a champion of democracy. On the Irish question, Arnold as against Gladstone, later writers like Carleton Stanley (*Matthew Arnold*, 1938) and W. Robbins ("Matthew Arnold and Ireland," *TQ*, 1947) continued to hold diametrically opposite views, Stanley as exponent of Arnold's prophetic insight and Robbins as defender of Gladstone and home rule. Although we have B. E. Lippincott's long chapter (somewhat slanted toward the liberal side) in *Victorian Critics of Democracy* (1938), Lionel Trilling's acute observations in his chapter, "Culture or Anarchy" in *Matthew Arnold*, and Otto Elias's full, well-balanced but at the same time pedantic and heavy-footed discussion in *Matthew Arnolds Politische*

Grundanschauungen (1931), the definitive work on Arnold's politics remains to be written. Arnold's hitherto not readily available pamphlet on the Italian question has now been published in a separate edition (Merle M. Bevington, *Matthew Arnold's England and the Italian Question*, 1953). Bevington supplies an introduction and notes, and in an appendix, James Fitzjames Stephen's *Saturday Review* article on the pamphlet.

EDUCATION. Since politics and education are not unallied, it need cause no surprise that the best brief work on Arnold's politics is J. Dover Wilson's "Matthew Arnold and the Educationists," in *The Social and Political Ideas of Some Representative Thinkers of the Victorian Age*, edited by F. J. C. Hearnshaw (1933). In the field of education proper, W. F. Connell's book, *The Educational Thought and Influence of Matthew Arnold* (1950), supersedes all other work. It is a systematic and thorough analysis. It places Arnold's theories against the contemporary educational background and illuminates both. In view of the importance that Arnold attached to education, it is fitting, perhaps, that this particular aspect of his work should be the first to receive anything like definitive treatment.

PHILOSOPHY AND RELIGION. Among Victorian philosophers the redoubtable F. H. Bradley in his scornful treatment of Arnold's theology (*Ethical Studies*, 1876, revised and expanded 1927) delights T. S. Eliot, who in *For Lancelot Andrewes* (1928) compliments Bradley on the finality of his criticism and the wit of his performance — an aping of Arnold's methods and tricks of speech. T. Sturge Moore, however, in "Matthew Arnold," *Essays and Studies by Members of the English Association* (1938), takes Bradley severely to task for distortion of Arnold's meaning, basing his criticism on a single chapter of *Literature and Dogma,* and misconception of the purpose of Arnold's books on theology. Basil Willey in *Nineteenth Century Studies: Coleridge to Matthew Arnold* (1949) regrets that Arnold's religious books are now little read, for they contain matter of importance for those who are concerned with preserving a rational religion. It is Willey's opinion that religion was Arnold's chief and central interest — all his efforts in criticism, politics, and education really led up to it. A full-length, scholarly treatment of Arnold and religion is long overdue. William Blackburn in his three admirable articles on backgrounds ("The Background of Arnold's *Literature and Dogma*," *MP*, 1945; "Matthew Arnold and the Oriel Noetics," *PQ*, 1946; and "Bishop Butler and the Design of Arnold's *Literature and Dogma*," *MLQ*, 1948), and John Hicks on Arnold's stoicism in *Critical Studies in Arnold, Emerson, and Newman*, by Hicks, E. E. Sandeen, and Alvan S. Ryan (1942) have made a beginning.

ARNOLD AND SCIENCE. On Arnold and science very little work has been done. Fred A. Dudley has contributed an exploratory article, "Matthew Arnold and Science" (*PMLA*, 1942), valuable for its definition of terms. Arnold used the word science in two senses. Of one he always approved: a thorough and systematic knowledge in any field, as opposed to irrational prejudice. Of the other he did not approve so uniformly: science in reference to a particular branch, such as physics or biology. F. E. Faverty's *Matthew Arnold the Ethnologist* (1951) is a discussion of Arnold's racial theories in the light of nineteenth-century classifications of the Celts, the Teutons, the Semites, and the Indo-Europeans. The title of the book is too restrictive, however. Many Victorian writers beside Arnold are treated and wider concepts are examined than those identified with the science of ethnology. The theme, in fact, is the whole confused but significant doctrine of cultural and racial traits which colored much nineteenth-century thinking.

LITERARY THEORY AND PRACTICE. Lionel Stevenson has recently said: "For half a century the critics have insisted on considering the Victorian poets only as sociologists and metaphysicians and then condemning them for their inadequacy in that role. Let us begin to do them justice as artists." It is pleasant to report that a number of recent critics have regarded Arnold as an artist. Among these one of the chief is E. K. Brown. His book, *Matthew Arnold: A Study in Conflict* (1948), following a lead from Geoffrey Tillotson's perceptive essay, "Matthew Arnold: the Critic and the Advocate" (first appearance in *Essays by Divers Hands*, edited by Gordon Bottomley, 1943; later included in G. Tillotson, *Criticism and the Nineteenth Century*, 1951) shows how often Arnold failed to practice the disinterestedness he preached. And where he failed to be disinterested, he failed as an artist. This is most apparent in the social essays. But the divided mind and spirit are evident in all the genres that Arnold practiced. In the poems, the conflict accounts for "the extraordinary success and extraordinary failure within the bounds of a single work," the beautifully accomplished style breaking suddenly into pieces. A similar view of Arnold's disinterestedness is taken by Everett L. Hunt in "Matthew Arnold: the Critic As Rhetorician" (*Quarterly Journal of Speech*, 1934). For all his praise of the objective critic and his attacks upon the rhetoricians, Arnold himself was primarily a rhetorician, attempting to persuade through intuitive rather than logical methods. It was the general reader for whom Arnold wrote with a learning greater than that of twentieth-century journalists, but less than that of twentieth-century professors. With increased specialization and the disappearance of the general reader, Arnold has lost his audience. Today he is reduced to the inglorious level of introducing college freshmen to culture.

Arnold's poetic diction and his prose style have also been analyzed by the critics. John Drinkwater in *Victorian Poetry* (1923) discovers in Arnold's poetic diction a seventeenth-century quality, something of the magic of Vaughan and Marvell. According to Bernard Groom in *On the Diction of Tennyson, Browning, and Arnold* (1939), Arnold's diction is "classical" as distinguished from the "traditional" and the "eccentric" diction of Tennyson and Browning respectively. And Arnold's habit of repeating expressions suggests limitation. The severest judgment on Arnold's diction is found, however, in F. W. Bateson's *English Poetry and the English Language* (1934). Bateson thinks that all mid-Victorian poetry, Tennyson's alone excepted, is badly written. And Arnold's verse specifically is deficient in poetic originality. "The sensibility is not of Arnold himself but of his age, and the style is an amalgam of the language that was then available for poetry, And what a language it was." As E. K. Brown suggests, a full-scale study of Arnold as a stylist in prose is worthy of a book. The most perceptive treatments of the subject thus far are Lewis Gates's in the introduction to his *Selections from the Prose Writings of Matthew Arnold* (1897) and E. K. Brown's own, in his *Matthew Arnold: a Study in Conflict.* They distinguish at least four styles in their author. John C. Major in "Matthew Arnold and Attic Prose Style" (*PMLA*, 1944) attempts an analysis of one type of style.

H. W. Garrod's "Matthew Arnold's 1853 Preface" (*RES*, 1941) is a significant contribution. Arnold's narrow poetic theory, Garrod argues, accounts for his failure in poetic practice. In attacking Keats and Shakespeare, he repudiated the influences that go to make up his own best poems. Between the "Scholar Gypsy" (1853) and "Thyrsis" (1866) lie "the 'Preface' and the desert." Douglas Bush underlines a similar paradox: that Arnold repudiated the Romantic Age while actually drawing nourishment from it (*Mythology and the Romantic Tradition*). George H. Ford in *Keats and the Victorians: a Study of His Influence and Rise to Fame, 1821–1895* (1944) devotes three chapters to Arnold. His thesis is that Arnold acts both as destroyer and preserver of Keats's reputation and influence. The 1853 "Preface" sets up standards in opposition to the practice of Keats and his Victorian successors. But in the *Study of Celtic Literature* and in the essay on Maurice de Guérin, Arnold pays Keats the highest tribute, ranking him with Shakespeare in natural magic, the Celtic strain in English poetry. In style and content Arnold's poetry as a whole is a deliberate departure from the Keats tradition. Among the Romantic poets Keats served as his "principal whipping-boy in matters of style." Arnold's chastened verse is a reaction to Keatsian exuberance. Furthermore, he minimized sensuousness, even to the point of excluding color. His verse-music also is a reaction to the smoothness of style established by Keats and developed by Tennyson. For their harmonies he substituted "a simpler, more intellectualized conversational style." All this holds true for the bulk of Arnold's minor work, yet in his best poems, "The Scholar Gypsy" and "Thyrsis," and in the uneven poems "Tristram and Iseult" and "The Church of Brou" the influence of Keats is pronounced. Thus Arnold turns upon himself, and ironically, the chief opponent of the Keats tradition himself succumbs. Indeed, Arnold's poetry is "the most convincing manifestation" of the importance of Keats's influence on Victorian literature.

In *The Alien Vision*, E. D. H. Johnson maintains that the dialogue of the mind within itself is a characteristic feature of Arnold's poetry. "The protagonists of his poems are invariably lonely and isolated figures, alien to their environment." Arnold accepts alienation and makes a virtue of it — the way of the Romantic poets. Alternating in his early poetry between involvement in and aloofness from his environment, Arnold failed to resolve his conflict. Some of his early poems and many of the letters to Clough attempt to "develop the aesthetic aspect of alienation." In the 1853 "Preface," according to Johnson, Arnold rejects the content and form of his earlier poetry and turns to objectivity and *architectonicè*. Poetry hereafter is regarded as a cultural agent. "The Empedoclean dialogue of the mind with itself was to be replaced by an outward communion between the artist and his public conducted on a no less elevated plane." In his rejection of introspection and in his pursuit of objectivity, Arnold took up narrative and dramatic forms. "Tristram and Iseult," "Sohrab and Rustum," "Balder Dead," and "Merope" show that he was temperamentally incapable of the change. All these poems lapse into the elegiac tone and are related to "The Scholar Gypsy," which is a refutation of most of the principles of the "Preface." "Arnold's myths are really studies in alienation, where the protagonists suffer in all innocence for their superiority to the Time Spirit." In his final chapter, Johnson discusses the transformation of the artist into the man of letters. If the age required an intellectual deliverance, it was Arnold the critic, not Arnold the poet, who would have to supply it. Yet even in the critical essays the subjects he preferred were the "foil'd circuitous" wanderers. In his prose no more than in his poetry was Arnold's conflict to be resolved.

Each of Johnson's main points had been made earlier in the literature on Arnold. His contribution lies in bringing all these theories together and in applying them to a considerable part of Arnold's work. The result, as P. F. Baum suggests in the present volume, is often a "seeing more deeply into the poet's mind." Yet the earlier literature on Arnold should have warned Johnson that his formula — the explanation of the poems on the basis of the artist's alienation from contemporary society — was an over-simplification. The rift between society and its artists is a phenomenon hardly peculiar to the early and mid-nineteenth century. Certainly the rift becomes more pronounced in the latter part of the nineteenth century and the early part of the twentieth. Johnson's thesis, therefore, becomes more convincing when applied, as in *The Last Romantics* (1949) by Graham Hough, to later authors.

REPUTATION AND INFLUENCE. A book on Tennyson and the reviewers appeared in 1952, and Swinburne's literary career and fame were properly chronicled some twenty years ago by C. K. Hyder. Arnold's reputation and influence offer materials even larger and more attractive in scope. As preliminary studies indicate,[3] his battles with the periodicals on social, political and literary questions were lively encounters, calling forth his best powers in irony and satire. In his controversies with the hosts of the orthodox over his religious heresies he gave better than was sent. E. K. Brown in "The French Reputation of Matthew Arnold" (*Studies in English by Members of University College, Toronto,* 1931) supplies evidence in plenty to support a basic law that between their foreign detractors and their eulogizers nations show more

[3] E. K. Brown, "The Critic as Xenophobe" (*SeR,* 1930); M. M. Bevington, *The Saturday Review, 1855–1868: Representative Educated Opinion in Victorian England* (1941); J. D. Jump, "Matthew Arnold and *The Saturday Review*" (*RES,* 1946), and "Matthew Arnold and *The Spectator*" (*RES,* 1949); and F. E. Faverty, *Matthew Arnold the Ethnologist* (1951).

interest in their detractors. Arnold the great friend of France has been given far less consideration in that country than Carlyle. In an important article, "Matthew Arnold and the *Academy*: a Note on English Criticism in the Eighteen-Seventies" (*PMLA*, 1953), Diderik Roll-Hansen shows that Arnold "had been consulted and had approved of the general plan of the new journal." It is one of the major ironies of his career, however, that because of his professional duties and his commitments to other periodicals, Arnold was able to contribute only a few articles to the *Academy*, the distinguished journal realizing his dream of a national organ which should bring about "a more centralized effort in intellectual matters," and carry England into the current of Continental thought.

Arnold is accused by T. S. Eliot of fathering the Decadents, Pater, and his disciples ("Arnold and Pater," *Bookman*, 1930). This paternity is disputed by Leonard Brown ("Matthew Arnold's Succession: 1850–1914," *SeR*, 1934) who emphatically disagrees with Eliot's idea that through Pater, Wilde can be traced to Arnold. Arnold's noblest bequest, according to Brown, was not his opinions but his attitudes, and these the Decadents ignored. His true heirs were the poets who had direct contact with his skepticism and therefore faced life with honesty and courage — Swinburne, Meredith, Hardy, De la Mare, and T. S. Eliot himself. That Eliot *is* a lineal descendant of Arnold is the contention also of M. L. S. Loring in "T. S. Eliot on Matthew Arnold" (*SeR*, 1935). Although Eliot himself will own no connection with Arnold, Loring feels that they are much alike, particularly in their views on the social purpose of criticism and the purpose of art. In a number of respects Eliot is a latter-day Arnold. Eliot's strictures on Arnold in *The Use of Poetry and the Use of Criticism* (1933) — that he is an undergraduate in philosophy and theology, a Philistine in religion; that he is an academic poet; that he is insensitive to style; that his definition of poetry as a criticism of life is meaningless — seem, therefore, to take on the nature of paradox. In a series of illuminating parallels, Douglas Bush (Chapter Fifteen of *Mythology and the Romantic Tradition*) summarizes the relationships between Eliot and Arnold:

> Though one would hesitate to suggest a transmigration of souls (certainly one would not suggest it to Mr. Eliot), and though fundamental differences are at least as marked as resemblances, no one else has come so close to being what Arnold was or what a twentieth-century Arnold might have been. While Mr. Eliot's classicism is less classical, more eclectic and modern, than Arnold's, as critics they are linked together by their fine taste, their cosmopolitan, anti-provincial, anti-romantic conception of literature, their faith in the living value of tradition, authority, standards, discipline. In both has been seen, rightly or wrongly, a cleavage between the groping, disillusioned, romantic poet — to speak only of Mr. Eliot's earlier secular poems — and the confident, dogmatic, classicist critic.

The disillusionment and pessimism of the two poets, according to Bush, have the same general origins. And in revolt from the mechanized and commercialized present, from "arid and ugly actuality," both turn to classic myth.

As early as 1897 Andrew Lang in "The Celtic Renaissance" (*Blackwood's*) traced the origin of the Celtic Revival to Renan and Arnold, the Moses and Aaron respectively of the movement. Further evidence on Arnold's part in this Renaissance is supplied by John V. Kelleher in "Matthew Arnold and the Celtic Revival" (*Perspectives of Criticism*, 1950) and F. E. Faverty in the fifth chapter of *Matthew Arnold the Ethnologist*.

Arnold was also the Patron Saint of Irving Babbitt and his circle, the American Neo-Humanists of the 1920's, as Everett L. Hunt convincingly demonstrates in "Matthew Arnold and His Critics" (*SeR*, 1936). Irving Babbitt, Norman Foerster, and Paul Elmer More were disciples of Arnold in their attitude toward Romanticism and in their defense of absolute standards of taste. Following Stuart P. Sherman's rehabilitation of Arnold (*Matthew Arnold, How to Know Him*, 1917), the Neo-Humanists developed the ethical side of his criticism to such an extreme that Arnold himself would probably have called them "Hebraists" (W. S. Knickerbocker, "Asides and

Soliloquies. Farewell to Neo-Humanism," *SeR*, 1930). And for the last forty years, university departments of English, American ones particularly, have been accused of deriving most of their critical opinions from one source — Matthew Arnold. Indeed, he "may even be said to have established the teaching of English as an academic profession" (Lionel Trilling, "Literature and Power," *Kenyon Review*, 1940).

In conclusion it can be said that Arnold's power to incite dissent is as strong today as ever. Everett L. Hunt in "Matthew Arnold and His Critics" shows that he is denounced and praised for different reasons by each critic. The basic quarrels of the critics are not with Arnold, but with each other, over the very nature of literature, criticism, religion, and society. Excellent illustrations are provided in Theodore Morrison's "Dover Beach Revisited. A New Fable for Critics" (*Harper's Magazine*, 1940) and in the 1953 exchange of asperities between F. W. Bateson ("The Function of Criticism at the Present Time," *Essays in Criticism*) and F. R. Leavis ("The Responsible Critic: or the Function of Criticism at any Time," *Scrutiny*). The title *Essays in Criticism* is singularly appropriate for the periodical that started its career at Oxford University a few years ago. Let us hope that in this case Oxford will not be the home of a lost cause.

A glance at the bibliographies for the last few decades reveals that Arnold's reputation in one or another of its facets has been assigned almost annually at some American or Canadian university as a thesis for the Master's or the Doctor's degree. Of these, the fullest and best, the one most deserving publication, is Marion Mainwaring's "Matthew Arnold's Influence and Reputation as a Literary Critic," a Radcliffe College doctoral dissertation, 1949. Miss Mainwaring presents a great deal of new information on Arnold the poet as well as on Arnold the critic, for, like almost all commentators on Arnold, she finds an absolute separation of his two major activities impossible:

The principal concern is with Arnold's literary criticism, but since his work was integrated as well as varied, and since many readers have been prejudiced in favor of or against his asethetic by their attitude towards his non-literary criticism, some consideration has inevitably been given his poetry and his writings on education, theology, politics, and sociology.

Although Arnold's contemporary influence is treated in great detail, and his posthumous career is given only in résumé, the history of certain theories and certain individual works is carried from the beginning to the present.

If all these scattered materials on Arnold's reputation and influence were brought together by some practiced hand, the result would be a fascinating and instructive account of the changes in culture and literary taste of the last one hundred years.[4]

[4] The limits in the criticism of Arnold's poetry are set at one extreme by T. Sturge Moore ("Matthew Arnold," *Essays and Studies by Member of the English Association,* 1938) for whom Arnold is the most satisfying of Victorian poets, and at the other extreme by J. D. Jump (*Matthew Arnold,* 1955) who insists that Arnold wrote only one great poem, "Dover Beach." Had his critical theories allowed him to rely oftener on symbolic landscapes, such as Dover, Berkshire, the Oxus, in which, says Jump, his deepest personal feelings were enlisted, he would have had greater artistic success. But in his pursuit of classical objectivity he excluded the subjective too rigidly. "As a result, too much of his work consists of uncreative ruminations and academic exercises."

6 ßᴥ

Algernon Charles Swinburne

Clyde K. Hyder

I. *Bibliography*

Nᴏʙᴏᴅʏ ɪs ɴᴏᴡ ᴛᴇᴍᴘᴛᴇᴅ to say that Swinburne was fortunate in his chief bibliographer, Thomas J. Wise, whose useful bibliography (1919–20; Bonchurch Edition, XX, 1927) cannot be trusted, though, like his *Swinburne Library* (1925; mainly based upon the earlier *Catalogue* of the Ashley Library, it cannot safely be neglected. The famous *Enquiry into the Nature of Certain Nineteenth Century Pamphlets* by Carter and Pollard (1934) identified three editions as forgeries — *Dead Love, Dolores, Siena* (one of the English editions); three other titles were rightly branded as suspect — *Laus Veneris, Cleopatra, An Appeal to England against the Execution of the Condemned Fenians* (the pamphlet, not the broadside). *The Firm of Charles Ottley, Landon and Co., Footnote to an Inquiry* (1948) named Wise as the culprit, demonstrating that *A Word for the Navy* (not the volume printed by George Redway, a true first edition), *The Question, The Jubilee,* and *Gathered Songs* are also spurious and that Wise falsely accused an earlier Swinburne bibliographer, R. H. Shepherd, in order to shield himself. Other writers (see especially Wilfred Partington, *Forging Ahead,* 1939) have raised the suspicion that certain "rarities" were really piracies — for instance, *Grace Darling, The Ballad of Bulgarie, Robert Burns: A Poem, A Sequence of Sonnets on the Death of Robert Browning.*

The student may ignore the older bibliographies by Wise (1897), Shepherd, Thomson, Vaughan, and O'Brien.[1] None of the bibliographies deal systematically with the manuscripts, a partial census of which has been compiled by J. S. Mayfield.

II. *Editions and Texts*

A large part of Swinburne's work is accessible only in the Bonchurch Edition (1925–27), the text of which is incomplete and shockingly corrupt. Without explanation Gosse and Wise changed the order of some poems and arbitrarily omitted others, as well as important prose writings like the *Dedicatory Epistle* to the first collected edition of the poems (1904) — an edition with a far more dependable text than theirs.[2]

Since 1925 other writings by Swinburne have been published. *Ballads of the English Border*, edited by W. A. Mac-Innes (1925), contains the poet's preface and the texts of twenty-six popular ballads, reconstructed on the assumption that one may combine passages from variant versions. Not without interest in relation to Swinburne's literary apprenticeship, the book is carelessly edited; the arrangement of texts is misleading.

Another aspect of Swinburne's apprenticeship was studied in G. Lafourcade's *Swinburne's "Hyperion" and Other Poems* (1927). The Introduction points out that, though he considered Keats supreme in his sphere, Swinburne conceived of that sphere as limited by lack of dominating moral ideas; [3]

---

[1] O'Brien's bibliography, in *A Pilgrimage of Pleasure* (1913), lists two published letters not listed by Wise (item 115, p. 167). Among the writings by Swinburne included in the volume is the early morality contributed to Mrs. Disney Leith's *The Children of the Chapel*.

[2] For some instances of editorial bungling in the Bonchurch Edition see the notes in Chew's *Swinburne*, pp. 151, 154, 286, 291. "The Sea-Swallows" was omitted from the text of *Poems and Ballads*; five poems were added. Prose passages on Congreve, Charles Wells, Webster, and Tourneur, and "Sir Henry Taylor on Shelley" were also among the omissions.

[3] Cf. Cecil Lang's text of a fragmentary essay in the Harvard Library ("Swinburne on Keats," *MLN*, 1949).

furthermore, the publication of the letters to Fanny Brawne affected him much as they did Arnold. In Swinburne's imitative poem we find fatality and a loosely "pantheistic" outlook instead of Keatsian ideas of beauty and progress. According to Lafourcade, the most lasting result of Swinburne's study of Keats appears in his diction, especially in the use of compounds.

In the second volume of *La Jeunesse de Swinburne* (1928), Lafourcade included extracts from "The Temple of Janus," as well as two contributions to the rare *Undergraduate Papers*. He also included a passage from the manuscript, *The Chronicle of Tebaldeo Tebaldei*, which he thought Swinburne had intended for his prose *Triameron*, a collection of stories planned but not completed. Randolph Hughes, who does not believe it was so intended, has edited the *Chronicle*, with an addition to Swinburne's title, in *Lucretia Borgia: The Chronicle of Tebaldeo Tebaldei* (1942) — according to its editor, "virtually a new study of the poet." He may claim originality of emphasis in discussing Swinburne's affinities with the Renaissance, at times overstressed. He dwells upon the poet's "anti-Platonism." One would find it easier to appreciate Hughes's study if the tone of his references to his predecessors were more gentlemanly. Wise's mistakes are often exasperating, but Hughes himself is not infallible.[4]

Hughes's purpose in *Lesbia Brandon by Algernon Charles Swinburne: An Historical and Critical Commentary Being Largely a Study (and Elevation) of Swinburne as a Novelist* (1952) is partly clear from the title. Though Swinburne had gifts which any novelist would envy, *Lesbia Brandon*, even after Hughes's laborious ordering of the text, is barely readable. But the imagery of some passages is strikingly imaginative, and the whole is not without biographical interest. Hughes's comments upon Swinburne's relationship to French novelists are well informed. The tone of the book, which runs to 618 pages, 189 of them devoted to Swinburne's text

---

[4] On pp. 64 and 65, for instance, is a bitter denunciation of Lafourcade and Wise for supposing (correctly) that in his youth Swinburne wrote fragments of a play on Cesare Borgia. On p. 73, *Dead Love* of 1864 is mentioned as if the edition of that date were not a forgery.

(interestingly enough, Hughes refers to Lafourcade's *La Jeunesse* as "huge" or "gargantuan" and accuses its author of being "wofully deficient in literary tact and delicacy"), is offensive: "I chivalrously warn anyone who thinks of entering the lists against me on behalf of Gosse — or any other persons I attack in this book — that this will be a perilous piece of charity." The most devastating rejoinder to the tiresomely reiterated strictures upon the accuracy of such writers as Gosse and Lafourcade was Cecil Lang's partial but extensive list of Hughes's blunders and misprints (*TLS,* 31 October 1952).[5]

Editions of Swinburne's "Changes of Aspect" and "Short Notes," by C. K. Hyder, appeared in *PMLA* (1943). The first of these reveals Swinburne's sensitiveness to the charge of inconsistency, defending his changing points of view on Ireland and on Byron, Tennyson, Arnold, W. B. Scott, Blake, Whitman; some passages touch upon the calling and character of poets. "Short Notes" are remarks on Ibsen, G. H. Lewes, and Arnold. Editorial comments include a discussion of Swinburne's invective which draws illustrations from his other works.

Some shorter writings by Swinburne cannot be fully discussed here.[6] Nor is there space to consider the volumes of

---

[5] Hughes is also responsible for "Greek Verses of Swinburne Hitherto Unpublished in England" (*Nineteenth Century and After,* 1937), a title making an unjustified claim, since W. R. Rutland had included the Greek verses originally appearing in *Le Tombeau de Théophile Gautier,* in his *Swinburne: A Nineteenth Century Hellene* (Oxford, 1931), along with a translation. In "Unpublished Swinburne" (*Life and Letters,* 1948) Hughes quotes some lines by Swinburne which, he believes, point to "an earlier, hitherto unnoticed love-affair."

[6] "Two Scenes from a Tragedy by Algernon Charles Swinburne," by E. H. W. Meyerstein, appeared in *The London Mercury* (1938). J. S. Mayfield has printed *A Roundel of Retreat* (1950) and six lines of a poem on Columbus (1944), and has deposited a photostatic copy of Swinburne's notebook in the Library of Congress and in the Brotherton Library at the University of Leeds. The appendix to J. Pope-Hennessy's *Monckton Milnes: The Flight of Youth* (1951) quotes Swinburne's French verses on the Marquis de Sade, "*Charenton en 1810,*" but the "undated love-song" cited in the same appendix is really an early version of Rossetti's "The Song of the Bower." Cecil Lang's "The First Chorus of Swinburne's *Atalanta*" (*Yale University Library Gazette,* 1953) reproduces "the holograph first version of the opening lines of the

selections from his work, though he is an author whom the beginning student would do well to read in selections.[7]

No satisfactory text of Swinburne's letters is now available. The selection edited by Gosse and Wise (1918) was reproduced in the Bonchurch Edition, together with some other letters, mostly addressed to W. M. Rossetti. The badly arranged letters in Mrs. Disney Leith's *The Boyhood of Algernon Swinburne* (1917) are both pleasant and revealing. Another extensive selection was prepared by Thomas Hake and Arthur Compton-Rickett (1918). Neither the text nor the dating in these three collections can be trusted. The Bonchurch Edition omits the important letters to the press. Cecil Lang is now preparing an edition of some 1,500 letters; he has given a foretaste of his quality as editor and commentator.[8]

Clearly, the textual study of Swinburne has been neglected, though it should be rewarding. J. S. Mayfield, who has examined many copies of the first edition of *Atalanta*, has found variant states unnoticed by Wise.

III. *Studies Primarily Biographical*

The merits and defects of Gosse's *Life* (1917; slightly revised for the Bonchurch Edition) are too well known to require extended treatment. It is readable and vivid, the work of a personal friend who possessed literary tact and skill, as well as a tendency to embellish, and whose reticences were doubtless due partly to loyalty and partly to notions of biographical candor different from ours. It cannot be ignored,

---

well-known invocation to Artemis." Miss F. E. Ratchford's "Swinburne at Work" (*SeR*, 1923) and Gosse's "The First Draft of Swinburne's *Anactoria*" (*MLR*, 1919) also study manuscripts for evidence on the poet's methods of composition.

[7] In recent years, selections, all without notes, have been edited by Richard Church, Henry Treece, Edward Shanks, Humphrey Hare. Though earlier annotated selections were edited by W. M. Payne and by W. O. Raymond, *The Best of Swinburne* (1937), edited by C. K. Hyder and Lewis Chase, seems to be the only annotated volume of selections now in print.

[8] In "Swinburne's Letters to Henry Arthur Bright" (*Yale University Library Gazette*, 1950) and in "ALS: Swinburne to William Michael Rossetti" (*Journal of the Rutgers University Library*, 1950).

but it cannot be fully trusted, for Gosse, who relied much upon oral sources, was disinclined to take pains in the verification of his statements, many of which have been disproved.[9]

Since the appearance of Gosse's pioneer biography, the most substantial contribution to our knowledge of Swinburne has been made by G. Lafourcade, the first volume of whose *La Jeunesse de Swinburne* (1928) is biographical. Lafourcade gives a fuller treatment than Gosse of such topics as Swinburne's family background, education, and friendships. He writes frankly of the poet's algolagnia. Lafourcade's later *Swinburne: A Literary Biography* (1932), though less important to the special student, supplies some new material.[10] In this and the earlier work, Lafourcade supplements and corrects Gosse — for instance, in regard to the poet's travels and the date and occasion of "The Death of Sir John Franklin." His discussion of *Songs before Sunrise* and of Swinburne's later career is more illuminating than Gosse's.

Because of its subtitle and its heavy indebtedness to Lafourcade, along with disregard of research by others, Humphrey Hare's *Swinburne: A Biographical Approach* (1949), may be mentioned here. Lafourcade was sometimes led astray by formulas; Hare oversimplifies what he found in Lafourcade. Swinburne's erotic sensibility is made the key to

[9] A recent article challenging Gosse's reliability is R. H. Super's "A Grain of Truth about Wordsworth and Browning, Landor and Swinburne" (*MLN*, 1952). Gosse's sketch in the *Dictionary of National Biography* gave currency to a false attribution of verses signed "A. C. S." His account of Swinburne's experiences in Normandy, in *Portraits and Sketches*, may profitably be compared with Lafourcade's. The attempt to link Gosse with Wise's forgeries has won little support. See, for instance, W. O. Raymond's *The Infinite Moment and Other Essays in Robert Browning* (1950); and cf. W. Partington's *Forging Ahead* (1939), especially pp. 168–169.

[10] Lafourcade's attribution to Swinburne of a criticism on himself which appeared in the *République des Lettres*, accepted by some reviewers, was based on flimsy evidence. Cecil Lang calls attention to a Swinburne letter (see Hake and Compton-Rickett, pp. 160–161) which indicates that Swinburne did not write the article or others by "Herbert Harvey." The poet mentions missing an issue containing (as he thought) a sequel to the article upon himself which was said in the article to be forthcoming, but which did not appear.

In reference to the canon, one may note here that some of Swinburne's contributions to the *Spectator* in 1862 are unidentified. See Chew's *Swinburne*, p. 48 n., and his earlier article (*MLN*, 1920).

an interpretation of *Atalanta,* described as "intellectualized algolagnia," the author alleging that after *Poems and Ballads* "the synthesis is abandoned and with it the theory of Art for Art's sake, . . . its necessary moral justification." Swinburne may have modified his theories about art, but he did not abandon them; his interest in Italy was older than his interest in the Marquis de Sade.

Hare unduly minimizes Swinburne's later work. In his earlier "Swinburne and 'Le vice anglais' " (*Horizon,* 1947; compare this title with that of an appendix in Praz's *The Romantic Agony*), Hare mentions the sense of isolation associated with Swinburne's sexual nature. But he does not take into account the effect of the poet's isolation, which did not diminish with the years — deafness, too, became a factor in his social life — the years that usually bring a loss of power; instead Hare attributes Swinburne's decline to the abandonment of "the algolagnic synthesis." Because of his dislike of Watts-Dunton, Gosse fostered the impression that Swinburne was overshadowed by his friend's personality. In an article whose title is taken from a phrase of Gosse's, " 'Within a Leyden jar': Swinburne and Watts-Dunton (1879–1909)" (*Horizon,* 1949), Hare repeats the old charge that Watts-Dunton caused the poet to turn against his youthful idols, such as Whitman and Baudelaire. But Swinburne's early opinion of Whitman was not one of unqualified approval,[11] and his alleged repudiation of Baudelaire — with whom, he said, he never had much in common — probably seemed to Swinburne a mere statement of fact; moreover, he doubtless resented being linked with Baudelaire by such persons as Robert Buchanan, who charged that the English poets of "the fleshly school" were mere imitators of the Frenchman.

Of the accounts of Swinburne and Watts-Dunton, the most delightful is Max Beerbohm's "No. 2. The Pines" — a work of art even if, like the pictures in his *Rossetti and His Circle*

[11] Cf. W. B. Cairns, "Swinburne's Opinion of Whitman" (*AL,* 1931); Lafourcade, "Swinburne and Walt Whitman" (*MLR,* 1927); Cecil Lang's "Swinburne and American Literature: with Six Hitherto Unpublished Letters" (*AL,* 1948). Lang's "A Further Note on Swinburne and Whitman" (*MLN,* 1949), lists the relevant books, with inscriptions, in Swinburne's library.

(1922), something of a caricature. Alfred Noyes's *Two Worlds for Memory* (1953) is more factual. Clara Watts-Dunton's *The Home Life of Swinburne* is naïve and anecdotal, but, like Mrs. Disney Leith's reminiscences, characterizes Swinburne as pleasant in his personal relations, thus tending to balance other observers' over-lurid descriptions. C. Kernahan's *Swinburne as I Knew Him* (1919) is also anecdotal. H. G. Wright's "Unpublished Letters from Theodore Watts-Dunton to Swinburne" (*RES*, 1934) illustrates Watts-Dunton's tact, incidentally showing that it was in 1872 (not 1873, as Gosse states) that he took over the management of his friend's business affairs. L. A. Marchand's "The Watts-Dunton Letter Books" (*Journal of the Rutgers University Library*, 1953) states that "the tendency if not the aim" of Watts-Dunton's last years with Swinburne "was to tame the wild bear he was proud to exhibit and to channel the poet's energies and his writing into safe and conventional paths."

Watts-Dunton has been accused of grooming Swinburne for the poet-laureateship — a position he would not have accepted. A behind-the-scenes account, "Swinburne and the Poet-Laureateship," by P. Knaplund (*TQ*, 1937) explains that Lord Acton called Gladstone's attention to the moral aspects of *Poems and Ballads*, as well as Swinburne's anti-Russian writings and advocacy of tyrannicide.

Among the books discussing Swinburne's other friendships are Helen R. Angeli's on D. G. Rossetti and on C. A. Howell. A study of John Nichol, by R. D. MacLeod, is reported to be under way. J. Pope-Hennessy's *Monckton Milnes: The Flight of Youth* (1951) modifies the picture of Lord Houghton and his influence in Lafourcade's *La Jeunesse*, emphasizing Swinburne's macabre sense of humor, as illustrated by his extravagant references to "the divine Marquis" even before he read the books lent to him by Lord Houghton.[12]

Gosse's story of the supposed central episode of Swinburne's emotional history was accepted by later writers, in-

---

[12] Lafourcade's conclusion (in *"L'Algolagnie de Swinburne," Hippocrate*, 1935, he supplied details) that Swinburne was *"un sado-masochiste"* has been attacked by Hughes, who argues that the poet was simply a masochist.

cluding Hughes, who, however, in his edition of *Lesbia Brandon* promised "definite evidence" of its falsity. J. S. Mayfield cites plenty of evidence to discredit the story (his mimeographed statement, 1953, was followed by "Swinburne's Boo"; published in *English Miscellany*, IV, and also in book form). He proves that Jane Faulkner was only ten years old in 1862, when Gosse thought Swinburne proposed to her, and was not married till 1871. Though Mayfield records a suggestion by B. Falk that "Gosse and Lafourcade must have mistaken Jane for an elder sister," he proposes no new candidate for Jane's role; his important discovery clears the way for further investigation.

Uncertainty also exists about the role of a woman fond of roles, Adah Menken. Falk's revised edition of his journalistic, sentimental, and undocumented biography of her (1952) adds nothing to our knowledge. With no evidence of the date when she and Swinburne met, he assumes that "Dolores" was inspired by her, though obviously it was rooted in the poet's reading and imagination. More inexcusably, he assumes that Swinburne's disavowal of "Dolorida" was a personal betrayal, whereas Swinburne was correct in saying that he had not contributed to an annual edited by A. M. Moore the lines in question, which appear in *Lesbia Brandon* and which were apparently copied as an inscription in Adah Menken's album. The title "Dolorida" had been used by Alfred de Vigny, and the name Dolores (in Latin, "pains," "sorrows") is an appropriate one for Swinburne's Anti-Madonna, "Our Lady of Pain," in "Dolores."

IV. *Sources of Inspiration*

Swinburne thought of books as living things; to consider them as sources of inspiration, in a category separate from that of experience, would have seemed to him arbitrary. The sale catalogue of his library and his letter on "The Hundred Best Books," as well as numerous literary allusions, bear witness to the catholicity of his reading.

His debt to both the Hebrews and the Greeks was vast.

But though his debt to the Bible and the Book of Common Prayer has not been adequately appraised, Swinburne's Hellenism has interested many students. Douglas Bush's treatment of Swinburne in *Mythology and the Romantic Tradition in English Poetry* shows command of the relevant scholarship and cites more references than can be mentioned here.[13] W. R. Rutland's *Swinburne: A Nineteenth Century Hellene* (1931) deals at length with the Meleager myth and with the relation of *Atalanta* to Greek drama, as well as with "the Hellenistic poems." Rutland is less accurate and polished than Bush but more generous in critical judgments. C. M. Bowra, obviously unschooled in certain revelations by Lafourcade or Praz, and, it may be, on that account less biased in his critical emphases, has praised *Atalanta* (*The Romantic Imagination*, 1949) as "profoundly and inescapably Greek," though pointing out that its author's love of the sea and of wild places, his delight in childhood and the family affections, his imagination and genius for language were important in shaping the play. In many ways Swinburne's experience was wholesome, even "normal," and Bowra's admirable criticism makes us wonder whether too much attention is not given to one component of that experience.

Like the Romantic poets of whom he was an heir and like his friends in the Pre-Raphaelite group, Swinburne was attracted to the medieval world. Lafourcade's *La Jeunesse* discusses the poet's study of Dante and of Villon. For the sources of the Arthurian poems, the student may turn first to S. C. Chew's *Swinburne* (1929). C. K. Hyder's "Swinburne and the Popular Ballad" (*PMLA*, 1934) is concerned with one of the earliest and most enduring of Swinburne's literary enthusiasms.[14]

[13] See especially the titles by Pound and Wier, listed in the bibliography to Hyder's *Swinburne's Literary Career and Fame*. Wier has also published an annotated edition of Swinburne's two classical plays (Ann Arbor [1922?]). Lafourcade's edition of *Atalanta* (1930) and his discussion in *La Jeunesse* should not be overlooked. The conflict of Hellenism and nineteenth-century culture is briefly surveyed in G. Highet's *The Classical Tradition* (1950; see especially Chapter 20) and in W. C. DeVane's "Browning and the Spirit of Greece" (in *Nineteenth-Century Studies*, ed. Herbert Davis *et al.*, 1940).

[14] Hyder's "Swinburne's *Laus Veneris* and the Tannhäuser Legend"

Swinburne's interest in the Renaissance has been discussed by Hughes (cited above); its chief literary manifestation was in his books on Elizabethan drama and his non-Hellenic plays. G. C. Spivey's "Swinburne's Use of Elizabethan Drama" (*SP*, 1944) lists literary devices thought to be borrowed from the Elizabethans; some of the parallels mentioned are unconvincing. Chew's chapter on the dramas considers sources. B. Ifor Evans in *English Poetry of the Later Nineteenth Century* (1933) includes some specific statements about the sources of *The Queen-Mother* and the plays on Mary Stuart.[15]

Swinburne's early verse shows his study of the eighteenth-century poets. His obligations to the Romantics need little comment. The author of *Hellas* and *Prometheus Unbound* was the object of lifelong enthusiasm to the author of *Songs before Sunrise*, as nearly all books on the latter explain. Also well known is the influence, personal and literary, of D. G. Rossetti and his circle. Several of the early poems now accessible in the Bonchurch Edition, as well as some in *Poems and Ballads*, show the influence of Rossetti and the more tangible influence of Morris. Differing views on the so-called Pre-Raphaelite phase of Swinburne's work are presented by Lafourcade and by T. E. Welby in *The Victorian Romantics 1850–70* (1929). And see also Chapter VII in the present volume.

Personal contacts and letters quickened Swinburne's devotion to his three great teachers — Landor, Hugo, Mazzini. W. B. D. Henderson's *Swinburne and Landor* (1918) perhaps

---

(*PMLA*, 1930) and "The Medieval Background of Swinburne's *The Leper*" (*PMLA*, 1931) may be cited here. In spite of some recent misguided comments, necrophilia plays no important part in "The Leper," which contains nothing unparalleled in medieval life and narrative. There may be a hint of necrophilia in the prose *Dead Love*, which, however, turns upon an evil spirit's dwelling in a human body — a widely diffused theme of which Swinburne could have learned from Dante (cf. the citations in Grandgent's edition of the *Commedia*, 1933, p. 296).

[15] Because of limitations of space the following can only be mentioned: E. Probst, *Der Einfluss Shakespeares auf die Stuart-Trilogie Swinburnes* (1935); Sir Archibald T. Strong's *Four Studies* (1933); Curtis Dahl's "Swinburne's Loyalty to the House of Stuart" (*SP*, 1949) ; and doctoral dissertations by Stella Heilbrunn (Chicago, 1915) and Josephine Chandler (California, 1935).

claims too much in attributing to Landor "the passionate love of liberty and contempt of tyrants which is one characteristic of *The Queen Mother*," though Henderson may be right in supposing the elder poet to have been responsible for Swinburne's advocacy of tyrannicide. Henderson identifies the foster-father of "Thalassius" as Landor. (When, during his visit to The Pines, Paul de Reul asked Swinburne who the old man of that poem and of the "Prelude" to *Songs before Sunrise* was, the poet replied, "Je ne sais pas . . . plutôt Landor.")

Like other critics, notably Lafourcade and Chew, Henderson also touches upon the influence of Mazzini on *Songs before Sunrise*. H. W. Rudman's *Italian Nationalism and English Letters* (1940) offers a broad perspective, though Rudman rather tantalizingly raises questions which he does not solve, such as the exact role of Swinburne's teacher at Oxford, Aurelio Saffi. Mazzini, whose charm and moral force won many disciples in England, perhaps more than Hugo imparted to Swinburne the vision of the universal Republic, the goal towards which humanity was believed to be moving.

The subject of Hugo's influence has been discussed at some length by Reul (*L'Œuvre de Swinburne*, 1922) and more briefly by Lafourcade and Chew. Parallels between *Les Châtiments* and *Songs before Sunrise* and *Songs of Two Nations* have been noted. Similarities have been found in the two poets' denunciations of Louis Napoleon and of the Pope. In rhyme and vocabulary, Swinburne's French songs are remarkably close to some passages in Hugo. Lafourcade thought the opening scene in *The Queen Mother* partly inspired by Hugo's *Le Roi s'amuse*. G. Jean-Aubry's *"Victor Hugo et Swinburne"* (*Revue Bleue*, 1936) is mainly concerned with personal relations and correspondence. Jean-Aubry errs in declaring that Swinburne's only translation of Hugo was that of "Les Enfants pauvres." Miss Ruth Faurot once pointed out to the author of this chapter that "Love" (Bonchurch Edition, II, 59) translates a song in Hugo's *Ruy Blas*. ("Love," by the way, is mentioned by Lafourcade as exemplifying the Pre-Raphaelite influence!)

Ludwig Richter's *Swinburne's* [*sic*] *Verhältnis zu Frankreich und Italien* (1911) is sketchy and superficial in its discussion of the relations between Swinburne and such writers as Hugo and Baudelaire. Swinburne himself thought that Reul, whose *Swinburne et la France* appeared in the poet's lifetime, had overemphasized Baudelaire's influence; a similar criticism has been made of a recent work, F. Delattre's *Charles Baudelaire et le jeune Swinburne* (1930). Harold Nicolson's "Swinburne and Baudelaire" (*Essays by Divers Hands* . . . , edited by G. K. Chesterton, 1926) compares the two poets' literary qualities. Swinburne's debt to other French writers, particularly Dumas, Balzac, and Gautier, is discussed in the two longer works edited by Hughes, mentioned above. Ruth Z. Temple's *The Critic's Alchemy* (1953) stresses Swinburne's indebtedness to Gautier and the relative soundness of his appreciation of French poetry. Lafourcade has dwelt upon the poet's borrowings from Sade, especially in "Dolores," "Anactoria," *Atalanta,* and *William Blake.* Cecil Lang finds that "Song before Death," in *Poems and Ballads,* translates a song in Sade's *Aline et Valcour.* Martha H. Shackford's "Swinburne and Delavigne" (*PMLA,* 1918) proposes "*Les Limbes*" as the source of "The Garden of Proserpine." K. L. Knickerbocker's "The Source of Swinburne's *Les Noyades*" suggests that Carlyle, not Louis Blanc as Richter thought, supplied the legend used in the poem. Eileen Souffrin (*Revue de littérature comparée,* 1950) writes of "*Swinburne et Banville*" (and see also her article cited in the concluding section). A few other articles on Swinburne's relations with foreign authors are listed in F. Baldensperger and W. P. Friederich, *Bibliography of Comparative Literature* (1950).

Since the study of sources has little value unless it helps one to explain or to judge an author's work, the mere fact that material was borrowed is of course less significant than the use made of it. Furthermore, no complete survey of Swinburne's sources is possible; clearly such a survey would embrace more than his reading. Mrs. Disney Leith tells of the effect of Handel's music on the poet during the composition of *Atalanta*; Swinburne's interest in Wagner is also acknowledged. His lifelong interest in painting helped to shape several poems and poetic passages — to say nothing of his criticism of art, in which he became an example for Pater. Though the influence of painting is manifest in such poems as "A Ballad of Life," "A Christmas Carol," "Before the Mirror," "Erotion," and "Cleopatra," no systematic study of it exists.[16]

V. *Swinburne's Thought and Art*

Swinburne's relations to his contemporaries and his use of contemporary ideas were complex for a poet sometimes said to have lived in isolation. The topic will repay study. A lecture by W. K. Clifford (*Lectures and Essays,* 1879) has influenced subsequent criticism of *Songs before Sunrise.* Clifford used "To Walt Whitman in America" and other poems to illustrate "cosmic emotion" — "emotion felt in regard to the universe or sum of things." He explains how Swinburne links evolution with freedom and with the ideal Republic. To a few later critics, Swinburne's describing man as "the master of things," in the "Hymn of Man," seems unforgivable; obsessed with recent events, they agree with Emerson: "Things are in the saddle, and ride mankind." One answer could reflect a point of view like that of Gilbert Murray, who declares that the Positivist venerates "not everything that is characteristic of Man, but that quality, or that effort, by which Man is morally and intellectually higher than the beasts" (quoted from "What is Permanent in Positivism," in *Stoic, Christian, and Humanist,* 1950). Moreover, the Positivist's disinterested altruism, which hopes for no reward, is much like that expressed in "The Pilgrims."

J. W. Beach's *The Concept of Nature in Nineteenth-Century English Poetry* (1936) gives a sympathetic exposition of

[16] T. E. Welby, whose *Victorian Romantics* includes a few pages on Simeon Solomon, seems correct in believing that Swinburne's "At a Month's End" preceded the design by the painter, despite the statement in the *DNB* article on Solomon.

Swinburne's outlook, though excluding from consideration his descriptive poetry and those poems, such as "A Nympholept," in which he deals with the more primitive feelings towards nature. For Beach, Swinburne is an English poet who has so well assimilated evolutionary ideas that he "has already invented a highly poetical vocabulary in which to render what is for him the spiritual gift of evolution, its bearing upon human conduct and destiny."

By a curiosity of criticism, the poet who mainly grounded his views in what he considered fundamental realities has been charged with lacking an "internal centre"; it is ironical that Meredith's phrase, applied to Swinburne before he had written any of his greater works, should have become fashionable, for Meredith's outlook is remarkably similar to Swinburne's. (What Meredith wrote in 1861 was, "I don't see any internal centre. . . .") Welby and others find the poet's "internal centre" to be his devotion to freedom. Herbert Dingle in *Science and Literary Criticism* (1949) thinks that it is "the passion for immersion in an infinite and indefinite environment."

As a critic, too, Swinburne had an "internal centre." Ruth C. Child's "Swinburne's Mature Standards of Criticism" (*PMLA*, 1937) collects passages indicating that he reserved his highest admiration for loftiness of thought and power of emotion — not merely skill of expression. T. E. Connolly's "Swinburne's Theory of Art" (*ELH*, 1952) rightly emphasizes the preëminence of Swinburne's republicanism over his art-for-art's-sake views, though Swinburne did not repudiate but rather modified the latter, stating that art for art's sake is sound as an affirmation but unsound as a prohibition of subjects like politics. A. J. Farmer's *Le Mouvement esthétique et "décadent" en Angleterre* (1931) and J. H. Buckley's *The Victorian Temper* (1951) help to clarify Swinburne's historic position in the "aesthetic movement." A. A. Löhrer's *Swinburne als Kritiker der Literatur* (1925) catalogues the poet's opinions on many authors. The citations referring to Americans may be supplemented by Cecil Lang's "Swinburne and American Literature: with Six Hitherto Unpublished

Letters" (*AL*, 1948).[17] Some of the longer studies listed in the final section, below, discuss Swinburne's criticism.

The more technical aspects of Swinburne's poetic art have probably been the subject of less disagreement than his ideas. Any appraisal of his technique should take into account what he himself thought of as the inner (rather than the merely external) music of verse. From a somewhat mechanical point of view, M. Kado's *Swinburnes Verskunst* (1911) makes an inventory of metrical forms under such headings as "lyric," "song," "ballad." A few pages in Saintsbury's *History of English Prosody* (1910) are more instructive. Lafourcade describes the meters used in *Poems and Ballads*. R. H. Fletcher's "The Metrical Forms Used by Certain Victorian Poets" (*JEGP*, 1908) furnishes some statistics, estimating that Swinburne used 420 metrical and stanzaic forms, almost twice as many as Tennyson (240) and Browning (200).

Swinburne's diction has been considered, not always in relation to his poetic effects, by Thomas, Drinkwater, Reul, Nicolson, Lafourcade, Chew, and others. An old-fashioned treatise, G. Serner's *On the Language of Swinburne's Lyrics and Epics* (1910), brings out the extent of the poet's archaisms and coinages in archaic patterns, as well as his fondness for compounds, especially participial compounds. Serner used an earlier study by H. W. F. Wollaeger. J. R. Firth's "Modes of Meaning" (in the English Association *Essays and Studies*, 1951) has a section on Swinburne, "the most phonetic of all English poets," emphasizing "idiosyncrasies which make it [Swinburne's language] so personal that it can be called Swinburnese." T. S. Eliot (*The Sacred Wood*, 1920) explains why Swinburne's "diffuseness" may, as in "The Triumph of Time," be considered a peculiar artistic achievement.

Most of Eliot's followers among "the new critics" have been anti-Romantic; perhaps partly for this reason and partly because of the nature of Swinburne's language, with an alleged lack of progression and correlation in his imagery, "explications" of his poems have not been numerous, though the first volume of the *Explicator* (1943) does contain a dis-

[17] Newton Arvin's "Swinburne as a Critic" (*SeR*, 1924) may also be cited.

cussion of "Autumn in Cornwall." Possibly the most curious explication of recent years is one of "Hertha," in E. M. W. Tillyard's *Five Poems* (1948). Tillyard assumes that "Hertha" and other poems were all "called forth" by Swinburne's "fury" against the Œcumenical Council (compare, however, Lafourcade, *Swinburne*, 1932, pp. 170–177). Though Tillyard's critical approach emphasizes historical backgrounds, some of his assertions are decidedly anachronistic. Swinburne's metaphor based on the Life-tree Yggdrasill becomes an excuse for accusing him of "something that would have appealed to Hitler and Rosenberg," though Tillyard could hardly deny that the general tenor of the poem, which insists on the freedom of the soul, would have been repugnant to both. The author of "Liberty and Loyalty" (Bonchurch Edition, XVI) was always a sincere believer in individualism — a point of difference between his views and Mazzini's. The attitude behind Tillyard's assault on "the cult of Truth" — Victorians who followed the leadings of conscience were unaware that it was a "cult" — is at least as likely to foster social irresponsibility as reverence for what Tillyard calls "the great abstraction." He is not judging Victorian thinkers in their own historical context but in accordance with a personal interpretation of what has happened since their time. One returns with relief to the explication of "Hertha" in Lafcadio Hearn's *Interpretations of Literature* (1917).[18]

VI. *General Criticism*

Among the more general critical works on Swinburne, those by Theodore Wratislaw, Edward Thomas, G. E. Woodberry, and John Drinkwater are mainly of historical interest and have been briefly considered elsewhere.[19] Paul de Reul's *L'Œuvre de Swinburne* (1922) is still worth consulting on such subjects as Swinburne's relation to French writers. It contains sections on Swinburne's music, imagination, and

[18] Gwen A. Jones, "Notes on Swinburne's 'Song of Italy'" (*MLN*, 1917) deserves mention, in passing, as helping to elucidate the historical allusions in the poem.

[19] In *Swinburne's Literary Career and Fame*, the bibliography of which lists books and articles not mentioned here.

ideas, as well as on the narrative poems, dramas, and criticism. Reul was also the author of *"Swinburne et la France"* (*La Grande Revue*, 1904). Alice Galimberti's *L'Aedo d'Italia* (1925) discusses, translates, and adapts Swinburne for Italian readers, as Reul does for the French, but is of less importance to English-speaking students.

Harold Nicolson's *Swinburne* (1926), like other studies, leans too heavily on Gosse's *Life* for its facts. Nicolson's thesis that the key to Swinburne's temperament lies in a pendulum-like oscillation between "the impulse towards revolt and the impulse towards submission" has more plausibility than many of the formulas fashionable in biographical writing, but occasionally it restricts his view of Swinburne's personal and literary qualities, as when he declares that *Love's Cross-Currents* illustrates "a curiously un-Swinburnian element of the mundane, the analytical, almost of the cynical" — a statement which hardly does justice to Swinburne's complexity. The most successful chapter deals with *Atalanta*. Though for reasons of temperament Nicolson must have found his subject not entirely compatible, his critical emphases may be commended.

T. E. Welby's *A Study of Swinburne* (1926), not to be confused with an inferior predecessor (1914), was based on more research than Nicolson's *Swinburne* and is more sympathetic, though it contains some repetition and other faults of organization. Like Nicolson, Welby believes that Swinburne's work is a "multiple, many-mooded offering to liberty apprehended in very many ways"; but he adds that "freedom for Swinburne is not a riot of impulses in a vacuum. It is that condition in which man becomes the conscious, voluntarily dedicated . . . instrument of the supreme purpose." He calls the author of *Songs before Sunrise* "a profoundly religious poet," since "a religious poet does not become irreligious" because he "says 'dear city of man' instead of 'dear city of Zeus.' " Welby is less reticent than Gosse about Swinburne's pathological side but declares, "With all his childishness, impishness, extravagance, all his freakishness and weaknesses, he was a very great man and a very great gentleman."

Volume I, *La Vie*, of Lafourcade's *La Jeunesse de Swinburne* has been discussed above, along with his later biography in English. Volume II, *L'Œuvre*, is, in spite of many inaccuracies and an annoying number of misprints, an essential work. No other writer has outlined so fully Swinburne's apprenticeship or the evolution of his artistic, political, and religious ideas. If the time limit (1867) seems arbitrary and the space given to certain juvenilia disproportionate, the book is usually informative. Though one may question the soundness of its main point (see the closing paragraphs of this chapter), it is often acute in its critical observations. Lafourcade called attention to the manuscript of *The Unhappy Revenge*, made Swinburne's authorship of "Modern Hellenism" seem plausible, and quoted from many unpublished letters and poems.

S. C. Chew's *Swinburne* (1929) appeared too soon after *La Jeunesse* to make use of its materials but is remarkable for a richness of detail due not only to assimilation of earlier researches but also the author's broad knowledge of Swinburne's milieu and of literature. It excels other studies in appreciation of *Songs before Sunrise* and in judicious and scholarly treatment of Swinburne's Arthurian poems, dramas, and criticism. The discussion of "Ave atque Vale" deserves special mention. Chew assigns to Swinburne the highest position among those poets whose work belongs exclusively to the second half of the nineteenth century. His article on Swinburne in *A Literary History of England*, edited by Albert C. Baugh (1948), is masterly in succinctness and knowledge.

Of the many short critiques of Swinburne, high rank must still be accorded to Oliver Elton's estimate in his *Survey of English Literature, 1780–1880*, IV (1920). This, together with some other twentieth-century criticism, is discussed in the last chapter of C. K. Hyder's *Swinburne's Literary Career and Fame* (1933), the concluding section of which summarizes the history of Swinburne's reputation to 1932. The book gives attention to Swinburne's response to criticism, especially in his invective.[20]

[20] Supplementary information may be found in Hyder's edition of "Changes

A noticeable lack is an adequate account of Swinburne's critical fortunes in Europe. In his centenary article (*RLC*, 1937), Henri Peyre writes of Swinburne's preëminence as a European poet, who like Byron and Poe deserves a place in the history of comparative literature — not only because he did much for the recognition of French poetry in England but also because he influenced such authors as Mallarmé, Verlaine, and Gide. Eileen Souffrin's *"Swinburne et sa légende en France"* (*RLC*, 1951) contains fresh material about the poet's reputation among French literary men, some of whom considered him *"un Edgar Poe 'fin de siècle'"*; curiously, while in England Swinburne was denounced for borrowing from the wicked French, in France he was often regarded as the representative of a vice characteristic of the English. (See also Baldensperger and Friederich, cited in section IV, above.) Mario Praz's *The Romantic Agony* (revised edition, 1951) mentions Swinburne's influence upon D'Annunzio and others. In "More Swinburne-D'Annunzio Parallels" (*PMLA*, 1940), C. S. Brown, Jr., deals with the extensive borrowings — more accurately, plagiarisms — of D'Annunzio, chiefly from Gabriel Mourey's prose translation of *Poems and Ballads*. Beulah B. Amram's "Swinburne and Carducci" (*Yale Review*, 1916) is primarily a comparison of the English and the Italian poet.

Of the critical articles which appeared on the occasion of Swinburne's centenary, two will be cited. E. K. Brown's "Swinburne: A Centenary Estimate" (*TQ*, 1937) seeks to define Swinburne's special qualities of rhythm and diction and praises his leading ideas: "the unity of man with nature, the dignity of humanity, the supreme value of liberty." Lafourcade's "Swinburne Vindicated" (*London Mercury*, 1938) proved to be that earnest student's final word in defense of the genuineness of Swinburne's sexual experience and there-

---

of Aspect" and "Short Notes," cited in section II. Sufficiently self-identifying are the titles of R. C. Beatty's "Swinburne and Bayard Taylor" (*PQ*, 1934), K. L. Knickerbocker's "Browning and Swinburne: An Episode" (*MLN*, 1947), J. A. Cassidy's "Robert Buchanan and the Fleshly Controversy" (*PMLA*, 1951), and Oscar Maurer's "Swinburne *vs.* Furnivall" (University of Texas *Studies in English*, 1952).

fore of the poems based upon that experience — and he rightly insists that Swinburne sang of many forms of love. In a passage about "sublimations," Lafourcade quotes from *Chastelard* "the most beautiful and moving lines [Swinburne] ever wrote," since "to show how he turned to account the strange though genuine material which lay at his disposal is to vindicate both the man and the artist." But if emotions are peripheral rather than central in human experience, their sincerity will hardly make the author who expresses them seem less remote from humanity.

Lafourcade thought Swinburne's affiliations to be with the moderns. Though the poet was responsible for some innovations, his art is usually considered a culminating point in the great century of Romanticism. The last generation has been one of anti-Romantic reaction, doubtless to some extent because of literary fashion and because of a misunderstanding of what Romanticism stood for, as Ernest Bernbaum and B. Ifor Evans (see especially the latter's *Tradition and Romanticism*, 1940) have convincingly argued. Critics of Swinburne may well choose grounds more strategic than Lafourcade's. They will admit the limitations and eccentricities of the poet's experience, but they will insist that a tree is not to be judged by its roots or a flower by the ordure which nourished it; nor will they dwell upon a part of that experience and disregard the whole. They will not admit that he lacked loftiness of thought or great power of imaginative perception. In a world too much besotted by specious pleaders for putting the human race into shackles, they will not concede that his vision of freedom as the very condition of the soul's growth lacks value. If his ideas or if a world-view such as is expressed, for instance, in what may be one of the most Lucretian, in scope, of nineteenth-century poems — "Genesis" — if this view offends various orthodoxies, so does the world-view of Lucretius himself, whose poetry has lasted during ages which have seen the decline and fall of many orthodoxies. Swinburne's kindest critics will not deny his weaknesses, but they will continue to defend the greatness of his art at its best.

7 ॐ

The Pre-Raphaelites

Howard Mumford Jones[*]

THE INITIAL PARADOX confronting the contemporary student of the Pre-Raphaelite movement is indicated by the fact that in any competent library the classification staff has great difficulty in determining whether a general book on this topic belongs under Fine Arts or under English Literature. A study like William Gaunt's *The Pre-Raphaelite Tragedy* (1942), though it is essentially a biography of Dante Gabriel Rossetti, may be listed under the history of painting, whereas R. L. Mégroz's *Dante Gabriel Rossetti* (1928), though it is subtitled "Painter Poet of Heaven and Earth," is ranked as a contribution to English literature. This confusion is symbolic of a precedent confusion of values: scholars who have interested themselves in the literary work of the Pre-Raphaelites, whoever the poets may be they so categorize, have commonly felt awkward in dealing with the work of Rossetti and Morris in the fine arts; and historians of British painting have usually assumed that comment on literary work is the business of professional literary scholars. Yet the Pre-Raphaelite movement is the leading example in British literary history of a fruitful union between literature and the graphic arts.

The initial difficulty shrouds a darker and deeper one of definition. What is Pre-Raphaelitism and who were the Pre-

* The author gratefully acknowledges the generous help of Miss Helen Willard of the Fogg Museum in preparing parts of this survey. Miss Willard is, however, in no way responsible for any of the judgments expressed.

Raphaelites? Literary comment tends thoughtlessly to identify the doctrine with Rossetti and in fact to confine member-
ship in the school to the Rossetti family with a few glancing
looks at William Morris. Other studies slide neatly over the
genuine difficulty of definition. The adjective, at any rate,
like many another enduring epithet, came after the fact and
in a spirit of derision. There is no reason to disbelieve Holman Hunt's account in a book which is basic to all relevant
scholarship, *Pre-Raphaelitism and the Pre-Raphaelite
Brotherhood* (two volumes, second edition revised from the
author's notes by M. E. Holman-Hunt, 1914). Hunt tells us
how at the Academy, when he and Millais began to find fault
with Raphael's cartoon of the "Transfiguration" "for its
grandiose disregard of the simplicity of truth, the pompous
posturing of the Apostles, and the unspiritual attitudinizing
of the Saviour," other students commented, "Then you are
Pre-Raphaelite," and that to this epithet as they later worked
side by side he and Millais "laughingly agreed." [1]

Before this weighty event became known, Rossetti, who
was to christen a transient "brotherhood" "PRB," was content to refer to radical painting as "Early Christian," an
epithet Hunt could not and would not accept, though his
renown was *par excellence* that of a "sacred painter." [2]

Rossetti seems to have had vaguely in mind both the German school that had Friedrich Overbeck (1789–1869) and
Peter von Cornelius (1783?–1867) as principal exemplars,
and the "early Christian" Italian painters, such as Orcagna.
But British holdings of the Nazarene paintings, then as now,
were negligible; [3] and neither Hunt, Millais nor Rossetti

---

[1] Hunt, I:68–69.

[2] Rossetti picked up the term from Ford Madox Brown. Hunt writes that
he objected to the term "as attached to a School called by the Germans
'Nazarene,' and as far from vitality as was modern classicism. . . . I insisted
that the designation 'Pre-Raphaelite' was more radically exact, and best expressed what we had agreed should be our principle." (Hunt, I:98).

[3] William Dyce (1806–1864), some of whose work has certain Pre-Raphaelite
characteristics but who was never a member of the group, was a student in
Rome during the twenties, where he became acquainted with the German
"Nazarenes." Ford Madox Brown, who visited Overbeck and Cornelius there,
apparently in 1844, seems to have been the only other person in any way as-

seems to have had a first-hand acquaintance with Italian primitives; [4] they had to content themselves with engravings for a long time. In this connection a remark by Clive Bell in his *Landmarks in Nineteenth-Century Painting* (1927, pp. 107–8) suggests a field of investigation. At the beginning of his unsympathetic discussion of the Pre-Raphaelites, he notes that Madame de Staël in *Corinne* (VIII, 3) and again in *De l'Allemagne* (II, 32) called attention to both the Nazarenes and the Italian primitives. Unfortunately Robert C. Whitford's *Madame de Staël's Literary Reputation in England* [5] does not go beyond 1831. Scholarship might be profitably employed in determining the development of a climate of English opinion favorable to "Christian" art before the appearance of Mrs. Jameson's *Memoirs of the Early Italian Painters* (two volumes, 1845) and her *Sacred and Legendary Art* (two volumes, 1848).[6] Studies of the Gothic revival in the nineteenth century scarcely touch this theme.

---

sociated with the Pre-Raphaelites to have had a first-hand acquaintance with the Nazarene painters. In view of the emphasis upon "nature" in the Pre-Raphaelite creed, Brown's comment that Overbeck never drew naked flesh from nature "on the principle of avoiding the sensuous in religious art" throws an interesting light on the difference between the two schools. See Ford M. Hueffer (Ford Madox Ford), *Ford Madox Brown: A Record of his Life and Work* (1896), pp. 44–45.

[4] "Scarcely anywhere in their writings (we must except one article by Mr. F. G. Stephens) do we find praise, or even mention, of most of the great pre-Raphaelite painters. Nothing of Mantegna, Botticelli, Bellini, Orcagna, Fra Angelico, Melozzo, Lippo Lippi, or Piero della Francesca. At a slightly later date Rossetti visited Bruges, and fell in love with Memling, but his letters even then reveal some very crude preferences." H. C. Marillier, *Dante Gabriel Rossetti*, 3d. ed. (1904), pp. 12–13. This is still the best guide to Rossetti's paintings and drawings. I assume that the Stephens article to which Marillier refers is that signed by "John Seward," "The Purpose and Tendency of Early Italian Art," in the second number of *The Germ*. The solitary footnote in the essay gives the "sources from which these examples are drawn," these being various histories of art and books of facsimiles, or reproductions at Somerset House and the Royal Academy, scarcely evidence of first-hand knowledge. For the identification of "John Seward" as Frederic George Stephens see William Sharp, *Dante Gabriel Rossetti* (1882), p. 76.

[5] *University of Illinois Studies in Language and Literature*, February 1918.

[6] In *A Hundred Years of British Painting, 1851–1951* (1951), p. 39, Hesketh Hubbard hints that "another German influence of the Brotherhood may well have been the woodcuts of Alfred Rethel, whose 'Dance of Death'

Critics contemporary with the movement sometimes tried to distinguish between "Pre-Raphaelism" and "Pre-Raphaelitism," but the difference is unimportant. What is of more consequence than either dialectical distinctions or the precise relation between the movement and the German Nazarene school is the original intent of Hunt and Millais, the only true begetters of Pre-Raphaelitism in the world of painting. Their purpose, if rightly understood, gives us a base from which to measure the departures of others. The classic statement is still that of Holman Hunt in his reminiscences; and though the conversations in *Pre-Raphaelitism and the Pre-Raphaelite Movement* have the air of the orations of Thucydides,[7] I see no reason to doubt their essential veracity. In the first place Hunt clung to his principles when others did

---

series, in which we can discern the mental darkness that was to overshadow their author, reached this country at about the time of the formation of the brotherhood." The parallel to Rossetti's mental breakdown is intriguing but, I fear, valueless.

The reference is to a pamphlet or broadside (the pictures appeared in both forms) entitled *Auch ein Todtentanz aus dem Jahre 1848 . . . Mit erklärendem Text von R. Reineck*, Leipzig, 1849, the pictures being six black-and-white variants on the dance-of-death motif, and the text being verses slightly better than doggerel. The designs were occasioned by the failure of the revolution of 1848 and are a satire on the fact that the dead found liberty, equality, and fraternity only in the grave. I find nothing specifically Christian in them nor, for that matter, in some other random prints on the same theme by the same artist. Aside from the fact that the *Todtentanz* was not published until 1849 and that Hunt and Millais had determined on their principles in 1847 and exhibited the first "Pre-Raphaelite" pictures in 1848, I know no way of validating the circulation of these designs in London. There is no entry for them in the British Museum Catalogue of Books. Realistic treatment of detail by the economic and powerful use of line is the only element these pictures might share with some Pre-Raphaelite art, but the Pre-Raphaelites, despite Rossetti's "morbidity," did not characteristically go in for the macabre. In his *The Dance of Death and the Macabre Spirit in European Literature* (1934), pp. 258–261, Leonard P. Kurtz discusses Rethel and his vogue but fails to connect the underlying philosophy of the pictures with the failure of the revolution of 1848. See note 22 below.

[7] "With regard to conversations with Millais, I cannot pretend to have recorded every exact word. But the illustrations and criticisms used, and the names of the works of art cited, are as fresh in my memory as if they had been spoken only yesterday, and therefore a revival of the conversational form of the interview seems to me the best way in which to convey an idea of what passed. . ." Hunt, I:56, note. But see also Hunt's "The Pre-Raphaelite Brotherhood," *Contemporary Review*, April–June, 1886.

not and was the more likely to remember their inception; and in the second place his book was preceded by *The Life and Letters of Sir John Everett Millais* (two volumes, 1899), which, said Hunt, "supplied the first accurate information about the relative positions of the first three active members of our Body." Hunt had the opportunity to check what he wrote with John G. Millais, both in Hunt's original edition (1905) and in notes used for the revision (1914). Rossetti of the commanding ways and persuasive personality may have later moved in on Millais and Hunt, organized the group, and taken over the movement in the minds of his partisans, but the governing principles of Pre-Raphaelitism as originally understood were the creation of Holman Hunt at twenty and John Everett Millais at eighteen.

Like other fiery young men these young men were in revolt. Scholarship has interested itself rather more in what they revolted against than in what they wanted, and this bias has not made for clear understanding. They were opposed, as every one is aware, to academy painting as young men always are — to conventionalism in coloring and design, to a theatrical representationalism, to the elder generation, in sum, and to its teacher, Sir "Sloshua," or rather to his teaching. Under his reign

came into vogue drooping branches of brown trees over a night-like sky, or a column with a curtain unnaturally arranged, as a background to a day-lit portrait; his feeble followers imitate this arrangement.

The first president of the Royal Academy was probably an "independent genius," but he had transmitted neither genius nor independence to his successors. The time had come for revolution, for change. "The backgrounds of pictures should be representative of nature"; "that delicate rendering of nature, which had led previous Schools to greatness"; "the more attentively I look at Nature the more I detect in it unexpected delights"; "it is simply fuller Nature we want" — these are the positive phrases that ring repeatedly in their conversations. And the concept is not that of Wordsworthian nature, albeit Hunt is by and by to find nature full of symbolism; it is the concept of nature exactly rendered, in the scientific spirit of the day. Hunt utters a series of illuminating rhetorical questions and afterwards discusses the way he proposes to paint apropos of "The Eve of St. Agnes"; both passages are of primary importance for understanding Pre-Raphaelitism.

Why should the highest light be always on the principal figure? Why make one corner of the picture always in shade? For what reason is the sky in a daylight picture made as black as night? And then about colour, why should the gradation go from the principal white, through yellow to pink and red, and so on to stronger colours? With all this subserviency to early examples, when the turn of violet comes, why does the courage of the modern imitator fail? If you notice, a clean purple is scarcely ever given in these days, and pure green is as much ignored (I:61).

Life is not long enough to drivel through a bad fashion, and begin again. The determination to save ourselves and Art must be made now we are young. I feel that is the only hope, at least for me. One's thoughts must stir before the hands can do. With my picture from "The Eve of St. Agnes" I am limited to night effect, but I purpose after this to paint an out-of-door picture, with a foreground and background, abjuring altogether brown foliage, smoky clouds, and dark corners, painting the whole out of doors, direct on the canvas itself, with every detail, and with the sunlight brightness of the day itself (I:62).

The exact rendering of nature — this was the central intention, an intention endorsed by a writer signing himself an Oxford Graduate in a book called *Modern Painters*, to which Hunt's attention had been drawn by a student named Telfer — "with whom, wherever he wanders, be everlasting peace" — and which Hunt managed to borrow from Cardinal Wiseman for twenty-four hours.[8] Scholarship is familiar with the enthusiasm for Ruskin among this generation of painters; what needs more detailed study is the effect upon these young

---

[8] Hunt, I:52. Wiseman was not named cardinal until 1850. He spent most of 1847 in Rome, returning in 1848 as the diplomatic representative of the Vatican. This seems to fix the time of the event as 1846. Hunt probably borrowed Vol. II of *Modern Painters*.

men of contemporary science.[9] For example, in the conversation about Raphael's cartoon the young rebels found an important fault in the "strained and meaningless action of the epileptic" depicted and Hunt supports his comment by three closely printed paragraphs from Sir Charles Bell, who had deplored Raphael's figure as "not natural" — i.e., lacking in medical precision.[10]

To us, children of an age of abstract and non-representational art, differences between pictures like Frith's "Derby Day," Opie's "The Schoolmistress," Mulready's "The Fight Interrupted," Landseer's "The Old Shepherd's Chief Mourner," and Maclise's "Girl at the Waterfall" on the one hand, and Hunt's "The Hireling Shepherd," Brown's "Work," Rossetti's "The Girlhood of Mary Virgin," and Millais' "Christ in the House of His Parents" are less important than their common characteristics as nineteenth-century narrative pictures.[11] Thus it is that a modernist like Clive Bell, in his *Landmarks in Nineteenth-Century Painting* (1927) dismisses all the Pre-Raphaelites as "worthless," as men who "put on the wrong track a number of promising young painters," inasmuch as "belief in representation, as the public understands it, is the infallible sign of a dolt." [12] But

[9] Among the more obvious titles of influential scientific works in the forties are Whewell, *Philosophy of the Inductive Sciences* (1840); Hugh Miller, *The Old Red Sandstone* (1841); Darwin, *Coral Reefs* (1842); Chambers, *Vestiges of Creation* (1844).

[10] Hunt, I:68. Hunt refers to the third edition of Bell's *The Anatomy and Philosophy of Expression* (1844), pp. 159–161. This influential work first appeared in 1806 and reached a second edition in 1824, but in 1840 Bell visited the Continent and, returning home, reworked the text so that the third edition was virtually a new and exciting book. He died in 1842; but a seventh edition appeared as late as 1877. His brother said the doctor was "a true lover of nature, and to trace the proofs of perfection and design in all the works of the Creator was to him a source of ever new delight." It will be remembered he wrote one of the Bridgewater Treatises, that concerning design in the human hand. The combination of piety and science undoubtedly appealed to Holman Hunt.

[11] Thus Sacheverell Sitwell's *Narrative Pictures: A Survey of English Genre and its Painters* (1937) opens with a reproduction of Millais' "The Blind Girl" and concludes smoothly with two pictures by James Tissot and two more by Walter Greaves.

[12] See his chapter, "The Pre-Raphaelites," *passim*.

if anything is clear about the Pre-Raphaelites, it is that they enormously desired to make the public believe in representation, only that it must be the right sort of representation.

If we find ourselves either baffled or merely amused by Dickens' famous onslaught on Millais' "Christ in the House of His Parents," which the novelist found "mean, odious, revolting and repulsive," it is because *we* are not put off by the "truth to nature" involved. But when Dickens sarcastically admitted that "the shavings which are strewn on the carpenter's floor are admirably painted," he was in truth admitting the central tenet of Pre-Raphaelitism, just as he was doing when he constructed an imaginary Pre-Raphaelite canvas in which "every brick in the house will be a portrait," "the man's boots will be copied with the utmost fidelity," and "the texture of his hands (including four chilblains, a whitlow, and ten dirty nails) will be a triumph." For Dickens, Pre-Raphaelitism ignored "all that has been done for the happiness and elevation of mankind during three or four centuries of slow . . . amelioration," it was the "great retrogressive principle," it was "desecration," it was a descent into "the lowest depths." Nor was Dickens sole and singular in these judgments, as a reading of the contemporary comments (excerpted in the life of Millais) on that controversial painting will show.[13] Indeed, when Ruskin came to the rescue of the beleaguered group in his famous letter to the *Times* for May 13, 1851,[14] the one element in Collins' forgotten "Convent Thoughts" that he selected for praise was the accuracy with which the water plant, Alisma Plantago, was drawn; and he admired the perspective skill of the group generally (a scientific problem), besides dwelling in this and his following communications upon a variety of details because of their representational accuracy.

The beginning of wisdom for modern scholarship in this confusing issue is to distinguish among responses to art as representational fidelity, not to confuse the response with

[13] John G. Millais, *The Life and Letters of John Everett Millais*, I:74–76.

[14] Reprinted in the Library Edition, ed. E. T. Cook and Alexander Wedderburn, XII (1904), pp. 319–323. The pamphlet entitled *Pre-Raphaelitism* has more to do with Turner than with Millais, Hunt and company.

the theory. To Dickens in 1851 the literalness of the Pre-Raphaelite canvases was repulsive because it was vulgar. To Clive Bell in 1927 the same work is repellent because it represents the vapid idealism of the amateur. *In medio tutissimus ibis.* A scholar who has properly estimated the true nature of Pre-Raphaelite painting for the light it can throw upon their literary work is Samuel C. Chew, when he writes:[15]

These young men would paint what they saw, not what the artists of the past who were held up to them as models had seen. They rejected various established principles of technique. Their special preoccupation was with problems of light. They altered the conventional proportions and distribution of light which academic theorists had legislated from the practice of Rembrandt. They discarded the use of bitumen as a ground work,[16] and instead of building up their lights from shade they built up their shades from light. They were thus feeling their way along the same line as that of the young Impressionists of France. But unlike the French group, so great was their devotion to religious, medieval, and romantic themes that their art was often subservient to literature. Moreover, while the French school, reacting against the newly invented art of photography, moved away from representation, the "P.R.B.," influenced by photography, became entangled in minute representationalism. Their meticulous attention to detail often involved the sacrifice of central emphasis; and when they first exhibited in 1849 this fidelity was thought to be unworthy of religious art and Millais was even accused of blasphemy.[17]

If the history of the arts were a matter of consistent de-

---

[15] *A Literary History of England* by Kemp Malone, Albert C. Baugh, Tucker Brooke, George Sherburn, and Samuel C. Chew (1948), p. 1422.

[16] The best discussion of the technique of Pre-Raphaelite painting so far as method and materials are concerned is that by Richard D. Buck in *Paintings and Drawings of the Pre-Raphaelites and their Circle* (1946), pp. 14–18.

[17] I diffidently venture to question whether the PRB as a group were influenced greatly by photography. It is true that Fox Talbot patented his calotype process in 1841 and published his *The Pencil of Nature* in 1844–46, but the price of the book was three guineas. I find no reference to book or author in the index to the biography of Millais or Hunt's reminiscences, and the Scott-Archer collodion process was not introduced until 1851. See W. Jerome Harrison, *A History of Photography* (1888), and C. E. Kenneth Mees, *Photography* (1937), Chap. I.

velopment, Ford Madox Brown would have been a member of the PRB and Robert Browning might have been assimilated to the literary campaign — Browning with his knowledge of Italian painting and his frank acceptance of contemporary speech and contemporary problems. But the arts do not develop consistently. Perhaps the two most significant remarks made by any Pre-Raphaelites were made by Morris and Rossetti: Morris, when he told W. J. Nairne, "To speak quite frankly I do not know what Marx's theory of value is, and I'm damned if I want to know";[18] and Rossetti, when he said he was not sure the earth really revolved around the sun, since "our senses did not tell us so, at any rate, and what then did it matter whether it did move or not?" [19] The first of these declarations cut off later Pre-Raphaelite thinking from the dynamism of an ideology that was to convulse Europe; and the second reveals that Rossetti understood nothing of nineteenth-century science and therefore could not comprehend the true intellectual basis of what Millais and Hunt were at the time working for. For Rossetti the careful objectivity of these men was no more than a phase of technique that was in its turn a phase of collecting "stunners."

Rossetti organized the PRB as part of the "jovial campaign," as Gaylord LeRoy has seen acutely,[20] but joviality is not the same thing as principle, and not a single member of the band aside from Hunt and Millais showed any real grasp of the theory or any long-run intention of carrying it through. Whether sculpture is properly within the Pre-Raphaelite pale is a nice question, but anyway Woolner, scarcely a Pre-Raphaelite, soon left for Australia; Deverell,

[18] J. Bruce Glasier, *William Morris and the Early Days of the Socialist Movement* (1921), p. 32. Morris went on to say: "Truth to say, my friends, I have tried to understand Marx's theory, but political economy is not in my line, and much of it appears to me to be dreary rubbish. But I am, I hope, a Socialist none the less."

[19] William Bell Scott, *Autobiographical Notes*, ed. W. Minto (2 vols., 1892), I:291. Rossetti was characteristically persuaded to accept the shocking theory when it was pointed out to him that it had proved satisfactory to Galileo, an Italian.

[20] *Perplexed Prophets* (1953), pp. 121–126.

the most promising and intelligent of the newcomers, died young; Collinson got himself entangled in theology and somnolence; Stephens abandoned art for art journalism; William Michael Rossetti never pretended to be more than the scribe and historian of the group; and Dante Gabriel Rossetti, after painting "Ecce Ancilla Domini" at least in the spirit of Hunt and Millais in 1850, began with "Borgia" and "How They Met Themselves" in 1851 to develop the lush and mannered style that became peculiarly his own. It is virtually symbolical that he could not complete his one picture of sociological comment, "Found," started in 1853. *The Germ* was subtitled "Thoughts towards Nature in Poetry, Literature and Art," but neither Tupper's two essays on "The Subject in Art," nor Ford Madox Brown's uninteresting "On the Mechanism of a Historical Picture," nor John Orchard's "Dialogue on Art" seems especially geared to revolutionary aesthetics, and it is characteristic that what one mostly remembers from this short-lived magazine is that it contained a number of poems and Rossetti's allegorical pastiche, "Hand and Soul." Perhaps one cannot hope that William Michael Rossetti in "The P.R.B. Journal," which ran from 1849 to 1853, could have recorded more shop talk by painters than he did, but what chiefly impresses one about its pages, with all their *lacunae*, is that it is mostly about literature, and that, though they "debated the propriety of having an article explanatory of the Principles of the P.R.B.," it was never written.[21] It is also characteristic that from 1851, when, in the general confusion, nobody quite knew what "P.R.B." might mean, though it was "determined that each of us should write a manifesto declaring the sense in which he accepts the name," no manifesto remains.

In London Rossetti had peremptorily destroyed the inner consistency of Pre-Raphaelitism, smothering it beneath a program of activism for its own sake. Simultaneously a spiritual denizen of England, of Italy, and of Bohemia, he could not, given the enigma of his own dark nature, do otherwise. But

[21] *Praeraphaelite Diaries and Letters*, ed. William Michael Rossetti (1900), pp. 205–309.

when we pass to the Oxford phase of Pre-Raphaelitism, beginning in 1855–56, not theory but the electric personality of Rossetti is the catalytic agent which, if it did not create the Oxford "Brotherhood," fused it into a creative whole. It is of course again true in one sense that the young men concerned — Morris, Burne-Jones, Cormell Price, Richard Watson Dixon, and the rest — had already come together. Already Morris had read aloud to this admiring circle his lost poem, "The Willow and the Red Cliff," and uttered the astonished remark, "Well, if this is poetry, it is very easy to write." Already in the magical summer of 1855 in France both he and Burne-Jones had decided to dedicate their lives to art; and the *Oxford and Cambridge Magazine* [22] had already been planned before Burne-Jones' crucial encounter with Rossetti in Great Titchfield Street late in December, 1855. But this time there was no antecedent theory to smother; the command from the Master was simply that everybody ought to be an artist, and the central immediate products were, so to speak, the Moxon *Tennyson* of 1857 [23] and the vanished Oxford Union frescoes of that same year. If in 1849 Pre-Raphaelitism had been principally a problem of the just representation of natural objects in a scientific spirit, by 1857 the notion of art as beautiful decoration was equally powerful and was to become more so. And since to the disciples of Ruskin, Victorianism *per se* could not be beautiful, in view of the richly literary context of later Pre-Raphaelitism, decoration turned

[22] One of the remarkable facts about this magazine is the paucity of material in it on the fine arts. Aside from a review of *Modern Painters*, Vol. III, pt. iv, and Morris' comment on French cathedrals, the only two essays on art in the twelve issues appear in August, 1856. One is on Rethel's "Death the Avenger" and "Death the Friend" (pp. 477–479); and one, by Vernon Lushington, "Two Pictures," discusses at long length what I take to be the watercolor version of "Dante's Dream" and Brown's "The Last of England." How remote the essayist was from the point of view of Hunt and Millais may be seen in the concluding paragraph, which praises the younger painters for having "chosen Man for their subject" and showing "how much of divine beauty and awe yet dwells and manifests itself in human forms."

[23] At the same time the importance of this publication can be over-estimated. Of the 54 illustrations (not counting the medallion of Tennyson by Woolner) only 30 are by the Pre-Raphaelites Millais (18), Hunt (7) and Rossetti (5); and it would be difficult for any but an expert to distinguish

backward to medievalism and inward to subjective romance.

It is not surprising that experts in art, though they may agree as to when and where Pre-Raphaelitism begins, cannot agree as to what or whom it includes and when it ends. The Fogg Museum exhibit of 1946 was confined to Brown, Burne-Jones, Holman Hunt, Millais, Albert Moore, Rossetti, Simeon Solomon, Frederic G. Stephens, and George F. Watts.[24] The catalogue of *The Samuel and Mary R. Bancroft English Pre-Raphaelite Collection* at Wilmington, Delaware, however, includes Brown, Edward Burne-Jones, Philip Burne-Jones, Walter Crane, George Du Maurier, Kate Greenaway, Millais, Albert Moore, Morris, Rossetti, Elizabeth Siddal, Frederick Sandys, Frederick Shields, Watts, William J. Stillman, and Marie Spartali. In the British Artist Series, Percy Bates, whose *The English Pre-Raphaelite Painters, Their Associates and Successors* reached a second edition in 1901, includes those in the Fogg catalogue, adds fifty, is casual about Watts, and in a final chapter on "Pre-Raphaelitism To-Day" concludes that "the principles of Pre-Raphaelitism remain as essentially true as when first promulgated," without ever making it quite clear what was promulgated. Robin Ironside's authoritative *Pre-Raphaelite Painters with a Descriptive Catalogue by John Gere* (1948) numbers twenty-four artists, yet it omits Woolner, who was a PRB, ignores Watts, and includes Sir Frederic Leighton. But if Sir Frederic Leighton, why not Alma-Tadema? If you list Walter Crane with Percy Bate, why omit Charles Sims, whose "The Wood Beyond the World" in the Tate Gallery was suggested by one of William Morris' romances? Why not include John Tenniel, whose

---

between the descriptive line of Maclise or Mulready and that of Millais as an illustrator. For further discussion of the Moxon *Tennyson* see George S. Layard, *Tennyson and his Pre-Raphaelite Illustrators* (1894), and Albert B. Friedman, "The Tennyson of 1857," *More Books* (1948), pp. 15–22.

What remains of the Oxford designs may be studied in *Oxford Union Society: The Story of the Painting of the Pictures on the Walls and the Decorations on the Ceiling of the Old Debating Hall (now the Library) in the Years 1857–8–9*. By W. Holman Hunt (1906); a collection of photographs (not by Hunt) with commentary.

[24] The only representation of William Morris was the Kelmscott Press books in the Houghton Library.

Alice illustrations curiously recall some of the engravings in the Moxon *Tennyson?* Why not Kate Greenaway?

Indeed, if one includes all that passes for Pre-Raphaelitism in the graphic arts, there is no relevant paradox of judgment that cannot be supported by excellent evidence on either side. The original intent was scientific realism — witness, among other things, Ruskin's careful studies of water and rocks; yet the majority of familiar Pre-Raphaelite pictures are romantic by almost any definition of romanticism — medieval revival, search for the remote and strange, delight in fantasy, subjectivism, abnormality, return to faith, what you will. But this statement is no sooner made than one's memory returns to such domestic scenes as Hunt's "The Awakening Conscience," [25] Brown's "Pretty Baa-Lambs," or Arthur Hughes' "Home from Work," and one realizes that the disillusioned social commentary of Brown's "Work" or Millais' sardonic pen-and-ink drawing, "The Race Meeting," silently fuses with Victorian sentimentalism. Consider, for example, Hughes' "Home from Sea," which is as teary as *The Wide, Wide World.* But making this comment, one then confronts Hunt's "The Hireling Shepherd" or William Bell Scott's "Coal and Iron" and realizes that Rossetti and Burne-Jones were not the only symbolists in the movement. The Pre-Raphaelites are literary painters — witness innumerable pictures suggested by Keats, Shakespeare, Malory, Dante, and the rest of a rich and riotous library; yet Stephens' "Mother and Child" is surely as "painty" as anything by Mary Cassatt on a similar theme, and so are Brett's landscapes or Martineau's "The Last Chapter," just as many of the hundreds of unlisted drawings by Rossetti, who apparently went in for tremendous self-discipline after the mid-fifties, are excellent as drawings. Rossetti is admirable as a designer for stained glass; and one has but to turn the pages of Gerald Crow's *William Morris: Designer* (1934) to be struck with astonishment that the road from Hunt's literal rendering of

---

[25] The agony on the woman's face was so realistically portrayed that it became unbearable to the owner, Sir Thomas Fairbairn, who persuaded Hunt to repaint her features.

the Dead Sea in "The Scapegoat" to the intricate formalism of the Kelmscott Chaucer, however inconsistent theory may be, is only forty years in the making. I do not know whether Watts is properly a Pre-Raphaelite, but the same hand that painted the mawkish "Hope" produced what is probably the most distinguished line of portraits in the Victorian era; and if Watts is to be ruled out, what of Millais' admirable "John Ruskin," painted in 1853–54?

Doubtless we should always strive to form clear ideas, but possibly classification, that characteristic vice of scholarship, may here mislead us. The wisest action may be to note that, for some miraculous reason, England participated in the wonderful flowering and culmination of genius which characterized the Continent in the fifties — Courbet, Berlioz, Wagner, Tolstoi, Baudelaire, Freytag, Gautier are the first names that come to mind — and that in this brilliant decade, which in London began with *In Memoriam* and concluded with both *The Origin of Species* and the *Rubáiyát*, groups of talented young men swirled and eddied around a central enigma named Rossetti, who took it as a matter of course that art is one of the primary functions of any intelligent human being. And the three literary masterpieces I have just named form, so to speak, the triangle in which their immense and contradictory energies were expressed — religion, science, exoticism. Even though they might adore *la belle dame sans merci* with Rossetti, even though they might repudiate contemporary culture with Morris, they were all children of the nineteenth century. Our difficulty is, indeed, that they were individualists *in* the nineteenth century, each of whom wore his rue with a difference. Doubtless the Frenchman, M. Gabriel Mourey, exaggerates; yet, trying to explain to his countrymen that there had been a Renaissance across the channel in terms of a splendid individualism, he wrote in 1895:

Un mouvement s'était produit en Angleterre, une vraie Renaissance qui devait rajeunir l'art tout entier de ce pays et dont le contre-coup commence à peine à se faire sentir en France: je veux parler de cette prodigieuse École préraphaélite qui rénova non seulement la poésie et la peinture anglaises, mais encore l'art industriel, l'art de le décoration et de l'ameublement, jusqu'à l'art du costume féminin, et la façon de sentir des intellectuels et des délicats . . . Quoique les origines de l'École préraphaélite. . . la personnalité justement glorieuse de Dante Gabriel Rossetti projette sur cette époque de l'art anglais une lumière mystérieuse et attirante, et provoque un enthousiasme qui ne va pas sans quelque injustice à l'endroit des camarades du peintre-poète, associés, de coeur et d'oeuvre, à la révolution esthétique que l'on sait.[26]

The dramatic instinct that led Frances Winwar to write *Poor Splendid Wings* (1933)[27] may be sounder than the scholar's analysis, inasmuch as the clash of personalities in the circle (or circles) is at least as crucial as aesthetic theory. However you group them, these artists were immensely conscious of themselves, immensely aware of adjacent human individualities. Not since Byron had the individual gesture seemed so important, not since the Keats circle had there been such an immense savoring of personalities. No doubt Ford Madox Ford's *Memories and Impressions* is impeachable on the score of absolute veracity, but it catches and holds this sense of rich and majestic self-determination, as in the anecdote of a call paid by Burne-Jones and his wife at Brown's studio, when

Lady Burne-Jones, with her peculiarly persuasive charm, whispered to me, unheard by Madox Brown, that I should light the studio gas, and I was striking a match when I was appalled to hear Madox Brown shout, in tones of extreme violence and of apparent alarm: "Damn and blast it all, Fordie! Do you want us all blown into the next world?"

Brown's excuse was there was a leak in the gas-pipe; the fact was, he was determined that the president of the Royal Academy, who accompanied the Burne-Joneses, should not see his picture. It was, says Ford on the next page and with no intention of irony, "satisfactory to me to think that there was

[26] Gabriel Mourey, *Passé le Détroit: la vie et l'art à Londres* (1895), pp. 133–135.
[27] The book is subtitled: The Rossettis and Their Circle.

among these distinguished and kindly men still so great a feeling of solidarity." [28]

Among such men every event is worth recording; hence, the tremendous letters that fly back and forth, the tremendous diaries which, it sometimes seems, every member of the Pre-Raphaelite groups felt duty bound to keep. Christina Rossetti commonly passes for being reticent, yet her *Family Letters*, even after being selected, excised, and doctored by William Michael Rossetti, make a book of 242 pages.[29] In September, 1869, Dante Gabriel Rossetti was at Penkill revising proof for the 1870 volume; he has to write to William to tell him about these important changes, and though William again excises the letter, it runs to more than three pages in the *Family Letters* [30] and has all the air of two specialists consulting over a difficult and delicate operation. Young Millais once presented a cousin with a picture of a female figure; her husband wanted one of the arms redrawn; and it takes Millais some 400 words of what is printed (how much of the letter is omitted I do not know) to deal with this, with piano-tuning, with his mother, the houseboy, and the smells of various bottles.[31] One sometimes feels that Bruce Glasier memorized every conversation he ever had with William Morris, and then went home and set it down. We shall not know about Swinburne's correspondence until Cecil Lang puts it in order, but we know that it is voluminous. Large sections of Ford M. Hueffer's (Ford Madox Ford) *Ford Madox Brown: A Record of his Life and Work* (1896) and of Amy Woolner's *Thomas Woolner, R.A., Sculptor and Poet* (1917) simply reprint letters, journals, and dictated fragments of autobiography. And there is William Allingham's *Diary* (edited by H.

---

[28] *Memories and Impressions* (1911), pp. 8–9.
[29] *The Family Letters of Christina Georgina Rossetti* (1908). Note the characteristic epigraph:
    'She stands there patient, nerved with inner might,
    Indomitable in her feebleness,
    Her face and will athirst against the light.'
Contrast this with the majestic control of poetesses over cab-drivers, in Ford, pp. 107–110.
[30] *Dante Gabriel Rossetti: His Family Letters* (2 vols., 1895), II:214–217.
[31] *Life and Letters of Sir John Millais*, I:192–193.

Allingham and D. Radford, 1907), not to speak of two volumes of correspondence in which he is concerned.[32] These are the principal books in this library of lives. One begins to wonder when these painters, sculptors, engravers, illustrators, poets and prose men had time to do their proper work.

On the base of this Olympian self-consciousness, affection and piety have raised one of the most remarkable biographical and autobiographical collections of the nineteenth century. The standard biographies or autobiographies of the leading painters are often in two massive volumes — Millais, Burne-Jones, William Bell Scott, Leighton, Watts (who requires three). J. W. Mackail's *Life of William Morris* (1899) requires two also; and as for William Michael Rossetti, faithful, discreet, and tireless, it takes him nine volumes to tell us all he knows, and these do not include his reprint of *The Germ* with its biographical preface (1901), nor his editing of his brother's poetical works in 1886, 1891, 1898–1901, 1904, and 1911, and of his sister's in 1904. One contemplates with a kind of awe the vast Library Edition of Ruskin in thirty-nine volumes (edited by Sir E. T. Cook and A. D. O. Wedderburn, 1902–12), steeped as it is in biography, autobiography, and reverence; or the equally impressive *Collected Works* of William Morris in twenty-four volumes (1910–15) edited by May Morris, who neverthless has energy and materials left over for a huge two-volume compilation, *William Morris: Artist, Writer, Socialist* (1936). In these days of "quickie" publishing, one feels that one is confronting the relics of the world before the flood.

Yet even Victorian voluminousness does not exhaust the manuscript material, and one of the tasks twentieth-century scholarship has rightly set itself is to make available many unpublished documents. I have spoken of Cecil Lang's projected complete edition of Swinburne's letters, which, when published, will supersede all existing collections.[33] Paull Franklin Baum's *Dante Gabriel Rossetti: An Analytical List*

[32] *Letters of D. G. Rossetti to William Allingham, 1854–1870*, ed. George Birkbeck Hill (1897); *Letters to William Allingham*, ed. H. Allingham and E. B. Williams (1911).

[33] Conveniently listed in *CBEL*, III, 320.

of Manuscripts in the Duke University Library (1931) is more than a calendar of papers, it reproduces a rich variety of prose and verse that permits us to see Rossetti at work in literature. The moderns have sought to fill in gaps in the Rossetti correspondence, as witness Oswald Doughty's *Letters of Dante Gabriel Rossetti to his Publisher, F. S. Ellis* (1928), Janet Troxell's *Three Rossettis: Unpublished Letters to and from Dante Gabriel, Christina, William* (1937), and Baum's *Dante Gabriel Rossetti's Letters to Fanny Cornforth* (1940), which, though the letters are uninteresting *per se*, is invaluable to the biographer.[34] Works like these are edited with scrupulous care; but there is apparently no way within the compass of modern publishing by which the vast numbers of letters, already in print but mutilated by Victorian decorum, can be reprinted with their missing portions restored.

These examples principally concern the Rossetti family. It is inevitable, I suppose, given the materials and the incessant conflict of testimony, that members of the Pre-Raphaelite circles should exist in the minds of general readers as personalities rather than as artists. Not even the Brownings have been subjected to more continuous biographical assault, usually in the name of modern psychology. Certainly many Pre-Raphaelites were problematical natures, and if they were not more eccentric than many another Victorian, what may be called the confessional habit among them — the strong outpouring on paper of personal views and intense emotions — made them seem so. We know too much about them to forget the human being and to concentrate on the art; and the distaste and adulation they aroused equally invite explanation and correction. The prefatory matter to Doughty's *Dante Gabriel Rossetti: A Victorian Romantic* (1949), at once the most detailed and stable of recent lives of this figure, deals justly, if briefly, with earlier lives of Rossetti. Even though it is lacking modern information about Rossetti's irregular amours, Arthur C. Benson's *Rossetti*

---

[34] With these should be associated Dante Gabriel Rossetti's letters to Alice Boyd as "chosen and arranged" by John Purves (*The Fortnightly Review*, 1 May 1928). Unfortunately the texts are not always complete.

(1904) is still a just appreciation. But Violet Hunt's *The Wife of Rossetti* (1932), Helen Rossetti Angeli's reply, *Dante Gabriel Rossetti: His Friends and Enemies* (1949), David Larg's *Trial by Virgins* (1933), Francis Bickley's *The Pre-Raphaelite Comedy* (1932), and William Gaunt's *The Pre-Raphaelite Tragedy* (1942) ring the changes on chloral, eroticism, abnormal psychology, jealousy, suspicion in greater or less degree, while at the same time they struggle to remember they are dealing with thinkers and artists. Not as detailed as Doughty's life, Mégroz's *Dante Gabriel Rossetti* more steadily retains as its central interest the inter-play of poet and painter in Rossetti's personality and career.

In 1928 the novelist Evelyn Waugh published *Rossetti: His Life and Works* (second edition, 1931). The intent of the book was to concentrate on the painting, and the mixed reception it received from general critical journals illustrates the perplexities of Pre-Raphaelite biography. Thomas Craven in the Herald-Tribune *Books* applauded the study as a needed corrective to "modern aesthetic science," saying that the author

supports his contention with admirable lucidity, defining his terms precisely, and translating the technical jargon of the fashionable aesthetic doctors into a language within the grasp of the general reader.

In *The Saturday Review of Literature* Arnold Whitridge found the book well worth reading both for the vivid picture it gave of Rossetti and also as a

much needed protest against certain tendencies in modern esthetic criticism. It is refreshing to find an author who is obviously sympathetic with modern art and who at the same time insists that the impulse to pictorial expression does not necessarily come from the contemplation of form, but quite possibly from "an emotional state of mind. . . ."

But Peter Quennell, writing in *The New Statesman*, would have none of this pedagogical nonsense. Not only did he deplore "Mr. Waugh's lengthy analysis of Rossetti's pictures," but he demanded "a collective, not a single portrait" of the Pre-Raphaelite group, inasmuch as the conduct of the pre-Raphaelite adventure, its enthusiasm and impetus, is, on the whole, more entertaining than its actual results.[35]

The one approach demands that a study of Pre-Raphaelitism shall serve as a stick to beat the dog of contemporaneity; the other apparently asks the retention of contemporary values and an "entertaining" biographical approach. The truth of Emerson's dictum that every scripture should be read in the light of the times that brought it forth disappears between two irreconcilables.

Christina Rossetti does not present the same biographical puzzles, though in another sense she is puzzling enough; and despite the flaccidity of its criticism and its inevitable decorum, Mackenzie Bell's *Christina Rossetti: A Biographical and Critical Study* (1898) is still unsurpassed, albeit Mary F. Sandars' *Life* (1930), equally decorous, is somewhat more penetrating in its critical comments. It seems to me, however, that the difficulty with three other modern biographies — Dorothy M. Stuart, *Christina Rossetti* (1930); Eleanor Walter Thomas, *Christina Georgina Rossetti* (1931); and Marya Zaturenska, *Christina Rossetti: A Portrait with Background* (1949) — is that they scrutinize her poetry mainly for biographical hints and for its religious views. One may, I trust, be forgiven for inquiring how criticism is forwarded by so flat a statement as: "What is derivative in Christina's religious poetry is that which has its source in the body of Christian teaching, mainly in the Bible"; or: "at the present time the world is writing and reading a great deal about mysticism, mysticism as a philosophy, as a religion, as the soul of poetry; especially in the last forty years, there has been an outpouring of mystic poetry." [36]

If recent studies of Morris have tended to swallow up the artist in the social reformer,[37] recent biographies of Ruskin

---

[35] Herald-Tribune *Books,* 2 Sept. 1928; *SRL,* 28 July 1928; *The New Statesman,* 12 May 1928.

[36] Thomas, pp. 193–194, 195–196.

[37] E.g., the opening sentence of the "Prelude" to Edward and Stephani Godwin, *Warrior Bard* (1947) runs: "To study the ideals of William Morris is now more than ever necessary if we are to gain the truly Socialist life

have tended to lose the reformer in the psychological "case." The reader who starts out in good faith with R. H. Wilenski's *John Ruskin: An Introduction to Further Study of his Life and Work* (1933) presently discovers from this biographer-critic that everything Ruskin wrote is to be referred to "the condition of his mind"; and if then he goes on to Amabel Williams-Ellis, *The Exquisite Tragedy* (1929), Sir William Milburne James's reply, *John Ruskin and Effie Gray* (1947),[38] David Larg's *John Ruskin* (1932), and Peter Quennell's *John Ruskin: Portrait of a Prophet* (1949),[39] he is involved in psychiatry.[40] It is a relief to anyone interested in literary history as such to come upon Derrick Leon's *Ruskin: The Great Victorian* (1949). New collections of Ruskin's letters need not here concern us; but it may be remarked that researches now going forward into the relation of Ruskin to his parents may change the basis of previous biographies and alter the assumptions upon which this psychotic personality has hitherto been analyzed.

Biography has its own values. Within its universe of discourse it may indeed be valuable to know why Mrs. Ruskin ran off with John Everett Millais, where Rossetti was the

---

which we all want." Cf. Lloyd Wendell Eshleman, *A Victorian Rebel* (1940), which is exactly the same book except for the title page as Lloyd Eric Grey, *William Morris: Prophet of England's New Order* (1949). Philip Henderson's *The Letters of William Morris to his Family and Friends* (1950) has a paragraph from "How I Became a Socialist" for epigraph, devotes about half its dozen illustrations to socialistic activity, and gives twice as much space to years 1871–1896 as it does to years 1849–1870; i.e., to the years of socialist activity. In better balance are lives by Paul Bloomfield (1934), Montague Weekly (1934), and Esther Meynell (1947). The last of these emphasizes Morris as craftsman.

[38] Entitled *Order of Release* in the London edition, 1948.

[39] In his prefatory matter Quennell says that to consider Ruskin's art criticism would require a separate treatise, that he cannot devote sufficient space to Ruskin the social reformer, and that he proposes to concentrate on the writer and the personality.

[40] Le Roy in his *Perplexed Prophets* has taken the trouble to look into professional analyses, and refers his readers to Louis J. Bragman, "The Case of John Ruskin: A Study of Cyclothymia" (*American Journal of Psychiatry*, March 1935); T. M. Mitchell's review of Wilenski (*British Journal of Medical Psychology*, December 1933); and Louise A. Nelson, "Why John Ruskin Never Learned How to Live" (*Mental Hygiene*, October 1928).

night of his wife's death, and whether Swinburne did or did not practise flagellation. It must be remarked, however, that the total impression left by many recent investigations into Pre-Raphaelite worthies has been to increase a sense that morbidity is characteristic of the group. Whether this approach is fair to their art is another matter. We know nothing of the human beings who wrote the Goliardic student songs of the Middle Ages, which, for all we can tell, may owe their flavor to anything from literary convention to perverted erotic tastes among their authors. It is at least arguable whether the overwhelming effect of Berlioz's "Symphonie Fantastique" is in any way increased by the discovery that the composer was in love with Miss Smithson, who made him very unhappy after she married him; nor do we quite dispose of Nietzsche's philosophy by the argument that he died a lunatic. Researches into the number and nature of Rossetti's models and mistresses undoubtedly throw some light on the meaning of *The House of Life*, but if we knew as little about the personal life of its author as we know about the personal life of Shakespeare, *The House of Life* like Shakespeare's *Sonnets* would still remain a great, a beautiful, and an enigmatic work of art. Biography may explicate without explaining, and one of the present embarrassments of scholarship is that we know too much about the poets and not enough about the poetry. It is also curious that the painters among the groups — by which I mean those whose claim to immortality rests primarily upon their work in the graphic arts — do not seem to occasion the same kind of psychoanalytic judgment as is occasioned by those who wrote poetry; yet on the evidence a case could be made out for delusions of persecution in the psyche of Ford Madox Brown, religious monomania as the driving force in Holman Hunt, and an inferiority complex as the explanation of Millais' selling out to society — that, or a guilt complex caused by his elopement. It all depends upon whose psyche is being analyzed.

If, after discussing the Pre-Raphaelites as painters and as personalities, we turn to their work as poets, the same difficulty of classification appears. There is no doubt of Dante

Gabriel Rossetti and of Christina; the early work of William Morris belongs, certainly, and probably the later work also; Swinburne has a vague Pre-Raphaelite phase — and after that we enter a cloud of doubt. The fact that Patmore and Meredith passed, as it were, through a Pre-Raphaelite penumbra does not of itself justify their inclusion, albeit argument can be made that Patmore's celebration of a domestic Eros is the complement of Rossetti's celebration of a more earthly deity; and that the sharp visual images which set "Modern Love" slightly part from Meredith's other work may be attributable to life among the painters. As for lesser men like William Allingham, Arthur O'Shaughnessy, William Bell Scott, Philip Bourke Marston, William Sharp, and John Payne, the problem arises of distributing praise or blame for their qualities among Tennyson, the Spasmodics, the Pre-Raphaelites, the Celtic revival, Browning, and the dawning aesthetic movement, to which, of course, Pre-Raphaelitism is in one sense a prelude.[41] Except for illustration, however, nothing is gained by departing from the broad highway as we turn to consider twentieth-century comment upon the principal, or, at any rate, less disputable, figures.

Perhaps the most astonishing fact that confronts the inquirer is that, outside of large libraries, it is virtually impossible to study Pre-Raphaelite poetry in scholarly texts except as the writers are represented in the gargantuan anthologies that now make literary study a heavy matter. The second fact is that the British are better off in the matter of texts in print than are the Americans. Paull Franklin Baum's epoch-making edition of *The House of Life* (1928) is still available, and so is John R. Wahl's edition of Rossetti's juvenile *Jan Van Hunks* (1952). But Baum's excellent edition of Rossetti's *Poems, Ballads and Sonnets* (1937), a model of judicious editing, is out of print; and American buyers are reduced to the undistinguished *Poems and Translations* in the Oxford Standard Authors series, if the book guides are reliable. The

---

[41] Professor Chew, in the chapter on "Rossetti and his Circle" already cited, includes at the end Andrew Lang, Austin Dobson, Edmund Gosse, and even Charles Stuart Calverley and James K. Stephen. But this is surely due to the desperation that overcomes good men while making textbooks.

British read Rossetti in an anthology by F. L. Lucas (1933); and the Australians a selection of his *Poems* (edited by Lillian Howarth, 1950).[42] As for Christina, she is virtually reduced to a World's Classics edition of *The Goblin Market, The Prince's Progress and Other Poems*, and to two editions of *Sing-Song* for juveniles. No reprints of William Morris have recently been made available in this country, albeit William Gaunt, Jack Lindsay, and H. M. Burton have edited selections presently in print in Great Britain, the latter combining Morris with Rossetti. Somewhat aside from this list is Janet Troxell's variorum edition of *Rossetti's Sister Helen* (1939), still available. D. S. R. Welland's *The Pre-Raphaelites in Literature and Art* (1953) is a mélange. The leading Pre-Raphaelites, for all but special students, have, it is clear, been reduced to anthology poets, and the usual penalties of exaggeration, misrepresentation, or misinterpretation follow.

Scholarship has done much to clarify the literary sources, English [43] and foreign,[44] of Dante Gabriel Rossetti's poems. Manuscript resources tell us something about his manner of

[42] The rather unsatisfactory edition of Rossetti in Everyman's Library has just (1954) been restored to print.

[43] Representative studies are: Kurt Horn, *Studien zum Dichterischen Entwicklungsgange Dante Gabriel Rossettis* (1909); James Routh, "Parallels in Coleridge, Keats, and Rossetti" (*MLN*, 1910 — unsatisfactory); Hill Shine, "The Influence of Keats upon Rossetti" (*ES*, 1927 — admirable); George Milner, "On Some Marginalia made by Dante Gabriel Rossetti in a copy of Keats's Poems" (*ES*, 1927); A. M. Turner, "Rossetti's Reading and his Critical Opinions" (*PMLA*, 1927); B. J. Morse, "Dante Gabriel Rossetti and William Blake" (*ES*, 1932); Elizabeth Jackson, "Notes on the Stanza of Rossetti's *The Blessed Damozel*" (*PMLA*, 1943); Dwight and Helen Culler, "The Sources of *The King's Tragedy*" (*SP*, 1944). Kerrson Preston, *Blake and Rossetti* (1944), is without value.

[44] For example, L. A. Willoughby, *Dante Gabriel Rossetti and German Literature* (1912); R. D. Waller, "The Blessed Damozel" (*MLR*, 1931); B. J. Morse, "Dante Gabriel Rossetti and Dante Alighieri" (*ES*, 1933); B. I. Evans, "Dante Gabriel Rossetti" (*English Poetry in the Later Nineteenth Century*, 1933); Paull F. Baum, *The Blessed Damozel: the unpublished manuscript texts and collation* (1937); Baum, "Rossetti's The Leaf" (*MLQ*, 1941); Baum, "Rossetti, 'The White Ship'" (*Library Notes: A Bulletin Issued for the Friends of Duke University Library*, 1948). I owe a number of these references to the kindness of Dr. Cecil Lang of Yale University, whose "The French Original of Rossetti's *John of Tours* and *My Father's Close*" (*PMLA*, 1949) is a model study.

composition,[45] and genetic analysis has proved especially fruitful in the case of "The Blessed Damozel." [46] Baum's edition of *The House of Life* inevitably antiquates early studies of the genesis, growth, and personal significance of this poem.

But these studies, solid as they are in many instances, together with others that are excursions into the history of ideas,[47] are not criticism, and especially do they fail to represent the application of modern criticism to a poet in many ways astonishingly contemporary in his psychological processes. What seems to be overlooked is the sound observation of Derek Patmore [48] that Rossetti was genuinely interested in creating a synthesis of poetry and painting. Much nineteenth-century criticism was so bemused by the conflict of ideality and sensualism, platonism and the exotic, contemporary problems and escape into the remote and fantastic, in Rossetti's work that what they said seems to us nowadays much beside the point.[49] From this general statement the chapter

[45] In addition to Mrs. Troxell's *Rossetti's Sister Helen* already cited, see her "The 'Trial Books' of Dante Gabriel Rossetti" (*Colophon*, Spring 1938); and Paull F. Baum, "The Bancroft Manuscript of Dante Gabriel Rossetti" (*MP*, 1941), with which compare Ruth C. Wallerstein, "The Bancroft Manuscripts of Rossetti's Sonnets" (*MLN*, 1929).

[46] R. D. Waller, "The Blessed Damozel" (*MLR*, 1931); K. L. Knickerbocker, "Rossetti's 'The Blessed Damozel'" (*SP*, 1932); J. A. Sanford, "The Morgan Library Manuscripts of Rossetti's 'The Blessed Damozel'" (*SP*, 1938). See also Baum, *supra*.

[47] Mary Suddard, in *Studies and Essays* (1912), advances the interesting idea that the Pre-Raphaelite movement in general and Rossetti in particular represent a sort of belated Renaissance. Of Rossetti she remarks that in twenty years (1860–1880) he condensed and transposed into another key the yield of four centuries, and she finds in the sonnets and songs of the *Poems* of 1870 the true Renaissance vitality and passion (pp. 261–278). William C. DeVane's "The Harlot and the Thoughtful Young Man" (*SP*, 1932), though it has its impulse in a desire to straighten out the Rossetti-Browning feud, identifies an intellectual formula in Victorian poetry.

[48] "The Pre-Raphaelites" (*The Spectator*, 1 October 1948).

[49] Consider, for example, the unruly vagueness of Stedman's statement that Rossetti's realism is "the spirit of beauty wandering within the confines of the . . . visible landscape" (*Victorian Poets*, 1875, pp. 357–366); or F. W. H. Myers' declaration that "Art and Religion, which no compression could amalgamate, may be Love expanded and interfused" (*Essays: Modern*, 1883, "Rossetti and the Religion of Beauty," pp. 312–334); or Stopford A. Brooke's coyness, confronted by the "apparent" sensuality of Rossetti's love poetry, the

on "The Rossettis" in the *Survey of English Literature, 1780–1880* (four volumes, 1920) by the Edwardian critic, Oliver Elton, should be excepted, for Elton escapes obvious moralizing and moves into the world in which art is a weighty original experience:

> Poets of Rossetti's studious tribe have always much cold-blooded technical work to get done; work as definite, and requiring as steady a hand, as that of a goldsmith, or of the Indian who inlays marble flower-petals into the marble tomb of an emperor. They rejoice in the sorting of coloured words, in bevelling the sentences, in blowing away the dust. It is the joy of decoration, which insensibly carries them away from natural forms into strangeness. (IV, 19)

This is rightly said and brings us back, as we should be brought back, to Rossetti the Pre-Raphaelite craftsman and decorator.[50] Critics came relatively late to understand that one of his fundamental notions is that poetry begins in fundamental brainwork.[51] Nor should it be forgotten that the present Poet Laureate has given us the comment of a craftsman upon a fellow craftsman in *Thanks before Going* (1946).

Doubtless it is unjust to declare that the interpretation of Rossetti (or of anybody else) takes a turn towards modernity with the appearance of one particular article, but the publi-

---

result of a sort of split personality, capable only in the "intense moment" (*Four Victorian Poets: A Study of Clough, Arnold, Rossetti, and Morris*, 1908, pp. 126–177). In S. N. Ghose, *Dante Gabriel Rossetti & Contemporary Criticism, 1849–1882* (1929) the reader may follow in chronological order the chief nineteenth-century comments on Rossetti's paintings and his poetry.

[50] There are those who take more seriously than I can the significance of "Hand and Soul" in *The Germ*. See B. J. Morse, "A Note on the Autobiographical Elements in Rossetti's 'Hand and Soul'" (*Anglia*, 1930); and Dom Thomas V. Moore, "Dante Gabriel Rossetti" (*Dublin Review*, 1937). And perhaps this is as good a place as any other to say that H. B. Forman's discussion of Rossetti in *Our Living Poets* (1871, pp. 187–228) is unexpectedly without an overpowering moral bias. Of the 1870 volume he says: "one knows at once that it is beautiful poetry, just as one knows and recognizes the benign presence of a beautiful-souled person." Read also his interesting discussion of the theme of laughter in "A Last Confession."

[51] See, e.g., Sir Walter Raleigh, "Dante Gabriel Rossetti" in *Chambers' Cyclopaedia of English Literature* (1904, III); and Albert E. Trombly, *Rossetti the Poet*, chap. I, "Fundamental Brainwork," in *University of Texas Bulletin*, No. 2060, 25 October 1920.

cation of Eva Tietz's perceptive study, "Das Malerische in Rossettis Dichtung" (*Anglia*, 1927), should have marked such an epoch. Dr. Tietz asked herself the question others should have asked earlier: what traces of the practice of a painter and designer are likely to linger in the poetry of a painter and a designer? She sorted out the answers into two unequal piles: one concerned with the choice of materials, and the other, with modes of recording experience. These latter she finds to be both linear and pictorial (*malerisch*). She looked beyond the mere dependence upon visuality (the problem is more than the *ut pictura poesis* of the eighteenth century) into questions of line, perspective, and depth, and into the inter-relation between light, color, and shadow on the one hand and modeling on the other, as in

> The shadows where the cheeks are thin

in "Jenny"; and in

>   turned
> Her gaze where Amelotte
> Knelt, — and the gold hair upon her back
> Quite still in all its threads, — the track
> Of her still shadow sharp and black

in "The Bride's Prelude." I am acquainted with no other study that thus sharply wrenches us out of the vague rhetoric of the late nineteenth century into the actual workings-out of Pre-Raphaelite theory in Rossetti's verse.

But Dr. Tietz could not do everything. What the further study of Rossetti needs is a closer analysis of his poetry in terms that the work of I. A. Richards and others has made familiar. In one sense we can well afford to return to the older mode of stylistic analysis for data.[52] From "My Sister's Sleep" to the late sonnets in *The House of Life* is a stylistic progression as astonishing as the movement of Pope's style from "Windsor Forest" to "The Epilogue to the Satires." If in its intense visuality, not to speak of sharpened hearing,

---

[52] Max Schoepe's *Der Vergleich bei Dante Gabriel Rossetti* (1914) has the mechanical accuracy one associates with German dissertations, but it offers the basis for a fruitful approach to imagery.

"My Sister's Sleep" has its relations to Keats and to Tennyson of the "Mariana" poems, so likewise it has its relations to "The Girlhood of Mary Virgin," just as "Jenny," in passages like

> rub your eyes for me, and shake
> My gold, in rising, from your hair,
> A Danaë for a moment there,

has its relations not merely to harlotry but also to "Mary Magdalene at the Door of Simon the Pharisee," for which a pen-and-ink drawing was made in 1858, the year Rossetti completely recast the poem. If Pre-Raphaelite painting moved from realism to decoration, Rossetti's poetry moved from the clarity of "The Blessed Damozel" —

> this earth
> Spins like a fretful midge.
>
> . . . . . .
>
> Time like a pulse shake fierce
> Through all the worlds.
>
> . . . . . .
>
> the curlèd moon
> Was like a little feather
> Fluttering far down the gulf —

to the synaesthesia which puts "Love's Nocturn," "The Stream's Secret," and many of the later sonnets among the more difficult work of the late Victorian world. Malory, Froissart, and mediaevalized classicism came in (as in the Oxford frescoes and Burne-Jones's androgynous figures illustrating Greek legend); Rossetti, whose mediaevalism had been Italianate, turned to the balladic narrative of "The King's Tragedy" and associated narrative verse. A fresh approach to Rossetti would reveal, I think, that in an age notable for didactic poetry, he is both a subtler moralist and a profounder thinker than may more celebrated bards, concealing his moral lesson so successfully in such magnificent figures as those in "Lost Days," " 'Retro Me, Sathana!' " "A Superscription," and "The One Hope" that casual readers do not think of him as a moralist at all. Consider, however, even in its somewhat too arduous fullness, the remarkable union of ethics and art in the prelude to *The House of Life*:

> A sonnet is a coin; its face reveals
> The Soul — its converse, to what Power 'tis due: —
> Whether for tribute to the august appeals
> Of life, or dower in Love's high retinue,
> It serve; or 'mid the dark wharf's cavernous breath,
> In Charon's palm it pay the toll to death,

six lines that concentrate imagery and meaning as intensely as does anything in T. S. Eliot. I do not know what impression much of Burne-Jones and most of Rossetti's later paintings make on others, but on me the impression is of a world in which time is frozen; and what strikes one reader, at any rate, is the failure of critics to deal with the parallel treatment of time in "The Burden of Nineveh" or such slow-motion poems as "Memorial Thresholds." Perhaps the supreme example of action transposed into inaction is the unfinished "The Bride's Prelude," unfinished because there was nothing to do with the poem except break it off. As in the early Morris, so in Rossetti: a typical poem has to do with the intense moment of preparation for action, or in the intense exhaustion that follows upon action, not (as with Scott or Longfellow) with action itself.

We need a study of Rossetti in another area — his imagery; something, say, as scrupulous and imaginative as Wolfgang Clemen's *The Development of Shakespeare's Imagery* (1951). And we need a parallel study in the case of Christina, who is generally considered the poetess *par excellence* of the nineteenth century, Mrs. Browning not having stood the test of time. But Christina's poetry is seldom approached as art; it is approached as autobiography, as religious monomania, as an example of the morbidity of children's verse in the death-conscious nineteenth century.[53] The three scholarly or critical inquiries of recent vintage that seem to begin by assuming

---

[53] It is amazing how vain repetitions condition most of the "scholarly" articles. See for examples, Justine F. de Wilde, *Christina Rossetti: Poet and Woman* (1923); Geoffrey W. Rossetti, "Christina Rossetti" (*The Criterion*, 1930); Dorothy M. Stuart, "Christina Rossetti" (*The English Association*,

she was an artist and not a moral convalescent are an essay by Walter de la Mare in *Transactions of the Royal Society of Literature* (1926); the second part of Fredegond Shove's *Christina Rossetti: A Study* (1931), which, though not profound criticism, at least approaches the poetry as poetry; and Friedrich Dubslaff, *Die Sprachform der Lyric Christina Rossettis* (1933), which, stiff and angular, sticks to the problem of her verse. Of the biographies I have already spoken.[54] I do not deny that fine things have been said of Christina as a lyric poet in general studies of poetry or of the century; but our present interest is to assess writing specially devoted to her.

The excessively literary origin of almost all of William Morris' verse except the songs of socialist propaganda has inevitably created a small library of source studies,[55] in which

---

Pamphlet No. 78, 1931); Elizabeth Belloc, "Christina Rossetti" (*The Catholic World*, 1942). Even Virginia Woolf sinks below herself in *The Second Common Reader* (1932). (Christina's faith "circles and clamps together these little songs," but her Pre-Raphaelite intensity, it seems, conflicts with her Anglo-Catholicism!) Two articles seem to me to stand out: In "The Sources of Christina Rossetti's *Goblin Market*" (*MLR*, 1933) B. I. Evans offers some sensible suggestions about the background and context of this poem, and B. J. Morse, for what it is worth, in "Some Notes on Christina Rossetti and Italy" (*Anglia*, 1931), demonstrates that Christina was not as insular in interest as legend declares. See also Barbara Garlitz, "Christina Rossetti's *Sing-Song* and Nineteenth-Century Children's Poetry" (*PMLA*, 1955).

[54] See above, p. 181.

[55] E.g., J. Riegel, *Die Quellen von William Morris' Dichtung 'The Earthly Paradise'* (1890); H. Bartels, *William Morris, The Story of Sigurd the Volsung and the Fall of the Niblungs: eine Studie über das Verhältnis des Epos zu den Quellen* (1906); G. H. Maynadier, *The Arthur of the English Poets* (1907); C. H. Herford, *Norse Myth in English Poetry* (1919); G. Apgar, "Morris's *The Lady of the Land*" (*Poet Lore*, 1922); G. T. McDowell, "The Treatment of the Volsungasaga by William Morris" (*Scandinavian Studies and Notes*, 1923); Stella P. Wilson, "William Morris and France" (*SAQ*, 1924); Lucien Wolff, "Le Sentiment Médiéval in Angleterre au XIXe Siècle et la première Poesie de William Morris" (*Revue Anglo-Américaine*, 1924–25); E. C. Kuester, *Mittelalter und Antike bei William Morris* (1928); Karl Litzenberg, "William Morris and Scandinavian Literature: A Bibliographical Essay" (*Scandinavian Studies and Notes*, 1935); Litzenberg, "Allusions to the Elder Edda in the 'Non-Norse' Poems of William Morris" (*ibid.*, 1936); Litzenberg, "William Morris and the Heimskringla" (*ibid.*, 1936); Litzenberg, "William Morris and the Burning of Njal" (*ibid.*, 1936) ; Litzenberg, "Tyrfing into Excalibur" (*ibid.*, 1938) ; Dorothy M. Hoare, *The Works of Morris and Yeats in Relation to Early Saga Literature* (1937); Clarice Short, "The Poetic Relationship of John Keats and William Morris" (*Cornell University Abstracts of Theses*, 1941); Short, "William

the Germans and the Germanic-minded have been especially diligent. The question of his socialism has evoked two types of inquiries: one devoted to a critical examination of his tenets, and the other what I can only characterize as settlement-house inquiry; that is, the assumption that Morris in a general way meant to uplift and to do good. I am not sure it is always possible to distinguish among these.[56] Inquiries into his work as a poet-craftsman are notably less numerous, possibly because it is felt that the simplicity of his verse offers no cruxes to interpretation.[57] In *Nineteenth Century Studies* (ed. Herbert Davis, William C. DeVane and R. C. Bald, 1940), Oscar Maurer, Jr., summarizes a controversy on "William Morris and the Poetry of Escape" which still haunts aesthetic evaluation: was *The Earthly Paradise* escape or sociological commentary? was it for the Philistines or for the Radicals? was it a flight into medievalism or was it concerned with the tensions and strains of Victorian England, elaborately disguised? Of Morris Mr. Mauer concluded, it seems to me a

---

Morris and Keats" (*PMLA*, 1944); Oscar Maurer, "Some Sources of William Morris's *The Wanderers*," (*University of Texas Studies in English*, 1950).

[56] For the biographies see above, p. 181. Inquiries more or less thorough into the intellectual basis of Morris' socialism would include the following: William Sinclair, "Socialism according to William Morris" (*Fortnightly Review*, 1910); G. R. S. Taylor, *Leaders of Socialism, Past and Present* (1910); E. Guyot, "Le Socialisme de William Morris," *Le Socialisme et l'Evolution de l'Angleterre contemporaine (1880–1911)* (1913); John Drinkwater, "William Morris and the State," *Prose Papers*, 1917; C. D. Burns, "William Morris and Industry," *The Principles of Revolution* (1920); G. Fritzsche, *William Morris' Sozialismus und Anarchistischer Kommunismus. Darstellung des Systems und Untersuchung der Quellen* (1927); (Mrs.) A. A. von Helmholtz Phelan, *Social Philosophy of William Morris* (1927) ; John M. Murry, "The Return to Fundamentals: Marx and Morris" (*Adelphi*, 1932); Murry, "William Morris" (*ibid.*, 1934) ; Bernard Wall, "William Morris and Karl Marx" (*Dublin Review*, 1938) ; Margaret R. Grennan, *William Morris, Medievalist and Revolutionary* (1945) .

It would be invidious to try to particularize essays presenting what I have called the settlement-house approach to Morris, but two of the more intelligent articles of recent vintage that illustrate it are Geoffrey Tillotson, "Morris and Machines" (*Fortnightly Review*, 1934), excellent in its comment on Morris' wrong-headed approach to craftsmanship versus the machine; and Margaret Cole, "The Fellowship of William Morris" (*Virginia Quarterly Review*, 1948), "Morris's Fellowship was Socialism."

[57] Any of the usual bibliographical listings will lead the reader to critical commentary; for example, the lists in Woods and Buckley, *Poetry of the Vic-*

touch hastily, that "when evasion became impossible for him, he left his generation behind." [58]

That Morris' poetry, though not his life, grows more and more remote from the original tenets of Pre-Raphaelitism seems to me an inescapable conclusion. One simple test is to contrast the "brown birds" which haunt his poetry with the demand for a conscientious specificity with which Millais and Hunt began. But inasmuch as Morris comes upon the stage of this world as a medievalist and a decorator (I recur to the Oxford Union designs) he cannot be fairly said to have departed from that which he never held. Rather may it be argued that he rediscovered the significance of the original tenets in his slow, dogged approach to the realities of English industrial life, which, characteristically, he came to by the roundabout road of the "Anti-Scrap" society and the problem of trying to forget six counties overhung with smoke.

One final observation in a commentary altogether too casual. It cannot be said that from 1800 to 1850 England was shut off from the Continent, but it can be said that the approach to foreign cultures alters perceptibly between the first half of the century and the second. Englishmen flock to Paris during the brief period of the Treaty of Amiens, but they do not take in Napoleonic romance. The visits of persons like Thackeray and Dickens to the Continent, especially where Latin culture is concerned, left them insular Britons to the end — consider the condescension with which Frenchmen and Italians are treated in the writings of either novelist. I forget who said of the Englishman of that generation that he took his bathtub and his national goddam around the earth, but the pitiless accuracy of Jules Verne's caricature, Phileas Fogg, in *Around the World in Eighty Days*, shows how impervious the Englishman seemed to other nationals. Or con-

---

torian Period; or in Stephens, Beck, and Snow, *Victorian and Later English Poets* (1934 and later). These are good working lists, and there are others.

[58] Contrast this with Walter Gropius' statement that in 1919 he was indebted to Morris, Ruskin, and the Deutscher Werkbund for his outlook, since they reunited the world of work with the world of the artist. Niklaus Pevsner, "English and German Art and their Inter-relations" (*German Life and Letters*, 1938).

sider Lady Hester Stanhope as pictured in Kinglake's *Eothen,* an eccentric Englishwoman among the Druses; though eccentric, she remains an Englishwoman to the end.

One of the great, dynamic contributions of the Pre-Raphaelites was to assist materially in altering English attitudes towards foreign cultures. Literary comment usually speaks of the exotic as if it represented some deviation from the highest moral law. But to be aware of the strange and the colorful may be as much a part of knowing the best that has been said and thought in the world as being aware of ethical commitments or philosophy. When the Pre-Raphaelites went all out for FitzGerald's version of Omar Khayyám, they helped to alter not only the British attitude towards foreign countries, but also the British attitude towards foreign art. The casual reader, as soon as his attention is called to it, must be aware of the devouring interest of the Pre-Raphaelite poets in translation. Rossetti produces some of the great standard versions of Romance literary masterpieces — Villon, Dante, the Italian poets before, and contemporary with, *The Divine Comedy.* The bulk of William Morris is either translation [59] or re-tellings in English verse of Continental tales. John Payne is now remembered only for his versions of Villon, Boccaccio, *The Arabian Nights,* and others. (It is easy, as I have discovered, to confuse him with James Payn!) Even Allingham's Irish fairy-lore and William Sharp's neo-Ossianism are a kind of translation. Rossetti said in 1865 (but I forget where):

Thinking in what order I love colours, found the following: (1) pure light warm green, (2) deep gold colour, (3) certain tints of grey, (4) shadowy or steel blue, (5) brown, with crimson tinge, (6) scarlet. Other colours (comparatively) only loveable according to the relations in which they are placed.

Possibly the restoration of these colors to English poetry, pos-

---

[59] See in this connection Geoffrey Riddlehough, "William Morris's Translation of the *Æneid*" (*JEGP,* 1937), and his "William Morris's Translation of the *Odyssey,*" in the same (1941). The fact that Morris's "Beowulf" is for most people unreadable and *Sigurd the Volsung* far too long should not obscure his great services as a conduit between the present and the past, and between the rest of the world and Great Britain.

sibly the reinvigoration of the search for color in life and art, for that strangeness which is no small part of beauty, and which, if it could not be found in London and in present time, could be found in Arabia or the mountains of the moon, or in that no man's land where the Sword put out to sea, and Jehane came all the way to part at last without a kiss — possibly this, rather than their relations to Aestheticism, the Decadence, Socialism, Symbolism, Freudianism, or any other solemn formula of scholarship is the true importance of the Pre-Raphaelites. With all their faults upon their heads — and their faults were many — they filled the cup of life to the brim.

8 ᗊ

Gerard Manley Hopkins

John Pick

I. *Bibliographical Materials*

ALTHOUGH GERARD MANLEY HOPKINS was rejected and neglected during his lifetime and although his single slim volume of poems was not published until 1918, almost thirty years after his death, the generations of critics since 1918 have probably directed more attention to him than to any other Victorian poet. The number of critiques, articles, essays, and books devoted to his contribution is now close to a thousand.

The most complete bibliographies appear in *Immortal Diamond: Studies in Gerard Manley Hopkins* (edited by Norman Weyand, 1949), which extends with thoroughness through 1944, and in "Forty Years of Criticism. A Chronological Check List of Criticism of the Works of Gerard Manley Hopkins from 1909 to 1949" in *Bulletin of Bibliography*, (1950). The ten-page bibliography in W. A. M. Peters' *Gerard Manley Hopkins: A Critical Essay towards the Understanding of his Poetry* (1948) is unreliable and inaccurate. And the most discriminatingly selective bibliography appears in "A Bibliographical Study of Hopkins Criticism, 1918–1949" (*Thought*, 1950) by Maurice Charney, who presents one hundred items.

The history of the Hopkins manuscripts — a history still tinged with mystery — as well as a catalogue of the unpublished manuscripts, is given by D. Anthony Bischoff in "The Manuscripts of Gerard Manley Hopkins" (*Thought*, Winter 1951–52).

Several surveys of Hopkins criticism have appeared. W. H. Gardner in the first volume of his *Gerard Manley Hopkins: A Study of Poetic Idiosyncrasy in Relation to Poetic Tradition* (1944) devotes a chapter, "Critics and Reviewers," to an evaluation through 1942. More recent is Maurice Charney's "A Bibliographical Study of Hopkins Criticism, 1918–1949" (*Thought*, 1950) which is carefully critical and usefully subdivided into such topics as trends, themes, sources and analogues, prosody, and style.

Because Hopkins often used words in their unfamiliar meanings or occasionally employed words in their provincial or dialectical usages and even revived archaisms or coined new words, a helpful aid is Raymond V. Schoder's "An Interpretive Glossary" in *Immortal Diamond: Studies in Gerard Manley Hopkins* (1949).

II. *Editions and Selections*

The first edition of *Poems of Gerard Manley Hopkins*, in 1918, edited by Robert Bridges, was followed by a second edition in 1930, with an introduction by Charles Williams and an appendix of additional poems, an edition which has been pirated. In 1948 this was superseded by the third edition, retaining Bridges' Preface and Notes for their historical importance but edited with additional poems, notes, and a critical and biographical introduction by W. H. Gardner. This printing includes nearly twice as many poems as the 1918 edition, but most of the additions are minor. Gardner, working with the manuscripts, corrects the chronology of earlier editions, makes additional collations and emendations, and restores some of the readings that Bridges had altered.

The first edition of the *Poems* appeared in 1918, but evaluations of Hopkins' character and of his objectives remained perilous until the middle and late thirties when four additional volumes of primary materials were published. Claude Colleer Abbott meticulously edited in 1935 (reprinted, 1955) *Letters of Gerard Manley Hopkins to Robert Bridges* and *The Correspondence of Gerard Manley Hopkins and Richard Watson Dixon,* and in 1938 *Further Letters.* The bulk of the latter volume is devoted to letters to Alexander Baillie and correspondence with Coventry Patmore, in addition to some letters to Newman and his school and college friends, but includes only a few family letters.

In 1937, Humphry House edited *The Note-Books and Papers of Gerard Manley Hopkins.* The volume, which became a mine for succeeding Hopkins scholars, includes generous portions of his diaries and journals, his essays, and examples of his sermons and commentaries. It is a model of editing and contains sketches, drawings, and even maps of the English and Welsh districts associated with Hopkins.

The search for Hopkinsiana has been strenuous. According to present information, the publication of two additions has been planned. Christopher Devlin is to edit all the diaries and journals, including 20,000 hitherto-unpublished words in three copybooks discovered in 1947 by D. Anthony Bischoff in a war-damaged room in London. More recently, the Hopkins family home has yielded an undisclosed number of manuscripts, including some fifty or more letters to the poet's mother; the material is now deposited at the Bodleian Library, and Abbott plans to edit the family letters. Since almost no family letters have hitherto been printed — only three to be exact — these recent discoveries will doubtlessly be important for closer understanding of Hopkins' life and character.

The various volumes of correspondence and notebooks were expensive, and gradually some went out of print. These facts, along with the widening acceptance of Hopkins, resulted in the appearance of three different volumes of selections in 1953.

An inexpensive *Selected Poems of Gerard Manley Hopkins,* edited with an introduction and notes by James Reeves, includes all the mature poems as well as two examples of earlier work and three specimens of later unfinished poems. Convinced that "readers of modern poetry are now so accustomed to accentual verse and 'the rhythm of common speech' that the marks may now be considered an unnecessary blemish," Reeves removed all accent marks, and unfortunately in doing so, in some cases he also removed the meaning from the poems. The edition is therefore not recommended.

The other two volumes of selections attempt to present representative poems and portions of the diaries, journals, letters, sermons, and commentaries. *Poems and Prose of Gerard Manley Hopkins,* edited by W. H. Gardner, has a chronological arrangement, while *A Hopkins Reader,* edited by John Pick, arranges the selections under various headings: observation of nature, poetic theory, practical criticism, religion, and the like. Gardner's book gives more space to the poems, while Pick's offers more of the prose.

III. *Biographical Studies*

No satisfactory biography of Hopkins exists, though the habit of quoting haphazardly from his letters and other sources of information about his life has seldom been resisted.

Certain special studies, such as Martin C. D'Arcy's "Gerard Manley Hopkins" in *Great Catholics,* edited by Claude Williamson (1939), Pick's *Gerard Manley Hopkins: Priest and Poet* (1942), and Martin C. Carroll's "Gerard Manley Hopkins and the Society of Jesus" (in *Immortal Diamond: Studies in Gerard Manley Hopkins,* 1949), are helpful for interpretations of separate aspects of the poet's life. This list could be extended considerably.

For some years following its publication in 1930, G. F. Lahey's *Gerard Manley Hopkins* had both the advantages and the disadvantages of being a pioneering work. But in attempting to do everything within the space of 150 pages, the book was merely an introduction. Quoting frequently and liberally from primary sources, this study whetted appetites while it left them unsatisfied and many found it sketchy, fragmentary, and disappointing.

The year 1944, the centenary of Hopkins' birth, evoked innumerable critical studies, and also Eleanor Ruggles' *Gerard Manley Hopkins: A Life*, which is still the only volume devoted primarily to biography. It is semi-popularized and has the quality of vivid readability. In its readability also lies its danger. Hopkins' life is fluently fictionalized and dramatized, though it would be too harsh to say that the work is a frustrated historical novel. It re-creates with a deceptive ease that can easily win the ordinary reader. But when Eleanor Ruggles indecisively faces difficult enigmas, she raises a paragraph of unanswered questions and leaves the reader to make his choice. This method leads to a subtle and almost unnoticeable kind of distortion.

The most balanced and carefully constructed brief biographies of the poet are those of Austin Warren in his introductory chapter to *Gerard Manley Hopkins by the Kenyon Critics* (1945) and W. H. Gardner's Introduction to the third edition of the *Poems* (1948). More detailed but not definitive are the biographical chapters scattered through both volumes of W. H. Gardner's *Gerard Manley Hopkins*.

The definitive biography of Hopkins is eventually to be a two-volume study. Humphry House until his unexpected death in 1955 was working at the pre-Jesuit years, 1844–68, and D. Anthony Bischoff is currently writing the later life of Hopkins.

IV. *History of Hopkins Criticism*

The advantage of a chronological survey of Hopkins criticism is that it is almost a history of the transition from Victorian to modern poetry. Above all, we learn again the truth of the observation that a poet often has to create the taste by which he is to be appreciated.

Hopkins died in 1889, and his poems were not published until 1918. But the criticism of his poetry started during his life among his small circle of friends, the three poets who constituted his public. The varying attitudes of Robert Bridges, Richard Watson Dixon, and Coventry Patmore are important and may be reconstructed in some detail by studying the various volumes of letters and correspondence already listed.

The least of these was the one who was most understanding and appreciative; for Dixon read the poems with "delight, astonishment, and admiration." He found them "amazingly original." He urged immediate publication. He felt the "power" of "The Wreck of the Deutschland," a poem which came to be a test for each of Hopkins' friends. Dixon perceived that something in Hopkins' life and character gave his poem a "rare charm," "something I cannot describe, but known to myself by the inadequate word *terrible pathos* — something of what you call temper in poetry: a right temper which goes to the point of the terrible: the terrible crystal."

Very different was the reaction of Patmore, a fellow-Catholic and experimentalist in verse, who preferred those poems that were least typical of Hopkins and most nearly approximated what he called "the ordinary rules of composition." Patmore granted that the "obscuring novelties" in time might become "additional delights" but yet "I do not think I could ever become sufficiently accustomed to your favourite poem, 'The Wreck of the Deutschland' to reconcile me to its strangeness."

But Bridges became for a long period the most influential and controversial critic of Hopkins, although strangely enough, his entire relationship with Hopkins has never been adequately explored. One of the initial difficulties is that Bridges destroyed his side of the correspondence and has therefore left himself open to criticism that may sometimes be unfair.

Bridges' lifelong friendship was very important to Hopkins in spite of the fact that there was little sympathy, either in religion or in poetry, between the two. Hopkins was conscious that, in a sense, Bridges was his most important audience; and Bridges' almost constant and discouraging criticism of Hopkins had the effect of making Hopkins consider with double care the effects he was trying to produce.

Hopkins apparently had to plead with Bridges to read "The Wreck of the Deutschland" a second time, and Bridges re-

torted that its sprung rhythm was "presumptuous jugglery."
Hopkins clearly hoped to convert Bridges to sprung rhythm;
the degree to which he influenced Bridges' own experiments
in sprung rhythm has not been sufficiently studied, and there
has even been the suggestion that Bridges delayed the edition
of Hopkins' poetry to put critics off the scent. A sound judgment can be possible only when all the facts are assembled,
and it appears that some of the evidence will always be
missing.

The only two poems that Hopkins submitted for publication were sent to the Jesuit periodical, *The Month*, which rejected them, and Bridges became during his lifetime the
custodian of the poems, carefully preserving them.

The story of the posthumous disposition of Hopkins' other
manuscripts is involved; scholars are relying on D. Anthony
Bischoff to clarify this area of Hopkins studies. The discovery
of Hopkins' will in 1947, almost sixty years after his death,
has added a note of drama to an already complicated situation (see "Hopkins' Manuscripts," by D. Anthony Bischoff,
Thought, Winter 1951–52).

Between the death of Hopkins in 1889 and the appearance
of the first edition of his poems in 1918, Bridges managed to
introduce several of Hopkins' poems — though sometimes in
truncated versions — into anthologies. This method of attempting to win a public for his dead friend seems com-
mendable, except that he adopted the habit of frightening
away readers by warning them in these anthologies that the
poems "not only sacrifice simplicity, but very often, among
verses of the rarest beauty, show a neglect of those canons of
taste which seem common to all poetry."

In 1909, probably embarrassed by the neglect of Hopkins
during his lifetime, and having tried to collect the scattered
manuscripts, the Reverend Joseph Keating, S.J., published a
series of three articles in *The Month*. And it has recently
been revealed that correspondence exists in which Father
Keating was thwarted by Bridges in publishing an edition of
Hopkins' poems in 1909. Until this correspondence is published, there can be no evaluation of the motives involved.

Nearly a decade later, in 1918, Bridges, then Poet Laureate, published the first edition of Hopkins' poems, and it became Bridges' most important piece of Hopkins criticism: he summarized his reflections after forty years of acquaintance with Hopkins' poetry. He had collated the manuscripts in his possession, had written notes for the poems, helpfully drawing upon explanations from Hopkins' letters, and it must be noted in Bridges' favor that not a single poem of major literary importance has been added in succeeding editions.

In his famous — to many later critics infamous — "Preface to Notes" (reprinted in all subsequent editions) the Poet Laureate set down in orderly fashion his final judgment of the poetry of Hopkins. It is no exaggeration to say that it presents the outlines of Hopkins criticism ever since that time, because all the scholarship since 1918 has tended either to accept Bridges' position, to qualify it, or eventually completely to reverse it. Future critics were to weigh every word and phrase of the "Preface to Notes."

Bridges hoped that readers could be led "to search out the rare" — and here Bridges seems to be indulging in an ambiguity — "masterly beauties that distinguish his work," but he felt it necessary "to put readers at their ease" by defining the "bad faults" of Hopkins.

The indictment starts with "faults of taste" under which he specifies "affectation in metaphor" and "perversion of human feeling" which he contends "are mostly efforts to force emotion into theological or sectarian channels" as in "the exaggerated Marianism of some pieces, or the naked encounter of sensualism and asceticism which hurts the 'Golden Echo.' "

Then he turns to "the rude shocks of his purely artistic wantonness . . . which a reader must have courage to face." These he classifies as "Oddity and Obscurity." The chief cause of the obscurity was "his habitual omission of the relative pronoun," a "license" Hopkins abused "beyond precedent." Another source of obscurity was "that in aiming at condensation" he used "words that are grammatically ambiguous"; he was insensitive "to the irrelevant suggestions that our numerous homophones cause"; and he "would seem even to welcome and seek artistic effect in the consequent confusion." Finally, some of the rhymes are "repellent," "freaks," and in these "his childishness is incredible" and "appalling." All these "blemishes . . . are of such quality and magnitude as to deny him even a hearing from those who love continuous literary decorum and are grown to be intolerant of its absence."

In the notes which followed, Bridges gave almost no help with Hopkins' first great poem, "The Wreck of the Deutschland," except to say, "the labour spent on this great metrical experiment must have served to establish the poet's prosody and perhaps his diction: therefore the poem stands logically as well as chronologically in the front of his book, like a great dragon folded in the gate to forbid all entrance, and confident in his strength from past success." And the editor admits, disarmingly enough that "he was himself shamefully worsted in a brave frontal assault, the more easily perhaps because both subject and treatment were distasteful to him." (Later one of Bridges' critics was to say that it was Bridges himself who "stands like a great dragon folded in the gate to forbid all entrance" to a sympathetic approach to Hopkins.)

But Bridges' "Preface to Notes" fortunately had been tucked away at the back of the book while at the front stood a warmly lyrical prefatory sonnet of dedication addressed to Hopkins and concluding:

> Go forth: amidst our chaffinch flock display
> Thy plumage of far wonder and heavenward flight!

Had the "Preface to Notes" stood in place of the sonnet it is difficult to see how reviewers would have dared pass the gate at all.

This little volume of 1918 was destined to affect deeply the course of modern poetry. Hopkins himself had written to Bridges of his poetry, "If you do not like it, it is because there is something you have not seen and I see . . . and if the whole world agreed to condemn it or see nothing in it I should only tell them to take a generation and come to me again."

Hopkins' premonition proved to be correct. Looking back at the 1920's, Sir Herbert Read in 1933 could write, "When the history of the last decade comes to be written by a dispassionate critic, no influence will rank in importance with that of Gerard Manley Hopkins."

Yet the first edition of 750 copies took ten years to exhaust. During the 1920's Hopkins was chiefly a "poets' poet" and the small sale appears to have been chiefly to writers; thus his influence was felt very soon on a generation that was rejecting both the Victorians and the Georgians. Between his death and the publication of his poetry a revolution had taken place: the imagists and *vers-libristes* had gained the ascendancy; and so, paradoxically, a poet was welcomed as a leader whose dates made him chronologically Victorian but whose poetry seemed at first sight a rejection of all traditions.

Reviews of first editions are seldom definitive. The one thing on which the critics were agreed was that Hopkins was difficult. But they varied widely; holding that he was not worth struggling over, or contending that the more his poetry was studied the more beauty was discovered. Bridges, too, was praised and attacked. One reviewer wrote of him as "the perfect devoted editor. Bouquets all go to him. Bridges is trying to breathe life into that which cannot live" (*Oxford Magazine*, 1919). To another his "Preface to Notes" was "This frank, lucid and just summary which makes appreciation easy" (*Everyman*, 1919). One critic cried out, "From our best friends deliver us, O Lord!" (Edward Sapir, *Poetry*, 1921). Thus wrote another: "Thirty years after the poet's death Dr. Bridges graciously permits us to inspect (for a fee of 12/6) the work of a greater thinker than himself" (*London Universe*, 1919).

The quarrel of the critics was on, and on such a variety of fronts as to be bewildering. Some were convinced that Bridges held a priori that emotion was forced if it "ran in theological channels" and that to complain of "exaggerated Marianism" was like complaining of the "exaggerated Beatricity of the *Divina Commedia*" (Frederick Page, *Dublin Review*, 1920). Hopkins' sprung rhythm evoked the comments:

"Any reader is to be forgiven who feels that life is too short to work through torment to the understanding of prosody" (Louise Imogen Guiney); and "The metrical effects which Mr. Hopkins studies with such assiduity do not seem to us to be worth the pains bestowed upon them" (*Spectator*, 1919). Yet other critics hailed him: "As a metrist he has no equal in English" (*Ave Maria*, 1919) and found in him "a rhythm which explicates meaning and makes it more intense" (John Middleton Murry, *Athenaeum*, 1919). To still another, "It is doubtful if the freest verse of our day is more sensitive in its rhythmic pulsations than the sprung verse of Hopkins" (Edward Sapir, *Poetry*, 1921).

The predominant note of the first reviews was frank confusion. Thus in a single review one could come across the remark that his poetry "produces the effect almost of idiocy" but that there are also "authentic fragments that we trust even when they bewilder us" (*TLS*, 1919).

The 1920's therefore tended to become years of violent rejection or of enthusiastic but often uncritical acceptance. It was also the decade during which Hopkins' poems began to be reprinted in anthologies of contemporary poetry and to be included in such surveys of recent writing as Laura Riding and Robert Graves' *A Survey of Modernist Poetry* (1927).

But the major historians of prosody tended to dismiss him with brief comment. T. S. Omond in a postscript classified Hopkins' sprung rhythm among the "fantastic new would-be developments of metre," and of the poems he said: "I cannot believe that these poems deserve or will receive attention from even the most determined seeker after novelties" (*English Metrists*, 1921). Saintsbury disposed of him in *The Cambridge History of English Literature* with a footnote, and in his *History of English Prosody* (1923), it is quite clear to him that Hopkins' poems "all were experiments," of rather doubtful importance.

There are many curiosities among this avalanche of early critiques of Hopkins. In an article entitled "Quality in Madness" (*Poetry*, 1929) Jessica North finds "a quality of authen-

ticity in his madness which many of the modernists lack."
The younger poets tended to welcome him, but such a writer
as T. Sturge Moore edited one of Hopkins' poems and con-
gratulated himself on having cut it in half: "Though as you
may decide, his lavish outlay in words attained more music,
my spare recension has retained most of his felicities, discarded his most ludicrous redundancies. . ." (*Criterion*,
1930).

The most important and influential criticism of Hopkins
starts with an article in 1926 by I. A. Richards (*Dial*, 1926;
see also *Practical Criticism*, 1930) and with William Empson's
Seven Types of Ambiguity (1930), interestingly anticipated
by Allan Porter ("Difficult Beauty," *Spectator*, 1926).

Richards trained upon Hopkins those methods of close examination of the text and critical exegesis for which he is
famous. Hopkins "may be described, without opposition, as
the most obscure of English verse writers," but unlike many
previous critics, Richards welcomed the difficulty. Indeed,
obscurity has a positive value and allows for "resistance" and
hence for more complex responses in the sensitive reader.
Consequently he approaches Hopkins enthusiastically as a
poet to be wrestled with, convinced that his subtleties will
yield great riches through careful critical analysis, and he
made "The Windhover" the focus of Hopkins criticism.
Richards had a profoundly salutary effect on later students of
Hopkins, though he probably misled them by dismissing
Hopkins' explanations of his prosody as excuses to allow himself "complete rhythmical freedom," and by approaching his
religious beliefs as "bundles of invested capital."

With the publication of Empson's *Seven Types of Ambiguity*, the poetry of Hopkins took on a new dimension and
became the happy hunting ground of the ambiguity seekers.
It cannot be denied that they made the text take on a richness that critics had not hitherto discovered. "The Windhover" for Empson illustrates "a clear sense of the Freudian
use of opposites, where two things thought of as incompatible
but desired intensely by different systems of judgment" are

brought into conjunction and "forced into open conflict before the reader."

The year 1930 — the period of the second edition of his poems and of the first volume devoted to a study of his life and art — became a turning point in Hopkins criticism. The reviewers' reception of the second edition differed markedly from that of the first, and it ran rapidly into more than a dozen printings. The number of articles produced in 1930–31 equalled the number produced during the entire preceding decade, and Hopkins was firmly established.

The second edition, adding a few early poems and later translations and fragments but nothing of major importance, was prefaced by a sympathetic and enthusiastic Introduction by Charles Williams, in direct contrast to the attitude of Bridges a dozen years before. In Hopkins' poetry, said Williams, "It is as if the imagination, seeking for expression, had found verb and substantive at one rush" and the defect is not with the poet but with the reader whose mind "cannot work at a quick enough rate." Hopkins "breaks now into joy, now into inquiry, now into a terror of fearful expectation, but always into song. . . . He was unique among the Victorians . . . because his purely poetic energy was so much greater." And more in the same vein.

Hardly a reviewer took issue with such assertions, and several of them made irreverent allusions to Bridges. The *Times Literary Supplement* (1930) called Hopkins "a true genius," "one of the major poets," "the most original of the poets of the nineteenth century," and for the young contemporary poet "full of strong powers (and an unexhausted technical prowess) which he feels he must assimiliate and possess." In America, Malcolm Cowley said: "He has more to teach the poets of today than either Tennyson or Browning" (*New York Herald Tribune Weekly Book Review*, 1931). Another reviewer went so far as to say, ". . . a careful reading . . . yields at once the poet's thought and the justification of his tortured syntax" (Justin O'Brien, *Bookman*, 1931). There was less loose talk about oddity, obscurity, and twisted prosody; some of the critics began to point out a relationship

between his neologisms, his "contorted grammar, his startling and baffling rhetoric" and his effort for inscape of his
emotions. They began to realize his poetry as an integrated
whole: ". . . a purposive colliding and jamming, an overlapping and telescoping of images and words in an effort towards
sustained music and sense" (Hildegarde Flanner, *New Republic*, 1931).

Gerard Manley Hopkins (1930) by G. F. Lahey was the
first critical-biographical volume, and about it some remarks
have already been made. Introductory rather than definitive,
it aroused deeper interest in his life and character. For the first
time it made available a larger group — for some had been
published in *The Month* (1909) and in *Dublin Review* (1920)
— of extracts from his letters and diaries. The critical sections
are the least adequate, and Father Lahey seems, surprisingly
enough, to echo Bridges in condemning some of Hopkins'
rhymes, tmesis, omissions of relatives, syncopation of words,
and marooning of prepositions. Indeed Father Lahey gal-
lantly pays as high tribute to Bridges as has ever been paid:

The staunch love and the highest literary appreciation of him
who was admittedly the best custodian of the poems, prevented
Dr. Bridges from flooding an unappreciative and uncomprehend-
ing literary public with the rays of so original a source of pure
poetry, so that he bided his time and with careful discrimination
slowly educated his future readers with selections given to anthologies. After almost thirty years of patient waiting he published
the slender volume of poems to which he added his own notes. . .

and of them the biographer added that they were "the creative criticism of a delicate poetic sensibility"!

In the most controversial sentences in the book, Father
Lahey spoke of the Dublin sonnets:

The celebrated "terrible sonnets" are only terrible in the same
way that the beauty of Christ is terrible. Only the strong pinions
of an eagle can realize the cherished happiness of such suffering.
It is a place where Golgotha and Tabor meet. Read in this light
his poems cease to be tragic.

Comments on and quarrels with this passage echo through
criticism for many years and take on several variations. Sir

Herbert Read in an important essay ("Gerard Manley Hopkins," *English Critical Essays, Twentieth Century* edited by P. M. Jones, 1933; and reprinted in *Defence of Shelley and Other Essays*, 1936, and in *Collected Essays in Literary Criticism*, 1938) built up a theory of poetry, elaborated with references to Hopkins (*Form in Modern Poetry*, 1933), that poetic sensibility is consistent only with a state of spiritual tension and acuity and that "true originality is due to a conflict between sensibility and belief." He went on to the conclusion that the tension is bridged by doubt. Hence he classified Hopkins' greatest poems, the "terrible sonnets," as poems of doubt. To him " 'The Windhover' is completely objective in its senseful catalogue but Hopkins gets over his scruples by dedicating his poem 'To Christ our Lord.' " It would seem that in this case the tension is between the poem and its dedication.

Sir Herbert's thesis that poetic activity is primarily the result of a conflict (or coexistence and counter-action) of sensibility and belief led him to suggest that Hopkins' Jesuit allegiance had a profound effect on his poetry: "Perhaps in actual intensity his poetry gained more than it lost by this step but one cannot help regretting the curtailment it suffered in range and quantity." Later Read withdrew the implication that there was "an open conflict between the poetic impulse and theological faith in Hopkins" (Gardner, *Gerard Manley Hopkins: A Study of Poetic Idiosyncrasy in Relation to Poetic Tradition*, I, 237), but presumably he continued to hold in modified form that the intensity of the later poetry had its origin in some kind of tension between sensibility and spirituality.

Sir Herbert's book, *Form in Modern Poetry* (1933), and his essays contained other valuable contributions, especially on Hopkins' use of language. He decided that "nothing could have made Hopkins's poetry popular in his day: it was necessary that it should first be absorbed by the sensibility of a new generation of poets," and after surveying contemporary poetry he concluded of Hopkins that "no influence whatsoever is so potent for the future of English poetry."

Probably even more influential on a generation of critics was F. R. Leavis, who in a chapter of *New Bearings in English Poetry* (1932) extended the work of Richards and presented what has been called the first thoroughgoing defence of Hopkins' style. He opens his essay with enthusiasm: "He was one of the most remarkable technical inventors who ever wrote, and he was a major poet. Had he received the attention that was his due the history of English poetry from the 'nineties onward would have been different." After fifty pages of analysis he concludes, equally enthusiastically, "He is likely to prove, for our time and the future, the only influential poet of the Victorian age and he seems to me the greatest." Almost everything that Leavis says is a direct contradiction to Bridges, of whom he comments, "What Dr. Bridges calls 'blemishes' are essential to Hopkins's aim and achievement," and he feels that Hopkins was a master in exploiting the resources and potentialities of English as a living language. The essay, including careful exegesis of half a dozen poems, remains twenty years later one of the best short introductions to the poetry of Hopkins.

In 1933 one of I. A. Richards' students, Elsie Phare, published her book *The Poetry of Gerard Manley Hopkins: A Survey and Commentary*, a volume long out of print. Like Richards and Leavis the author tends to disregard Hopkins' prosody (for evidence of interest in Hopkins' metrics during the same year, however, see a controversy in *TLS*, 16, 23 February, and 2, 9 March, 1933). Miss Phare's method is loose, rambling, and informal, but she makes a number of contributions. By a multitude of comparisons she tries to determine the "school" or "tribe" to which he belongs, and her book has many paraphrases of the poems. Her exegesis is frequently skillful though occasionally subjective or merely impressionistic. Some poems are spoiled by the "naked encounter between sensuousness and asceticism." However, Miss Phare's most frequently recurring criticism is that Hopkins artificially forces and exaggerates his emotional responses. In such a case the poem must have "a significance for him which it lacks for the reader." She confesses that her tendency is to think "that becoming a Jesuit must involve some unnatural or undesirable deformation." Hopkins' emotions, therefore, tend to be unnatural to her, and yet she very frequently attempts critical sympathy.

T. S. Eliot has never reversed his very qualified estimate of Hopkins which he made briefly in *After Strange Gods* (1934), the same year that Edith Sitwell in *Aspects of Modern Poetry* was to praise him so highly. Still another poet during the same year, C. Day Lewis, called him "among the great technical innovators in verse" and his sprung rhythm "one of the best gifts to posterity" (*A Hope for Poetry*, 1934). To Day Lewis, "He is a true revolutionary poet, for his imagination was always breaking up and melting down the inherited forms of language, fusing them into new possibilities, hammering them into new shapes."

Ever since 1918 this emphasis on Hopkins the revolutionary has been the predominant note of criticism. To Day Lewis, for instance, his poetry "is difficult to connect with anything in the past. . . . Hopkins remains without affinities." Terence Heywood objected to this presentation of him as having "entered the world by a kind of parthenogenesis" (*English*, 1940; see also Th. Tillemans, "Is Hopkins a Modern Poet?" *English Studies*, 1942), but it was not until the Kenyon critics (1944) and Gardner (1944) that a balance was struck.

In 1935 several important contributions appeared in a Hopkins issue of *New Verse* (No. 14, April 1935). In addition to Humphry House's "A Note on Hopkins' Religious Life," suggesting that Jesuit discipline intensified an already scrupulous strain, especially notable is Christopher Devlin's essay "Gerard Hopkins and Duns Scotus," the first article to explore the parallelism between the medieval Franciscan philosopher and the nineteenth-century poet. Charles Madge and Geoffrey Grigson contributed articles on Hopkins' imagery with important comparisons, developed for the first time, between Hopkins and Whitman, and there was also an article by Ll. Wyn Griffith on Welsh influences, a topic to be further developed by later critics.

The Hopkins issue of *New Verse* is very difficult to obtain, as is a little book also published in 1935 in an edition of 300 copies: *The Mind and Poetry of Gerard Manley Hopkins* by Bernard Kelly. Humphry House in *New Verse* had pointed out what critics were reluctantly coming to realize, that Hopkins' religious experience was "the direct origin of some of his greatest poems"; Bernard Kelly concentrates on the intensity and psychological actuality of his spiritual vision and opposes both Bridges and Read in holding that a true asceticism welcomes both the delight of the senses and of transcendant reality. And continuing the study of Hopkins' religious experience, Christopher Devlin, in "The Ignatian Inspiration of Gerard Manley Hopkins" (*Blackfriars*, 1935) discussed the pervading influence, barely mentioned heretofore, of the *Spiritual Exercises* of St. Ignatius on the poet's character and verse. Devlin held that the Exercises "were not the occasion but the origin of Hopkins' poetic experience."

All of Hopkins scholarship was put on a firmer footing in the middle thirties by the publication of *The Letters of Gerard Manley Hopkins to Robert Bridges* and *The Correspondence of Gerard Manley Hopkins and Richard Watson Dixon* in 1935, *The Note-Books and Papers of Gerard Manley Hopkins* in 1937, and *Further Letters of Gerard Manley Hopkins* in 1938. These volumes raised his stature considerably. In his letters and other prose works many critics now found the same disciplined honesty and intensity of conviction as in his poems. Now scholars could study his diaries and see in them the raw materials of his poetry. They offered adequate explanations of his prosody, his literary methods, and his ideals of poetry. Now they might discover a new Hopkins in his literary criticism and they learned about the multiplicity of his interests, much about his struggles, and a good deal about his character. Hopkins scholarship has by no means as yet exhausted these volumes.

In the flood of reviews and short articles which appeared almost immediately there was a new admiration. Bonamy Dobrée, for instance: "The more one reads Hopkins the more complex does he become, and the greater in stature"

(*Spectator*, 1938). And publication of these books is responsible for such articles as that of C. K. Ogden on "Sprung Rhythm" (*Psyche*, 1936), Charles Trueblood's "The Esthetics of Gerard Manley Hopkins" (*Poetry*, 1937), John F. Waterhouse's "Gerard Manley Hopkins and Music" (*Music and Letters*, 1937), and Terence Heywood's "Hopkins's Ancestry" (*Poetry*, 1939) — each article speaking with an authority which had previously been impossible.

During this period the two most articulate voices of dissent were those of G. M. Young and D. S. MacColl. To the former Hopkins was an admirable poet "but his theories on metre [seemed] to be as demonstrably wrong as those of any speculator who has led a multitude into the wilderness to perish," while he illustrated Ruskin's judgment of Reynolds: that he was "born to teach all truth by his practice and all error by his doctrine." Indeed Young found Hopkins' ignorance on the subject of metre was "so profound that he was not aware there was anything to know" ("Forty Years of Verse," *London Mercury*, 1936, reprinted in part in G. M. Young, *Daylight and Champaign*, 1937).

No less forthright was D. S. MacColl's statement after reading *Further Letters*: "It is high time that the bubble so assiduously blown around Hopkins's mistaken views on prosody should be pricked" ("Patmore and Hopkins: Sense and Nonsense in English Prosody," *London Mercury*, 1938). It was not until later that critics became more aware of the high degree to which his aesthetic theory was in harmony with his creative practice.

One has only to acquire a cursory knowledge of Hopkins scholarship to realize the possibilities it affords for conflicting estimates of his poetry. But if the publication of his poetry had stirred controversy, the publication of his letters added fuel to the flames.

The storm that centered around his prose was almost entirely devoted to some aspect of a single problem: did his Jesuit life kill the poet in him or did it enrich his poetry? Abetted by Abbott's introductions to the volumes, with such statements as "It is our good fortune that his name belongs to literature and not to hagiography," and "But what is possible to the resolved will of Milton the heretic was beyond the power of Hopkins the priest," and with the new mass of evidence, the critics dashed in to quote now one passage, now another. The battle over Bridges' "Preface to Notes" had not been hotter. C. Day Lewis dismissed the problem bluntly: "His religious vocation puts a wall between his life and ours only reminiscent of the wall of a madhouse" (*New Republic*, 1935).

There were those who took the position of G. W. Stonier: "Religion did not stifle the poet in Hopkins for without religion he could hardly have written many of his best poems" (*New Statesman and Nation*, 1935); and of Egerton Clarke: "The habit of mind and will which was fostered in his life as a Jesuit transformed his work. Under that influence it developed, changing from mere experimental versification into an authentic utterance. . ." (*Dublin Review*, 1936). David Daiches, who also gives a reasoned explanation of Hopkins' innovations in language, implied that his religious values were so secure that he was enabled to concentrate on expression, communication and the art of poetry (*New Literary Values*, 1936).

The most trenchant voice of opposition to such views was that of John Gould Fletcher: "To an artist of Hopkins's sort, dogmatic theology, though it may be of assistance in first orientating and disciplining his mind, always ends by finally destroying it. Art, and perhaps more particularly poetry, is a heresy which ends in being more valuable to a man than any orthodoxy whatsoever . . ." (*American Review*, 1936).

In the midst of all the talk about the unhappy, repressed, and frustrated Jesuit, an essay particularly outstanding for taking a multiplicity of factors into consideration is Martin C. D'Arcy's "Gerard Manley Hopkins" in *Great Catholics*, edited by Claude Williamson, 1939. D'Arcy does not shy away from "unresolved tensions" and the tendency in Hopkins toward scrupulousness, nor does he minimize "the war within" which was so evident in his letters and which found expression in his greatest poetry.

Minor stirs were created in the 1930's by critics quick to pick up references to Communism in his letters (for instance, Babette Deutsch, *This is Modern Poetry*, 1935), which often were linked with the suggestion that he started out as a young Communist and eventually conformed to a Tory conservatism. While such views were extreme, they had the virtue of bringing attention to Hopkins' social thought, briefly but well summarized by F. O. Matthiessen (*American Renaissance*, 1941), who also dealt perceptively with the recurring comparison between Whitman and Hopkins, emphasizing Hopkins' more highly disciplined art. The most recent treatment of the subject, suggesting more actual and positive influence of Whitman on Hopkins than former critics had, is by William Darby Templeman ("Hopkins and Whitman: Evidence of Influence and Ethics," *PQ*, 1954).

There were those also, who, after reading the letters and going back to the poetry, detected Freudian phrases everywhere (already noted in *New Verse*, 1935, by Grigson and Madge) and by isolating these elements built up interpretations of Hopkins as a martyr to torture, accepted masochistically at the hands of severe Jesuit discipline — and worse. Philip Henderson (*The Poet and Society*, 1939) not only sees Communism everywhere, but detects in Hopkins obvious Freudian significances.

John Pick's *Gerard Manley Hopkins: Priest and Poet*, 1942 (anticipated by his articles in *Month*, 1940), was an attempt to make a thoroughgoing study of the relationships between Hopkins' life and poetry on the one hand and his religious ideals and standards on the other. The latter, Pick contended, are expressed in *The Spiritual Exercises*, which became the chief formative influence on attitudes expressed in the mature poetry. He grants that the poet's dedication to Jesuit life was at least in part responsible for the small quantity of his production but asserts that it correspondingly gained in intensity and in those very qualities which every critic has granted as constituting his greatness.

That Pick's thesis has not been universally accepted may be judged from an article by T. Weiss ("Gerard Manley

Hopkins: Realist on Parnassus," *Accent*, 1945) in which he holds that Hopkins' life "proves not only the ruthlessness of art in its exposure of the basic inacceptability for him of religion, but also the common incompatibility today between art and religion. An art as piercing and rigorously honest as Hopkins' could allow him little contentment with what became for him increasingly evasion." Weiss concludes that if we can with some certainty conjecture that the opium of speculation proved Coleridge's undoing, likewise religion was the opium of Hopkins.

In 1944 one hundred years had passed since the birth of Hopkins, though barely twenty-five had elapsed since his first poems were available to the public. Eleanor Ruggles' *Gerard Manley Hopkins: A Life* has already been commented on. The centenary year was signalized, as might be expected, by the major periodicals, which carried nearly a hundred anniversary articles and reviews. Notable among these was Vincent Turner's "Gerard Manley Hopkins: A Centenary Article" (*Dublin Review*, 1944). Special issues of *Kenyon Review* (Summer and Autumn 1944) were devoted to Hopkins, and the articles were reprinted, with the edition of an introductory biographical sketch by Austin Warren and an article by F. R. Leavis from *Scrutiny* (1944), in a collected volume called *Gerard Manley Hopkins by the Kenyon Critics* (1945).

Several generalizations may be made about this notable book. The assumption behind each of the contributions is that Hopkins has assumed a permanent position in English letters and that what remains is to define exactly his place. Next, all of the critics take almost for granted that his religion contributed to his greatness. Leavis, for instance, brings the volume to a close with: "Hopkins's religious interests are bound up with the presence in his poetry of a vigour of mind that puts him in another world from the other Victorians. It is a vitality of thought, a vigour of thinking intelligence, that is at the same time a vitality of concreteness."

A further observation may be made: while the predominant tendency of earlier critics had been to think of Hopkins as almost totally lacking in any Victorian elements, the Kenyon contributors emphasize those aspects in which he was a poet of his own time. This is not true merely of Arthur Mizener's essay, which is labelled "Victorian Hopkins."

The longest and most detailed of the chapters is "Sprung Rhythm" by Harold Whitehall. According to Whitehall, Hopkins' sprung rhythm is not accentual but dipodic. Critics have not been willing to accept his contentions (see Brewster Ghiselin, "Reading Sprung Rhythm," *Poetry*, 1947; Sister Marcella Marie Holloway, *The Prosodic Theory of Gerard Manley Hopkins*, Doctoral Dissertation, Catholic University of America, 1947; Walter Ong, "Hopkins' Sprung Rhythm and the Life of English Poetry," in *Immortal Diamond, 1949*; Margaret Stobie, "Patmore's Theory and Hopkins' Practice," *TQ*, 1949).

However, these criticisms of Whitehall, as Ghiselin has pointed out, do not invalidate the importance of some of his assertions about the integration of technical devices accompanying dipodic rhythm that apply equally to accentual verse: that in accentual or sense-stress verse, alliteration, internal rhyme, word repetition, and assonance there are organic and functional components to reinforce or "overstress" the rhythmic pattern and that syntactical abbreviations, climactic appositions, tmesis and marooned prepositions, even word compounds, interlock.

Still another centenary tribute likewise took the form of a collection of articles, *Immortal Diamond: Studies in Gerard Manley Hopkins*, edited by Norman Weyand, though this collection by a dozen American Jesuits was delayed, because of wartime conditions, until 1949. Like many symposia, it is uneven in quality. The importance of the "Glossary of Difficult Words" and the Bibliography has already been pointed out. "Gerard Manley Hopkins and the Society of Jesus" by Martin C. Carroll, in the absence of a definitive life of Hopkins, is valuable for sketching the typical training of a Jesuit, though it may oversimplify the problems of the priest and the poet in the real as distinguished from the ideal order. As might be expected, it is where doctrinal points are concerned that the book makes important contributions, and helpful aid is given in Maurice M. McNamee's "Hopkins: Poet of Nature and of the Supernatural," and in Robert B. Boyle's "The Thought Structure of 'The Wreck of the Deutschland.'" The editor has contributed an appendix entitled "The Historical Basis of 'The Wreck of the Deutschland' and 'The Loss of the Eurydice,'" giving the newspaper and eyewitness accounts of the two tragedies. As is almost inevitable, there is one chapter devoted to an analysis of what has been Hopkins' most discussed poem, "What does 'The Windhover' Mean?" by Raymond V. Schoder, who gives a thoroughly Ignatian interpretation. The article summarizes most of the previous interpretations, principally those by Richards, Empson, Leavis, Phare, Sargent, Kelly, Pick, Ruggles, McLuhan, and Grady. His own position is that the poem is not so much one of renunciation, stoic sacrifice, indecisive inner conflict, as of victory and triumph.[1]

An eighty-page chapter, the longest and one of the best in the volume, is "Hopkins' Sprung Rhythm and the Life of English Poetry" by Walter Ong, an essay built up with great care and with a multiplicity of examples. According to Ong, Hopkins found the source of sprung rhythm running like an undercurrent in English poetry and speech wherever sense stress or interpretive stress was found. It was "a rhythm still inherent in the language and only suppressed by an artificially sustained tradition" — a rhythm deeply grounded and rooted in the genius of the English language.

Ong's emphasis on the organic quality of Hopkins' poetry is one that critics had been increasingly emphasizing. This essay was written during the year both Whitehall and Gardner were to put forth the same thesis. The introduction, for instance, of rhyme into sense-stress verse gives it a different function from that in ordinary running rhythm; the line end-

[1] The poem has continued to attract critics, and the most recent articles are those of Robert R. Boyle, "A Footnote on 'The Windhover'" (*America*, 1949); F. R. Leavis, "The Windhover" (*Scrutiny*, 1950); Frederick L. Gwynn, "Hopkins' 'The Windhover': A New Simplification" (*MLN*, 1950); and Carl R. Woodring, "Once More 'The Windhover'" (*Western Review*, 1950).

ings are less marked and exact rhymes therefore have less purpose. Further, sense-stress or sprung rhythm calls for alliteration, assonance, crowding out of relatives and the dramatic suppression of words, the telescoping of grammatical structure — not ornamentally but because with these devices the interpretive stress mounts in value. Bridges failed to appreciate Hopkins, Ong contends, because he refused to regard Hopkins' rhythm as an organic whole and hence the kind of "bickering" that was evidenced in his "Preface to Notes" in 1918.

The centenary year also brought forth the first installment of a two-volume study which is the most definitive work on Hopkins thus far, the work by W. H. Gardner entitled, accurately if a trifle awkwardly, *Gerard Manley Hopkins (1884–1889): A Study of Poetic Idiosyncrasy in Relation to Poetic Tradition.* Volume I appeared in England in 1944 and in America in 1948; Volume II in both countries in 1949.

Gardner had himself been the author, starting in 1935, of several of the most significant articles on Hopkins: "The Wreck of the Deutschland" (*Essays and Studies,* 1935); "A Note on Hopkins and Duns Scotus" (*Scrutiny,* 1936); "The Religious Problem in Gerard Manley Hopkins" (*Scrutiny,* 1937); "Gerard Manley Hopkins as a Cywyddwr" (*Transactions of the Honourable Society of Cymmrodorion,* 1940). His new study took into careful consideration not only these articles but all that favorable or other unfavorable critics had to say about Hopkins up to this time.

The key to his comprehensiveness is indicated by the subtitle of his work: "A Study of Poetic Idiosyncrasy in Relation to Poetic Tradition." His purpose is to show that Hopkins was both traditionalist and revolutionary; that his poetry, at first sight so odd and eccentric in matters of style and rhythm, is in fact deeply rooted in European traditions. For example, Hopkins called most of his poems "sonnets," and in a chapter on "Sonnet Morphology" Gardner demonstrates how Hopkins did not abandon the Petrarchan form but developed its latent possibilities. (See also Lois Pitchford, "The Curtal Sonnets of Gerard Manley Hopkins," *MLN,* 1953.) Thus his practice was "to infuse a new spirit into the old form without destroying its identity." The same comment, Gardner would hold, can be applied to his metrics, his imagery, and his thought. Primarily critical rather than biographical, the book has adequate chapters on Hopkins' life, relating him to his family and friendships, to his social, cultural, artistic, political, economic and religious backgrounds. Gardner also deals with the influences of Scotus and *The Spiritual Exercises*, and with the evolution and growth of his poetry.

On the ever-recurrent problem of the relation of the priest to the poet, Gardner, without agreeing with Sir Herbert Read, holds that there was a "lifelong tension between the two vocations, between the religious and the artistic-creative, between personality and character." To him, Hopkins never achieved *permanent* balance and harmony between his conflicting ideals, desires, and impulses, and the study of his poetry is in part a study of the extent to which he achieved such balance. Gardner holds that some of the religious apologists of Hopkins have underestimated the complexity of the conflicts within the man. In most cases, however, "what threatened to be a serious dislocation was to become in many ways a successful coalition of energies."

His chapters on prosody and on meter are very detailed and especially significant because he refuses to isolate sprung rhythm not merely from the semantic rhythm but from all the numerous highly wrought devices which Hopkins used to fuse his poems into organic wholes.

Gardner treats the usually emphasized influences of Old English metrics and makes a detailed study of the impact of Greek melic and choral verse (see also W. B. Stanford, "Gerard Manley Hopkins and Aeschylus," *Studies*, 1941) and of Welsh poetry (drawing partly on G. Lilly, "Welsh Influence in the Poetry of Gerard Manley Hopkins," *MLR*, 1943), which influenced the poet in the direction of syntactic dislocation or interruption, thus imparting vigor and dramatic immediacy to poetry.

Particularly valuable is Gardner's emphasis on the disciplined quality of Hopkins' poetry and on the means he used to try to avoid the pitfalls usually accompanying sprung rhythm: "Sprung rhythm tends to degenerate into doggerel or even bad prose" when it is written "without the strict architectonic and elaborate phonal devices which Hopkins employs." Further chapters are devoted to his diction and syntax, his themes and his imagery, along with careful examination of his vocabulary.

A whole series of chapters is devoted to a chronological survey of his poetry, from the earliest verse (the first study of these poems to make clear Hopkins' early ability to handle conventional forms) to his final and last production, and including even the more important fragments. Occasionally an entire chapter is devoted to a single poem, as in the case of "The Wreck of the Deutschland." Here Gardner's distance from Bridges can be judged by his assertion that it "stands like a great overture at the beginning of his mature work, rich in themes which are taken up, developed and varied, sometimes more than once, in the subsequent poems."

In these chapters, with exegesis accompanied by sensitive paraphrase, he gives frequent scansions, and there are elaborate footnotes and appendices. Gardner tries to qualify the comments of such critics as those who have made Hopkins into the only Victorian influential in modern poetry, pointing out in a chapter devoted to "Hopkins and Modern Poetry" the importance of Browning, of Whitman, and of several other figures and movements just as formative as Hopkins. Significant, too, are his comments on the difference between sprung rhythm and free verse, whence came a confusion of which critics and poets had alike been guilty.

A final "Epilogue" attempts to summarize Hopkins' limitations and failures, his contributions and accomplishments. For Gardner the latter far outweigh the former: "After an intensive reading of Hopkins, most other English poetry seems outwardly facile and in varying degrees inadequate."

It would be folly to contend that the fifteen chapters of the two volumes are equally successful. "Hopkins as Reader and Critic," for instance, falls short. But it is as competent as the attempts of M. G. Lloyd Thomas ("Hopkins as Critic," *Essays and Studies,* 1946) and Anne Treneer ("The Criticism of G. M. Hopkins," *The Penguin New Writing,* No. 40, edited by John Lehman, 1950). Gardner's is a reasoned admiration, and in his enthusiasm he has discovered much that escaped previous critics, though one reviewer of his work perhaps goes too far when he says, "He has sunk himself so long and so sympathetically in his subject that what were jarring flaws at first glance have now become elusive beauties."

The chief defect of Gardner's two volumes is an organizational one. Separate chapters are really separate essays, and there is repetition and backtracking. This was partly due to the unusual circumstances under which the work was published: Volume I appeared during the war as a selection of the most important chapters, and then additional chapters, later revised, were printed as the second volume. No mere rearrangement of the chapters, however, would succeed in making it an organic whole. But it does remain as the most comprehensively inclusive work that has been published on Hopkins, and the best summation of Hopkins' basic contributions to poetry.

The third edition of the *Poems,* which Gardner edited in 1948, draws on the findings of the two volumes and together they have established Gardner as the leading Hopkins scholar of our time.

In 1947, between the publication of Gardner's two volumes, several articles of worth appeared. *Philological Quarterly* (1947) carried two articles with the same title, "The Poetic Theory of Gerard Manley Hopkins." That by John K. Mathison is helpful in bringing together many of the scattered comments of Hopkins; the other, by Selma Jeanne Cohen, concentrates on the relationship between his poetic theory and his theology. This article is an attempt at a valuable synthesis but probably goes too far in relating poetic inspiration and grace, and it is perilously close to identifying poetry and prayer. Another article, "Philosophical Themes in G. M. Hopkins," by James Collins (*Thought,* 1947), ranges so widely amid philosophical ideas scattered throughout his prose, that it is suggestive rather than definitive.

More extended than the three articles above, but like Cohen's and Mathison's an attempt at synthesis, is the doctoral dissertation of Sister Marcella Marie Holloway, *The Prosodic Theory of Gerard Manley Hopkins,* published in 1947. From all the sources available she attempts a synthesis of his metrical theories apart from his practice. Thoroughgoing as it attempts to be, the thesis probably must be supplemented by Gardner's second volume in regard to the further influences of Greek and Welsh prosodic practice on Hopkins' theories.

In 1948 an almost useless book appeared, *Gerard Manley Hopkins: The Man and the Poet* by K. R. Srinivasa Iyengar, published by the Indian Branch of the Oxford University Press. Much of the book had originally appeared in 1938 in *The New Review* of Calcutta, and the book was ready for press in 1939. Publication was delayed by the war, and the author resisted too firmly the temptation to revise extensively so that he might take advantage of the numerous special critical studies which appeared during the ten years from 1938 to 1948.

This judgment may be harsh, and the book does stand as an instance of how widespread interest in Hopkins has become in countries other than England or America; for instance, in the same year, 1948, appeared *Gerard Manley Hopkins: Gedichte* with a long introduction by Irene Behn. Among the most recent examples of the acceptance of Hopkins in other countries are *Hopkinsiana: la vida, la obra y la supervivencia de Gerard Manley Hopkins* by José Manuel Gutiérrez, which resulted in an extended interchange of letters in *TLS* during 1954 and 1955 about the meanings of "The Windhover"; and French translations by Pierre Leyris (*La Nouvelle N. R. F.,* August 1953).

In 1948 a major critical work appeared, *Gerard Manley Hopkins: A Critical Essay towards the Understanding of His Poetry* by W. A. M. Peters, dealing in detail with a single aspect of Hopkins and making this aspect the key to all of his poetry. Much had been written previously of "inscape" and Duns Scotus; important earlier studies had been Christopher Devlin's "Gerard Hopkins and Duns Scotus," W. H. Gardner's "A Note on Hopkins and Duns Scotus" (*Scrutiny,* 1936), and Devlin's "An Essay on Scotus" (*Month,* 1946); but here was an entire book devoted to showing that inscape explains why Hopkins wrote exactly as he did.

Peters sets out to show that his "obscurity and oddity," his deviations from common usage, his syntactical or grammatical idiosyncrasies, and all that is baffling to the ordinary reader are not the result of "artistic wantonness," as Bridges contended, but are the logically integrated outcome of his theory of inscape.

Hopkins had said, "Inscape is what I above all aim at in poetry" and he called it "the very soul of art," but nowhere did he define inscape in precise philosophical and metaphysical terms. Almost every critic who has dealt with inscape has attempted a definition. After surveying all of Hopkins' variant uses of the term, Peters formulates his own: "the unified complex of those sensible qualities of the object of perception that strike us as inseparably belonging to and most typical of it, so that through the knowledge of this unified complex of sense-data we may gain an insight into the individual essence of the object." Like previous critics he holds that it was Scotus who, though not the originator of Hopkins' views, confirmed his devotion to inscape.

As a poet Hopkins was trying to capture the sharply individualized uniqueness of his experiences and the finished poem must have a corresponding individuation. Hence Hopkins said, "Poetry must have, down to its least separable part, an individualising touch." With such a view a merely conventional use of language was incompatible. Ordinarily most words, with the exception of proper names, are universal terms, but inscape involves a distinct, individualized meaning for each word. Hence Hopkins resorts, for instance, to impersonation and frequently omits the article or relative, thus in effect making the common noun into a kind of proper name. Adjectives he uses not descriptively but *restrictively;*

hence the long groups of adjectives placed before the noun in such poems as "The Windhover."

In his desire for inscape he employs words in unfamiliar meaning, words in themselves unfamiliar, dialect usages or newly formed compounds, or he revives dead suffixes or coins new words, usually analogous formations. And sprung rhythm, in which the scansion of each poem is uniquely different, is the natural embodiment of this desire. Always there is a reason for what he does, and the reason is always the same: the inscape of his experiences.

All this is set forth by Peters with logical progression and with a host of examples, including even an examination of Hopkins' use of the hyphen and of punctuation in order to achieve inscape. Throughout, Peters' contention is that the poetic experience for Hopkins, no matter how distinctive, would lose its individuality if it were expressed in conventional forms, and he likes to quote Hopkins to the effect that the result of admiring masterpieces was to make him admire — and then do otherwise.

He finds great richness in Hopkins' use of homophones, which Bridges had objected to, and he delights in "the convergence of multiple meanings." This would seem to be one of the most difficult things to reconcile with inscape as individually unique and sharply precise, and it raises the whole question initiated by Richards and Empson as to whether ambiguity was a part of Hopkins' intention.

Peters chooses to ignore the factor of literary tradition and thus inevitably exaggerates the uniqueness of Hopkins. While W. H. Gardner had attempted to suggest the complexity of "idiosyncrasy in relation to poetic tradition," Peters isolates the absolute individuality of the poet and he seems unaware of the solipsistic subjectivity toward which his thesis carries him.

However, even if he insists too strongly on making everything in Hopkins fit his central thesis, he has explored so thoroughly certain aspects of Hopkins' use of language that whoever will finally write the balanced and comprehensively definitive book about Hopkins' poetry will have to draw on **Peters.**

The relation of Duns Scotus to Hopkins has continued to interest critics. Marjorie D. Coogan introduced minor qualifications in a redefinition of inscape ("Inscape and Instress: Further Analogies with Scotus," *PMLA,* 1950). Very far-reaching in its implications is a tentative article by Christopher Devlin ("Time's Eunuch," *Month,* 1949) which relates Scotus so intimately to Hopkins' inspiration that the falling-off of his productivity is attributed to his abandonment of Scotism as a speculative system and is conjecturally used as an explanation for much of the feeling of frustration in his later poems.

Related problems are tenuously and subtly explored by Devlin in two further articles of the following year ("The Image and the Word I & II," *Month,* February and March, 1950; see also the interchange of correspondence on these articles between Devlin and Gardner, *Month,* Sept. 1950). Scotus was one of the most abstruse of philosophers, and these are difficult articles, but their far-reaching importance is that they touch on Hopkins' whole metaphysic as well as aesthetic, though in the form in which they appear not all the ramifications have been worked out.

The general trend from 1918 until today has been toward the growing acceptance of Hopkins, and within the past half-dozen years almost the only extended and violent attack on his poetry has been by Yvor Winters ("The Poetry of Gerard Manley Hopkins," *Hudson Review,* I, Winter and Spring 1949; for an extended reply see J. H. Johnston, "Reply to Yvor Winters," *Renascence: A Critical Journal of Letters,* II, Spring 1950). After fifty deflating pages, Winters grudgingly places Hopkins as low as he dares, among "the twelve or fourteen best British poets of the nineteenth century." But even this is an index to the change that has taken place in criticism since 1918.

Hopkins has undoubtedly been both underrated and over-praised, and one thing alone seems certain: he continues to be a controversial figure and the only nineteenth-century poet who appears in the anthologies of both the Victorians and the Moderns — for both are now almost equally eager to claim him.

9 ह∼

The Later Victorian Poets

Lionel Stevenson

THE PERSPECTIVE of time is still strangely uncertain with regard to the significance of the many competent poets who flourished during the final third of the nineteenth century. Instead of two or three dominant figures, there were a score or more of varied writers, whose reputations both then and now are difficult to define and to correlate. Research scholars of the present generation have concentrated upon a few of the poets and have done little with others. One group, in particular, who may be called the "Tennysonians" and who were unquestionably the most widely admired in their own day, are now virtually forgotten. This group included Robert Buchanan, Lewis Morris, Edwin Arnold, Alfred Austin, and William Watson. Austin, the prolific laureate, has recently been made the subject of a thorough biographical study, which attempts to place him in his literary and political *milieu — Alfred Austin: Victorian,* by Norton Crowell (1953). But otherwise the school of Tennyson remains unexplored territory.

In the present chapter, fifteen of the "late Victorians" are considered. Several fairly distinct "schools" or "groups" or "movements" are recognizable; but the effort to classify the fifteen poets in any way has proved impracticable, in view of the overlapping and complex relationships among them. Francis Thompson, for instance, belongs primarily in the Roman Catholic group with Patmore and Alice Meynell, and yet he has much in common with the Aesthetic group that

stemmed from Pater and included Wilde, Dowson, and Johnson. Accordingly the poets are arranged merely in the chronological order of age, from Patmore to Dowson — a span of
forty-four years.

COVENTRY PATMORE (1823–1896)

The biography of Coventry Patmore has gone through several distinct phases. Soon after his death he was made the subject of a ponderous two-volume "official" biography, *The
Memoirs and Correspondence of Coventry Patmore*, by Basil
Champneys (1900). This book provided the formal picture
of the poet's life, and quoted liberally from his letters and
journals; but its author, an architect, was unskilled in writing and was further handicapped by the fact that the widow
and children of his subject were alive. The whole emotional
life of this highly emotional poet was therefore slighted: his
relations with his three wives were mentioned in the most
conventional terms, and his senile infatuation for Alice Meynell was ignored.

Five years later Edmund Gosse did a short biographical
sketch for the series named Literary Lives (1905). Not for
the first or last time, Gosse was torn between his instinct to
make an incisive biographical portrait and his respect for
discretion, and hence he was not able to make full use of his
knowledge of Patmore's complex personality.

During the next generation Patmore perhaps more intensely than any of his contemporaries suffered from the
general contempt toward all things "Victorian," because as
author of *The Angel in the House* he was regarded as the
extreme spokesman of sentimental domesticity. Thirty years
after Gosse's book, a young writer named Derek Patmore
awoke to the fact that his great-grandfather had been a man
of some literary stature, and in 1935 he published *Portrait of
My Family*, confessing frankly that

it was not until I went to New York, at the age of nineteen, that
I became interested in the subject. Over there, everybody seemed
to know more about my family than I knew myself! . . . In

mortification at my own ignorance and partly in self-defense, I determined to read his poems, and learn something about his life.

After discovering Champneys' biography in the Columbia University Library, the young Patmore became so intrigued that he searched for family documents after his return to England. His book was youthfully naïve and unnecessarily jaunty, but it used many of Patmore's letters to his third wife and revealed several new aspects of the poet's character.

During the next dozen years Victorianism grew respectable and the late-Victorian school of Roman Catholic poetry came into fashion. Besides, Derek Patmore matured; and his great-uncle, the last surviving son of the poet, died. Hence a complete revision of the biography was undertaken, and came out in 1949 as *The Life and Times of Coventry Patmore*. It is based upon much more extensive research than its predecessor, and maintains a soundly objective attitude. "When this book first appeared," the author remarks, "the revival of interest in Coventry Patmore and his poems had only just begun after a long eclipse. . . . A new generation has now arisen. . . . For them, Coventry Patmore is no longer the slightly ridiculous poet of matrimony, but a mystic and a religious poet of the highest order."

This change in critical estimation had been started by two books that appeared during the three decades of Patmore's general disfavor. The first was *The Idea of Coventry Patmore*, by Osbert Burdett (1921). With somewhat ponderous thoroughness Burdett expounded his thesis that Patmore

is one of the few poets who had a system of thought. . . . Though this fact has been admitted, his theory has not been studied, partly because no one has given serious attention to his idea, partly because the detail which it introduced into his epic has been judged adversely by his critics on the ground that poetry, even on the grand scale of the epic, was incapable without degradation of assimilating the contemporary atmosphere which it was his main endeavour to express. He is one of the few poets who have tried to build a philosophy of life out of the experiences of love; and his attempt is original because it is not, as were previous attempts, based upon any disregard or arbitrary manipulation of the facts, but was inspired by an unusually frank admission of them. If we value this poetical honesty, we shall study the attempt in a fair light. If not, the difficulties resulting from the honesty will appear unnecessary because they could have been evaded. . . .

There have been two previous attempts to make love the basis of a comprehensive philosophy. The first was made by Plato, the second by Dante. Each of his predecessors influenced Coventry Patmore, but he differed in a capital point from both. . . . Each theory idealized one aspect of human relations. Plato chose the friend, Dante the unmarried woman, Patmore the wife.

The second important critical work was *Patmore: A Study in Poetry* (1933). It was written by Frederick Page, an enthusiast who had devoted years to collecting information about Patmore and his circle and who had contributed useful facts and acute criticism both to Burdett's book and to Derek Patmore's. The gentle irony of Page's style can be illustrated by his introductory allusion to Burdett's pretentious claims:

Patmore's poetry lends itself to the facile and intricate systematization by the summarist and the student that one may maliciously and usefully disturb and postpone. . . . Whether his poetry is seen through the reversed telescope of writers of handbooks, or through Mr. Osbert Burdett's microscope, equally it is not seen as poetry.

To correct this imbalance, Page devotes much of his attention to Patmore's artistic technique in *The Angel in the House* and *The Unknown Eros*. He asserts that "The alternation of preludes and idyls constitutes an art-form unique in English, although perhaps owing something to Wither's *Faire Virtue*." Page suggests that "the very close connexion of *The Angel in the House* and *Faire Virtue*" would repay a more thorough analysis than he was able to give it.

Probably the best critical essay on Patmore is the one which Sir Herbert Read contributed to *The Great Victorians*, edited by H. J. and Hugh Massingham (1932) and which was later reprinted in Sir Herbert's volume, *In Defence of Shelley, and Other Essays* (1936). Admitting "the intermittency of his inspiration" and the "ugly inversions and elisions" even in his best poetry, Sir Herbert nevertheless concludes that in the Odes "the thought is irredeemably fused in the expression, and the result is true poetry of the rarest and perhaps the highest kind — metaphysical poetry such as has been written by Lucretius, Dante, Donne, Crashaw, and Wordsworth."

Other essays which discuss Patmore and his poetry with some authority are by Shane Leslie, in *Studies in Sublime Failure* (1932), and by F. L. Lucas, in *Ten Victorian Poets* (1940). The most recent article is "Prophet without Responsibility: A Study of Coventry Patmore," by J. M. Cohen (*Essays in Criticism*, 1951). A stimulating study, though cranky and exaggerated, as its subtitle implies, is "Patmore and Hopkins: Sense and Nonsense in English Poetry," by D. S. MacColl (*London Mercury*, 1938). Attacking Hopkins's "mistaken views on prosody," MacColl declares that

Coventry Patmore is the only English poet who has understood what he himself and his brother poets were doing when they wrote verse. . . . Patmore had arrived at the truth and expounded it . . . in an article printed by the *North British Review* in 1857, and reprinted as an introduction to his volume of poems, *Amelia*, etc., published in 1878.

Patmore's great innovation was to discard the concept of the metrical "foot" and substitute that of the musical "bar," measured from stress to stress. MacColl asserts that Bridges and Hopkins made a "theoretical mess" of Patmore's principle, and that Hopkins only gradually grasped its true import as he grew older.

In the *Princeton University Library Chronicle* (1952), Robert B. Martin reports upon a collection of more than 200 letters and items associated with Patmore which is now at Princeton.

GEORGE MEREDITH (1828–1909)

Students of George Meredith are abundantly supplied with bibliographical data through two monumental volumes compiled by Maurice Buxton Forman: *A Bibliography of the Writings in Prose and Verse of George Meredith* (1922) and

Meredithiana (1924), the latter listing every scrap of second-ary material that had appeared in print up to the date of its publication.

One of the immediate desiderata in the study of Meredith is a dependable edition of the letters, and Professor C. L. Cline of the University of Texas is preparing one. The two volumes edited by Meredith's son (1912) suffer from every sort of editorial misdemeanor — misreadings, misdatings, un-indicated omissions, suppressed names. A number of letters in the largest extant collection of Meredithiana were printed in *A Catalogue of the Altschul Collection of George Meredith in the Yale University Library,* edited by Bertha Coolidge (1931), but this, too, is not free of errors; and many letters have come into the Altschul Collection since the catalogue was compiled.

The first book which offered any biographical information about Meredith was *George Meredith in Anecdote and Crit-icism,* by J. A. Hammerton (1909), reissued two years later, with revisions, as *George Meredith: His Life and Art in Anec-dote and Criticism.* This was a scissors-and-paste job, made up largely from reviews of his books and from other articles in periodicals. A serious attempt at a biography was made by S. M. Ellis, who had experience in writing about other Vic-torian novelists; both the merits and the defects of his book — *George Meredith: His Life and Friends in Relation to his Work* (1919) — spring from the fact that his father had been Meredith's first cousin. He was able to supply many details of family history not previously available, but this led to undue emphasis on Meredith's early life and to distortion of trivial details in order to exalt the Ellis family at Meredith's expense. Annoyed by his allegations, Meredith's heirs took advantage of the fact that Ellis had padded his book with excessive quotation, and brought suit for infringement of copyright. The book was recalled from circulation and a new edition was issued, reduced about sixty per cent by omission of the quoted passages. Except for a few letters, there was nothing of informational value in the excisions.

French academic thoroughness and accuracy marked the

book by René Galland, *George Meredith: Les cinquante pre-mières années (1828–1878)* (1923). Galland had worked on the book for years, and consulted surviving members of the family, who supplied him with authentic details. Nothing so favorable can be said about *The Life of George Meredith,* by "R. E. Sencourt" (R. E. Gordon George), which came out in the centennial year, 1928. It contains fantastic errors of fact and of interpretation, and is colored throughout by its writer's idiosyncrasies. There is better writing in Siegfried Sassoon's book, *Meredith* (1948), but as a biography it is ill-proportioned and sketchy, in consequence of Sassoon's lack of experience in methods of research. He had access to the large collection of data assembled by M. Buxton Forman and then owned by the publishing firm of Constable, but he seems to have dipped into it at random instead of making a sys-tematic study. The only full-scale biography based upon ex-tensive investigation of all available evidence is *The Ordeal of George Meredith,* by Lionel Stevenson (1953).

For the study of Meredith's reputation there are two help-ful volumes: *George Meredith: Some Early Appreciations,* compiled by Maurice Buxton Forman (1909), and *George Meredith and British Criticism,* by René Galland (1923).

Most of the general studies of Meredith's writings have con-centrated upon his novels and need not be discussed here. The only book devoted solely to his poetry is *The Poetry and Philosophy of George Meredith,* by George Macaulay Trevel-yan (1906), which retains its value after nearly half a century and is indispensable as an introduction to Meredith's poetical work. Nevertheless, its title reveals an emphasis which was prevalent at the time but which has contributed to a surviving notion that Meredith's poetry was solemnly didactic. The same point of view dominated the book by Constantin Pho-tiadès, *George Meredith: sa vie, son imagination, son art, sa doctrine* (1910), translated by Arthur Price as *George Mer-edith: His Life, Genius, and Teaching* (1913); the references to Meredith's poems in this book deal mainly with their philosophic content. In *George Meredith, Novelist, Poet, Re-former,* by M. Sturge Henderson (1907), four chapters on

Meredith's poetry were supplied by Basil de Sélincourt, three dealing with the ideas in his poems and one on "Meredith as artist and craftsman." Mrs. Sturge Henderson herself wrote the chapter on *Modern Love*, almost the first to deal perceptively with that important poem. Twenty years later this book was revised and reissued as *The Writings and Life of George Meredith*, by Mary Sturge Gretton (1926), with some of de Sélincourt's comments absorbed into the main body of the book, which now received a chronological arrangement. The chapter on "Meredith's Poetry" in *George Meredith*, by J. H. E. Crees (1918), is totally commonplace.

Essays of general appreciation include two by Sir E. K. Chambers in *A Sheaf of Studies* (1942), "Meredith's *Modern Love*" and "Meredith's Nature Poetry" (both originally printed in journals many years earlier), and one by Chauncey B. Tinker in *Essays in Retrospect* (1948), "Meredith's Poetry," which first came out as preface to the catalogue of the Altschul Collection.

The connection between the ideas in Meredith's poetry and the current scientific thought of his day is explored in a chapter of *Darwin among the Poets*, by Lionel Stevenson (1932), and in a chapter of *Scientific Thought in Poetry*, by Ralph B. Crum (1931). Further relevant points can be found in an article by James Stone, "Meredith and Goethe" (*TQ*, 1952).

Meredith's highly idiosyncratic use of symbolism and other figurative devices ought to be of interest to modern critics; but the only extant study of it is to be found in a dissertation by Hildegarde Littman, *Das dichterische Bild in der Lyric George Merediths und Thomas Hardys im Zusammenhang mit ihrer Weltanschauung* (1938). The same book was issued also as Volume VI of *Schweizer anglistische Arbeiten* under the simpler title of *Die Metapher in Merediths und Hardys Lyrik*. It classifies the principal symbols used by each poet.

The special notice accorded to *Modern Love* among Meredith's poems, first observable in the chapter on his poetry in Richard Le Gallienne's early book, *George Meredith: Some Characteristics* (1890), and reiterated by Harriet Monroe in an article on "Meredith as a Poet" in *Poetry* (1928), in which she terms that poem his "one masterpiece," has gained new impetus from the introduction supplied by C. Day Lewis for an edition of the poem published in 1948. There is a useful article by William T. Going, "A Note on 'My Lady' of *Modern Love*" in (*MLQ*, 1946), which challenges Sencourt's assertion that the "lady" was Janet Duff Gordon; Mr. Going argues that this portion of the poem is not to be interpreted as literally autobiographical.

JAMES THOMSON (1834–1882)

The first biographical information about Thomson was provided by his loyal friend Bertram Dobell in an introduction to the posthumous volume of Thomson's work, *A Voice from the Nile*, in 1884. This memoir was enlarged when prefixed to the complete edition of the *Poetical Works* in 1895. Meanwhile Henry S. Salt had written *The Life of James Thomson* (1889), a book which printed a good deal of material from Thomson's letters and journals. By 1910 this biography had long been out of print, and so Dobell reissued his own sketch in a small volume, *The Laureate of Pessimism*, omitting some passages but also adding a good many.

A conventional German doctoral dissertation came out in 1906, *James Thomson der jüngere, sein Leben und seine Werke*, by Josefine Weissel (*Wiener Beiträge zur englischen Philologie*, 24). J. E. Meeker's book, *The Life and Poetry of James Thomson* (1917), is undistinguished and sometimes undependable; and David Worcester's Harvard thesis, "James Thomson the Second: Studies in the Life and Poetry of B.V.," is available only in abstract in *Harvard University Summaries of Theses* (1934).

The most recent and thorough book is *James Thomson (B.V.): A Critical Study*, by Imogene B. Walker (1950). She announces her intention, somewhat portentously, thus:

I have considered the influences on, events in, and conditions of Thomson's life; his honest, analytical, philosophic cast of mind; his sympathetic and imaginative temperament; his works both as outgrowths and as evidence of the above; and the development and final statement of his philosophy. This philosophy, as expressed in his writings, is the result of his life, his cast of mind, and his temperament, plus the times in which he lived. . . . These five strands I have endeavoured to weave into a whole that the relations between them may become apparent, letting first one and then another dominate as chronology dictates.

Mrs. Walker was given access to unpublished notebooks, diaries, and letters in the possession of Percy Dobell, and she has produced an adequate and intelligent book, though some areas of the author's biography are left without much detail.

One of these areas had already received full treatment in a special study of real value and interest by Marjorie L. Reyburn: "James Thomson in Central City" (*University of Colorado Studies,* Series B, 1940). Using previously unpublished material from Thomson's personal diary and business journal and from the court records of Gilpin County, along with the recollections of an old inhabitant, Miss Reyburn gives a full account of Thomson's fantastic expedition to Colorado.

Probably the best general consideration of Thomson is the chapter in *Genius and Disaster* (1925), by Jeannette Marks. Also helpful is "James Thomson and his *City of Dreadful Night,*" by N. Hardy Wallis, in *Essays by Divers Hands* (1935). Attention should be directed to the introduction by Gordon Hall Gerould in *Poems of James Thomson* (B.V.) (1927), and the one by Edmund Blunden in an edition of *The City of Dreadful Night and Other Poems* (1932).

There have been several studies of the origins of his pessimistic philosophy: "Les Sources du pessimisme de Thomson," by Henri Peyre (*Revue Anglo-Américaine,* 1924–25); "Poets and Pessimism," by Benjamin M. Woodbridge (*Romanic Review,* 1944); and "Leopardi and *The City of Dreadful Night,*" by Lyman A. Cotten (*SP,* 1945). Two other academic studies deserve mention. "An Angel in the City of Dreadful Night," by H. Hoffman (*SeR,* 1924), deals with the influence of Shelley. "Blake's Nebuchadnezzar in *The City of Dreadful Night,*" by George M. Harper (*SP,* 1953), suggests that both the imagery and the ideas in Thomson's Canto xviii are derived from Blake's poems and his drawing of Nebuchadnezzar.

THOMAS HARDY (1840–1928)

An earlier bibliographical source for Hardy, *A Bibliography of the Works of Thomas Hardy*, by A. P. Webb (1916), has now been replaced by *Thomas Hardy: A Bibliographical Study*, by Richard Little Purdy (1954), a thorough, accurate, and well-organized work, which also supplies many details of Hardy's life which are not to be found in the biographies. For secondary material, an excellent compilation is *The First Hundred Years of Thomas Hardy, 1840–1940: a Centenary Bibliography of Hardiana*, by Carl J. Weber (1942).

The official biography of Hardy was nominally by his widow, Florence Emily, and came out in two volumes, *The Early Life* (1928) and *The Later Years* (1930). Actually it seems to have been written wholly by Hardy himself and left for posthumous publication. While it supplies much essential information, it is exasperating because of its omissions and evasions, and the style is undistinguished. The first published biography, *The Life of Thomas Hardy*, by Ernest Brennecke (1925), was handicapped by lack of data, being an unauthorized work written within the subject's lifetime. For scholarly accuracy and a well-balanced survey of the available facts, the only dependable book is *Hardy of Wessex*, by Carl J. Weber (1940). Edmund Blunden's *Thomas Hardy* in the English Men of Letters series (1942) is a pleasant brief sketch but adds nothing of biographical significance.

The Letters of Thomas Hardy, edited by Carl J. Weber (1954), is a less comprehensive book than its title implies, being confined to about 120 letters in the Colby College library, some of them of slight importance. A complete collection of the correspondence is still in the future.

Most of the books on Hardy's writing deal primarily with the novels, but since 1920 several have included discussion of his poetry also. Samuel C. Chew entitled his book *Thomas Hardy, Poet and Novelist* (1921; revised, 1928). A chapter on the poetry, written by J. E. Barton, was added to a new edition of Lionel Johnson's book, *The Art of Thomas Hardy*, in 1923. The poems supplied most of the material for Ernest Brennecke's account of the author's philosophical ideas, *Thomas Hardy's Universe: A Study of a Poet's Mind* (1924). H. C. Duffin had published a book in 1916 entitled *Thomas Hardy: A Study of the Wessex Novels*; when a third and revised edition came out in 1937, the subtitle was changed to read "A Study of the Wessex Novels, the Poems, and *The Dynasts*." One of the better general books on his writings is *Thomas Hardy: A Study of his Writings and their Background*, by W. R. Rutland (1938). There is a good deal of reference to the poems in the book by Harvey C. Webster, *On a Darkling Plain: The Art and Thought of Thomas Hardy* (1947). A group of modern American critics announced their opinions of both the prose and the poetry in the "Hardy Centennial Issue" of the *Southern Review* (1940). The latest long book, *Thomas Hardy: A Critical Study* (1954), by Evelyn Hardy (no relation), makes some use of manuscript sources, but is not noteworthy for accuracy of detail, acuteness of judgment, or mastery of recent research in the field. Its main value for students of Hardy's poetry is the careful linking of individual poems with events of his life and passages in his novels. She also makes some good comments on his poetic imagery.

It was the era of disillusionment after the first World War that brought recognition to Hardy as a poet, and consequently the studies devoted exclusively to his poetry began to appear at that time. In 1919 John Middleton Murry, in the *Athenaeum*, declared that Hardy's poetry is at least as important as his novels. This influential essay was reprinted, with the title "The Poetry of Thomas Hardy," in Murry's book, *Aspects of Literature* (1920). Robert M. Smith wrote a good article on "Philosophy in Thomas Hardy's Poetry" (*North American Review*, 1924). John Livingston Lowes contrasted Hardy's attitude toward Nature with Meredith's in "Two Readings of Earth" (*Yale Review*, 1926; reprinted in *Essays in Appreciation*, 1936). F. L. Lucas included Hardy among his *Ten Victorian Poets* (1940). Perhaps the best of the general essays on the subject is the introduction by G. M. Young to *Selected Poems of Thomas Hardy* in the Golden Treasury series (1940). There are two essays on Hardy's poetry in R. P. Blackmur's volume, *The Expense of Greatness* (1940), one of them reprinted from the recent *Southern Review* centennial issue; and another of the essays from that issue, by Allen Tate, was included in Tate's *Reason in Madness* (1941). V. H. Collins contributed an essay on "The Love Poetry of Thomas Hardy" to *Essays and Studies by Members of the English Association* (1942). "The Dramatic Element in Hardy's Poetry" was dealt with by Marguerite Roberts in *Queen's Quarterly* (1944).

E. C. Hickson published a University of Pennsylvania dissertation on *The Versification of Thomas Hardy* (1931), and Hildegarde Littman analyzed his metaphors in the Bern dissertation which is described above in the section on Meredith. The most important book devoted wholly to Hardy as a poet is *The Poetry of Thomas Hardy*, by James G. Southworth (1947). While attempting to keep an impartial attitude, Professor Southworth admits that he became less enthusiastic about Hardy as a poet as he wrote the book: "I belong to a different age from those who have written largely about Hardy, and I cannot share their exuberance. Where they see victory, I sense defeat; where they see vision, I sense shortsightedness."

The first part of Southworth's book undertakes "to synthesize Hardy's poetic aesthetic as well as his poetic thought. . . . It becomes increasingly clear that Hardy formulated no philosophical system, nor did he intend to do so." Part II is devoted to the poet's technical methods, examining his prosody in detail and attempting to define his prosodic theory. The author claims to be the first to study the revisions that Hardy made in the manuscripts of his poems. The final section of the book is "an attempt at a general evaluation of Hardy's achievement as a poet, not as a thinker." Expressing the opinion that *The Dynasts* is "fragmentary as a work of art," Southworth did not treat that work in detail, in order to avoid overlapping with the book by Amiya C. Chakravarty.

In recent years the greatest attention has centered upon that epic-drama. Amiya C. Chakravarty devoted a whole volume to *"The Dynasts" and the Post-War Age in Poetry* (1938); about two-thirds of the book gives a detailed analysis of the poem, and the remaining portion advances the theory that the work gained great significance through the events of the first World War and the subsequent rise of dictators — significance that Hardy could not have foreseen when writing what he considered to be the reconstruction of a past era and of a vanished system.

Annette B. Hopkins dealt with *"The Dynasts* and the Course of History"* (*SAQ*, 1945). Harold Orel discussed the epic qualities of the poem in *"The Dynasts* and *Paradise Lost"* (*SAQ*, 1953). George Witter Sherman suggested one of the imaginative sources for it in "The Influence of London on *The Dynasts"* (*PMLA*, 1948). A specific origin, in *The Drama of Kings,* by Robert Buchanan, was proposed by Hoxie Neale Fairchild, in "The Immediate Source of *The Dynasts"* (*PMLA*, 1952); and a sequel to this article, in the same journal (1954), "The Original Source of Hardy's *Dynasts,"* by John A. Cassidy, went back to Hugo's *Légende des Siècles.* Another element in the epic-drama was discussed by E. A. Horsman, "The Language of *The Dynasts"* (*Durham University Journal,* 1949). As 1954 was the semi-centennial of the first volume of *The Dynasts,* several articles undertook a general reassessment. A leading article in *TLS* (15 January, 1954), "Hardy after Fifty Years," declared that the time has now come when his poetry can be judged fairly. Richard Church wrote on "Thomas Hardy as Revealed in *The Dynasts"* in *Études Anglaises* (1954). In *"The Dynasts,* a Prophecy" (*SAQ,* 1954), Jacob Korg followed the main idea of Chakravarty's book (without mentioning it) by saying that Hardy's theory that "war, which has always been considered as an instrument of human policy, was itself making an instrument of men . . . was practically unintelligible to the Edwardian world which received it," but "has gained authority from recent history."

ROBERT BRIDGES (1844–1930)

Robert Seymour Bridges is one of the few minor Victorian poets to be accorded a full and accurate bibliography, that by George L. Mackay (1933). On the other hand, Bridges' long life was so uniformly pleasant and uneventful that an extensive account of it is not seriously needed; and therefore no attempt has been made to defy the request in his will that no biography should be written. His richest satisfactions, and perhaps his greatest significance, lay in his relationships with literary friends; hence the truest picture of his life can be derived from his correspondence with them and his generous tributes to their memory. His recollections of Digby Mackworth Dolben, Richard Watson Dixon, and Henry Bradley were assembled in a small volume under the title *Three Friends* (1932). *The Correspondence of Robert Bridges and Henry Bradley, 1900–1927* came out in 1940. And the first volume of *The Letters of Gerard Manley Hopkins*, edited by Claude Colleer Abbott (1940), consisted wholly of "Letters to Robert Bridges." A few years later, another batch of correspondence was edited by Derek Patmore in "Coventry Patmore and Robert Bridges: Some Letters" (*Fortnightly Review*, 1948).

Several of Bridges' younger contemporaries have recorded their acquaintance with him. One of these is Edward Thompson, whose slim book, *Robert Bridges, 1844–1930*, came out in 1945. This book offers a general survey of Bridges' poetry, with copious quotations, but it is the personal anecdotes that make it interesting. Logan Pearsall Smith wrote his recollections of Bridges in Tract XXXV of the Society for Pure English (1931). George Gordon gave some agreeable memories and comments in two lectures which were later published: the Rede lecture of 1931, printed in *The Lives of Authors* (1950), and his final lecture in the Oxford Chair of Poetry, 1938, printed in *The Discipline of Letters* (1946), the latter discussing Bridges' relations with Hopkins. Simon Nowell-Smith traced the special topic of Bridges' long association with the Clarendon Press in "A Poet in Walton Street," in *Essays*

Mainly on the Nineteenth Century Presented to Sir Humphrey Milford (1948).

The first separate monograph on Bridges was by F. E. Brett Young, *Robert Bridges: A Critical Study* (1914). It was a useful defense of Bridges as a lyric poet at the time when his appointment as Poet Laureate had invoked a deluge of stupid journalistic abuse; but it showed little understanding of his dramatic work. A very sketchy book by T. M. Kelshall, *Robert Bridges, Poet Laureate* (1924), was inaccurate as to facts and indiscriminate in its praise.

The appearance of *The Testament of Beauty* in 1929 resulted in an immediate re-estimation of Bridges' importance and of his essential qualities. The philosophical content of the book, its wide range of learned reference, and its experiments in prosody all combined to render it a challenge to scholars. Nowell C. Smith brought out a very useful guidebook, *Notes on "The Testament of Beauty,"* in 1931 and revised it for a new edition in 1940. Smith did not get very far in analyzing the philosophic theme of the poem, but he traced a great many sources and explained obscure allusions with accuracy and thoroughness. Mabel L. V. Hughes adopted a different approach in *Everyman's "Testament of Beauty"* (1942); her earnestly religious disquisition adds nothing for a genuine understanding of the poem. Finally, a detailed study of its technical aspects has been made in the University of Pennsylvania dissertation of Elizabeth Cox Wright, *Metaphor, Sound, and Meaning: A Study of Robert Bridges' "Testament of Beauty"* (1952).

The one indispensable book on Bridges, however, is that by Albert J. Guérard, *Robert Bridges: A Study of Traditionalism in Poetry* (1942). With scholarly thoroughness, critical acumen, and a luminous style, Guérard offers not only "the first exhaustive critical study of Bridges' poetry," but also "a study and defence of traditionalism." His thesis is that

far from being a learned formalist, primarily interested in prosodic exercises, Bridges seems to me to have been one of the most impressive as well as one of the most serious poets of the last hundred years. . . . The way in which Bridges used very diverse masters in his lyrics, plays, and philosophical poems may illustrate not only the manner in which a poet perfects his style but also some of the workings of the creative imagination.

Guérard presents precise evidence as to sources and analogues, much of it embodied in the text of his chapters, and further data in an appendix. Another appendix gives a detailed study of Bridges' prosody.

Of strictly academic studies, the earliest in date is a German dissertation by Alfred Gilde, *Die dramatische Behandlung der Rückkehr des Odysseus bei Nicholas Rowe, Robert Bridges, und Stephen Phillips* (1903), and the most meticulous is *On the Language of Robert Bridges' Poetry*, by Tatsu Sasaki (1932). On his general philosophy, the most careful articles are those by J. Gordon Eaker on "Robert Bridges' Concept of Nature" (*PMLA*, 1939), and by Andrew J. Green on "Robert Bridges and the Spiritual Animal" (*Philosophical Review*, 1944). "Bridges' Classical Prosody: New Verses and Variants" was the subject of an article in *TLS* by Simon Nowell-Smith (28 August 1943), quoting material from manuscript copies made by Lionel Muirhead, a friend of Bridges.

Several good general appreciations of the poet came out about the time when *The Testament of Beauty* was published or at the time of his death a year later. Edward Davison's essay "In Praise of the Poet Laureate" was in *Fortnightly Review* (1928); Arthur Waugh's "Robert Bridges" was in the same periodical (1930); and Oliver Elton's "Robert Bridges and *The Testament of Beauty*" (English Association Pamphlet, 1932) was reprinted in his *Essays and Addresses* (1939).

A short article by Adam Fox on "English Landscape in Robert Bridges" (*English*, 1942), emphasized that

Bridges was not a romantic, and at the same time he was not a reactionary. He thought new effects might be got in poetry by mastering the medium, that is the words with which poets work, and he came in course of time to feel that new effects could only be had through new methods. . . . The scene for him brings its own enjoyment, and that enjoyment he seeks to communicate.

The same point of view appears in the most recent essay, "The Road Not Taken: A Study of the Poetry of Robert Bridges," by J. M. Cohen (*Cambridge Journal,* 1951). Dwelling on Bridges' essential classicism, Cohen asserts that

as a lyric poet he remains to be rediscovered; a succeeding generation may find his the outstanding poetry published between Thomson's *City of Dreadful Night* (1880) and Yeats' *Green Helmet* volume (1910). . . . The *Shropshire Lad* is the product of a much less profound and anonymous emotion than Bridges'.

ALICE MEYNELL (1847–1922)

A competent study of Alice Meynell's work and her relationship with various contemporaries can be found in *Mrs. Meynell and her Literary Generation,* by Anna K. Tuell (1925). A full and graceful account of her life, avoiding many of the faults of family biographies, was the work of her daughter, Viola Meynell: *Alice Meynell: A Memoir* (1929). Some features of this book receive more explicit treatment or acquire different emphasis through a more recent publication by the same author, *Francis Thompson and Wilfrid Meynell* (1952).

Critical essays on Mrs. Meynell's poetry have been restrained and gentle, in harmony with their subject. The best of them are "The Multitude: An Appreciation of Alice Meynell," by Jeannette Marks (*North American Review,* 1923); "The Poems of Alice Meynell," by Osbert Burdett (*Critical Essays,* 1925); "Alice Meynell," by Katherine Tynan (*Catholic World,* 1929); and "Alice Meynell and her Circle," by Theodore Maynard (*Catholic World,* 1931).

The centennial of Mrs. Meynell's birth brought out a considerable body of material. The *Alice Meynell Centenary Exhibition Catalogue,* published by the Cambridge University Press (1947), included useful bibliographical data, quotations from unpublished letters, etc. A more extensive volume is its American counterpart, *Alice Meynell Centenary Tribute: A Symposium Opening an Exhibition of Alice Meynell Manuscripts, Letters, First and Rare Editions* (1947). Edited by Terence L. Connolly, S.J., it contains "A.M., A Personal

Tribute," by Robert Francis Wilberforce, "Reminiscences of Mrs. Meynell through her Prose," by Anna K. Tuell, "Alice Meynell, Poet of my Delight," by Sister Mary Madeleva, and also a report on the Alice Meynell Collection at Boston College and "A Short-title List of Published Volumes, 1875–1947," these last two contributions by Fr. Connolly.

V. Sackville-West supplied a perceptive introduction to *Alice Meynell: Prose and Poetry, Centennial Volume* (1947). Two articles of some value came out in the *Poetry Review* of that year, one by Sir George Rostrevor Hamilton (325–330) and the other by her son Sir Francis Meynell (477–485). The *Dublin Review* also printed two articles at that time in Number 441, one by G. K. Chesterton (3–12) and the other by her daughter Viola (13–19).

Various minor details of Mrs. Meynell's poems have been elucidated in short articles by Frances Price in *Notes and Queries*, 1943–1950, *passim*.

WILLIAM ERNEST HENLEY (1849–1903)

A full biography of Henley was long planned by his friend and disciple, Charles Whibley, who collected a mass of material for the purpose but died in 1930 with only a rough draft of three chapters written. Henley has therefore been receiving his first significant study only within the past decade. Two earlier books about him were brief sentimental tributes — *William Ernest Henley*, by L. Cope Cornford (1913), and *W. E. Henley: a Memoir*, by Kennedy Williamson (1930). In 1945 Jerome H. Buckley published *William Ernest Henley: A Study in the "Counter-decadence" of the 'Nineties*, and four years later came *W. E. Henley* by "John Connell" (John Henry Robertson). These two volumes, one American, the other English, complement each other effectively. Buckley, attempting "the first general criticism of Henley's life and work," announces that he has "deliberately slighted anecdote and personal melodrama, in order to relate Henley to a broader social, aesthetic, and intellectual background." He starts with a good chapter on "The Victorian Activist Philosophies" and uses Henley as the outstanding representative of this school. Connell, on the other hand, had access to Whibley's notes and drafts and to the six large volumes of Henley's letters that Whibley had bound in chronological order. Accordingly his book is largely biographical, with much quotation from letters. The incompleteness of his data, however, was soon proved to him; in consequence of a talk that he gave on the BBC he came into possession of a large collection of Henley correspondence that Henley's widow had left to a friend. Connell reported on this new material in three articles in the *National and English Review* (1951). There is also an article by J. H. Hallam, "Some Early Letters and Verses of W. E. Henley" (*Blackwood's*, 1943), recounting a friendship between the poet and a London coffee-house keeper in 1872–79, which gave Henley his knowledge of Cockney slang. Hitherto unpublished poems in the National Library of Scotland were edited by W. M. Parker under the title, "W. E. Henley: Twenty-five New Poems: A Centenary Discovery" (*Poetry Review*, 1949).

Critical essays include one by Marietta Neff on "The Place of Henley" (*North American Review*, 1920), which points out that though Henley regarded himself as a rebel and innovator he was influenced by many forces. W. B. Nichols took a similar line in "The Influence of Henley" in *Poetry Review* (1921), declaring that Henley could have had little or no effect upon the Georgian generation in their free-verse experiments because none of them seemed to be acquainted with his work. Alfred Noyes contributed an appreciation of "Henley — Last of the Buccaneers" to the New York *Bookman* (1916). This reappeared with slight changes in the *Contemporary Review* (1922), and in his book, *Some Aspects of Modern Poetry* (1924). Noyes praised Henley as "our first, our only, our unapproachable portrait-painter in English verse." On the other hand, a strongly antagonistic evaluation was given by Arthur Symons in "The Revival of Henley" (*London Quarterly Review*, 1922).

Dealing with Henley's prose and his journalism are two essays of some value, one by Horace Gregory, "On William Ernest Henley's Editorial Career," in *The Shield of Achilles*

(1944), and one by Morris U. Schappes, "William Ernest Henley's Principles of Criticism," in *PMLA* (1931). Fuller study of this topic must depend upon the identification of the great quantity of reviews and essays that Henley published anonymously in many papers.

ROBERT LOUIS STEVENSON (1850–1894)

A veritable library of books and articles about Robert Louis Stevenson has accumulated during the past half-century, but relatively little of it can be accorded the name of "research" and far less of it can be regarded as bearing directly on his poetry. The standard bibliography was compiled by William F. Prideaux (new edition, edited and enlarged by Mrs. Luther S. Livingston, 1917). Currently in course of publication, under the editorship of George L. MacKay, is a monumental three-volume catalogue of the works by and about Stevenson in the Beinecke collection, Yale University Library (Volumes I–II, Printed Books, Pamphlets, Broadsides, etc., 1951–52). A general report on "The Edwin J. Beinecke Collection of Robert Louis Stevenson," by Marjorie Gray Wynne, appeared in the *Yale University Library Gazette* (1952).

The cornerstone of Stevenson biography is still the two-volume *Life* by Graham Balfour (1901), and the principal walls are the four volumes of *Letters*, edited by Sidney Colvin (1912). A new and complete collection of the letters is now being edited by Professor Bradford A. Booth. In recent years assiduous admirers have devoted whole books to each epoch of Stevenson's life — Edinburgh, Switzerland, California, Samoa. The adulation of earlier biographers and critics rendered Stevenson a natural target for the debunkers during the twenties, and his life was subjected to a combination of psychoanalysis and gossip-mongering by George S. Hellman in *The True Stevenson* (1925) and by J. A. Steuart in *Robert Louis Stevenson, Man and Writer* (two volumes, 1926). Some of the scandalous rumors that they unearthed are now discounted, but a better-balanced portrayal of Stevenson was made possible by their assault on the old sanctification of him.

An extensive recent biography is *Voyage to Windward*,

by J. C. Furnas (1951), and an intelligent modern estimate of Stevenson's work can be found in the volume on him by David Daiches in the Makers of Modern Literature series (1947).

For the study of Stevenson's poems, it is essential to use the edition prepared by Janet Adam Smith (1951). The need for a thorough revision of his text with recourse to manuscripts was clearly shown through a correspondence in *TLS* (29 August 1929; 26 December 1929; 30 January 1930), which brought out a few of the misreadings in *New Poems and Variant Readings* (1918). Miss Adam Smith has established a text that often differs significantly from previous printings of the poems.

The one modern scholar who has spoken out strongly upon the significance of Stevenson's poetry is H. W. Garrod. His essay on "The Poetry of Robert Louis Stevenson," in *The Profession of Poetry and Other Lectures* (1929), reprinted in *Essays Mainly on the Nineteenth Century Presented to Sir Humphrey Milford* (1928), makes several interesting assertions:

For the secondary account in which the poetry of Stevenson is held, Lang, I fancy, has some responsibility. Yet the real michief began, perhaps, with Stevenson himself. Stevenson practiced self-depreciation as an art; and it is an art which no poet can afford. . . .

It can hardly, I think, be accident that the three Victorian poets who wrought the disintegration of Victorian poetic diction were all of them novelists. The greatest of them I take to be Stevenson. But "prosators" they are, all of them. . . .

He took from Matthew Arnold . . . his blank verse. I am bold to say that it is the best part of his poetry. . . . Of the blank-verse lyric . . . I count Stevenson . . . a supreme master.

The poems . . . influenced deeply two poets who, till the other day, counted a good deal with the young — Housman and Rupert Brooke. . . . When I am asked what poets we have had since Matthew Arnold, I say still always, Stevenson, Housman, Brooke.

One of Stevenson's poetic disciples, Alfred Noyes, included an essay on him in his book, *Some Aspects of Modern Poetry*

(1924), and Hugh Richards contributed an article on "Robert Louis Stevenson and his poetry" to the *London Quarterly and Holborn Review* (1932).

A Marburg dissertation by Hermann Alberts, *Der Optimismus des englischen Dichters Robert Louis Stevenson* (1928), presents the fairly obvious facts about his philosophic attitudes. The historical authenticity of the story used in his poem "Ticonderoga" is dealt with in an article by David A. Randall in *New Colophon* (1949).

OSCAR WILDE (1854–1900)

The prolific output of books on Oscar Wilde shows little sign of diminishing. It is true that the last of his personal friends is now dead, and so presumably there is an end to the string of controversial books of recollections, wherein Shaw, Sherard, Harris, Douglas, Ross, and others gave their conflicting reports. But a new generation continues to be fascinated by the man's psychological peculiarities and by his paradoxes and epigrams.

A *Bibliography of Oscar Wilde* was compiled by "Stuart Mason" (C. S. Millard) in 1914. But in spite of the extensive records printed by Wilde's associates and acquaintances, no thorough and objective biography of him has as yet been published. *Oscar Wilde*, by Gustaf J. Renier (1932) gives a reasonably well balanced study of the principal influences that shaped his career. *Oscar Wilde and the Yellow Nineties*, by Frances Winwar (1940), and *Oscar Wilde: His Life and Wit*, by Hesketh Pearson (1946), are popular works designed for easy reading. The background of his boyhood is vividly presented in *The Wildes of Merrion Square*, by Patrick Byrne (1953), and an intimate picture of his tragic later life can be found in *Son of Oscar Wilde*, by Vyvyan Holland (1955). His letters are now being collected for publication by Allan Wade.

George Woodcock's book, *The Paradox of Oscar Wilde* (1949), presents the view of a clever young modern. In it and in most of the works mentioned above his poetry is discussed incidentally, but specialized studies of it in English are few. An article by Edouard Roditi, "Oscar Wilde's Poetry as Art

History" (*Poetry,* 1947), was later used as the first chapter of Roditi's book on Wilde in the Makers of Modern Literature series (1948). In emphasizing the influence of Whistler and the Impressionists, Roditi followed the same line as Gerda Eichbaum in her article, "Die impressionistischen Fruhge-dichte Oscar Wildes unter besonderer Berücksichtigung des Einflusses von James MacNeill Whistler" (*Die neueren Sprache,* 1932).

It is remarkable that virtually all the detailed investigation of Wilde's poetry that has been made is in German. Bernhard Fehr published "Studien zu Oscar Wildes Gedichten" in *Palaestra* (1918). Helene Richter dealt with most of the poems in a long and exhaustive article, "Oscar Wildes Persönlichkeit in seinen Gedichten" (*ES,* 1920). In spite of its title, an article by Stefan von Ullman, "Synästhesien in den dichterischen Werken von Oscar Wilde" (*ES,* 1938), deals mainly with the prose; but its analysis of certain types of imagery is also applicable to the poetry.

Only one of Wilde's poems has been subject to separate examination. Bernhard Fehr wrote on "Oscar Wildes 'The Harlot's House'" (*Archiv für das Studium der neueren Sprachen und Literaturen,* 1916), tracing the influence of Poe and of various French authors; and J. D. Thomas presented evidence as to the date and circumstances in which the poem was written in "The Composition of Wilde's 'The Harlot's House'" (*MLN,* 1950).

JOHN DAVIDSON (1857–1909)

In John Davidson's will he requested the destruction of his letters and prohibited the writing of his biography. Though his life was a picturesque and tragic one, the ban has been respected. The only academic treatment of Davidson in English is a University of Pennsylvania dissertation by Hayim Fineman, *John Davidson: A Study of the Relation of his Ideas to his Poetry* (1916). It is a relatively brief and superficial treatise. Fineman links him with the imperialistic swagger of his time and with the realistic poetry about London slums, but makes claims for his originality:

He had a point of view and a depth of emotion altogether his own; he tried to stem the tide of French influence and endeavored to construct a new basis for English poetry. Out of his own experience and the scientific thought of his own time he attempted to create 'a new dwelling place for the human imagination.' This he did with a passion and energy in the presence of which the writings of most of his contemporaries pale.

Much of Fineman's essay is concerned with Davidson's interpretation of Nietzsche, which Fineman considers to be a subjective and sometimes inconsistent affiliation: "in his later work he passes the Nietzschean ideas through a materialistic crucible so that they practically become amplifications of his own point of view." This aspect of his work is examined more fully in *John Davidson und sein geistiges Werden unter dem Einfluss Nietzsches,* by Gertrud von Petzold (1928).

An essay by Milton Bronner, "John Davidson: Poet of Anarchy" (*Forum,* 1910), emphasizes the autobiographic element in his poetry, and deplores the megalomania that affected his later work: "Both by actual performance and by what is here foreshadowed and indicated, one sees what a powerful poet of the masses Davidson might have become had his attention remained concentrated on this phase of existence."

Edward J. O'Brien wrote an introduction to *The Man Forbid,* a collection of Davidson's critical essays (1910), in which he suggested that Davidson "succeeded in founding a school in contemporary English composition . . . whose chief exponent today is Mr. Gilbert Chesterton." He attributed Davidson's attitude to his innate Scottish individualism and love of disputation. This idea was carried out more fully by R. M. Wenley in an introduction to the Modern Library edition of Davidson's poems (1924). Wenley had known Davidson when they were fellow-students, and he elaborates the early formative influences of Scottish Calvinist theology and of the philosophical ferment at Glasgow University under Nichol and the Caird brothers.

"The Religious Significance of John Davidson" was discussed by A. J. Maries in the *Westminster Review* (1913). An essay by D. R. Lock, "John Davidson and the Poetry of the

'Nineties' " (*London Quarterly and Holborn Review*, 1936), reappeared (under the pen-name of "Petronius Applejoy") as "A View of John Davidson against a 'Nineties Background" in the *Catholic World* (1942). Lock emphasizes the stylistic influence of Henley and asserts that all of Davidson's best imaginative work was done before the close of the nineties.

The largest and richest collection of Davidson material is at Princeton and is described in "The Quest for John Davidson," by J. Benjamin Townsend (*Princeton University Library Chronicle*, 1952).

FRANCIS THOMPSON (1859–1907)

There is a larger body of writing about Francis Thompson than about most of his contemporaries of comparable stature; but much of it is of limited scholarly value, for several reasons. The chief biographical source is the Meynell family, who wrote about him with much literary grace and sensitive affection but were inevitably influenced by their intricate personal relationship with him. Other writers have been sentimentally moved by Thompson's pathetic life and unworldly charm. Still others approach his work strictly from the direction of Roman Catholic liturgy and doctrine. He has been the subject of several doctoral dissertations, beginning with one by George Ashton Beacock at Marburg in 1912, which made a detailed study of his metrical techniques and of his vocabulary. Another German dissertation is "Francis Thompsons dichterische Entwicklung: ein biographische-psychologischer Versuch," by Alfons Martz, at Münster (1932). Recent American dissertations which presumably bring scholarly thoroughness and impartiality to the subject are available only in abstracts: "Francis Thompson: His Theory of Poetry," by Norman Thomas Wayland, a St. Louis University dissertation (*Microfilm Abstracts*, 1940); "Francis Thompson: His Poetry in Relation to the Ideas of his Day," by Kathleen Flesch Torbert (*Summaries of Doctoral Dissertations, University of Wisconsin*, 1950), and "Francis Thompson's Philosophical Poetry: An Evaluation," by Catherine Carolin Weaver, a University of Michigan dissertation (*Microfilm Abstracts*, 1951).

The official *Life of Francis Thompson,* by Everard Meynell (1913), is one of the best-written biographies of its generation, and gives a delightful picture of the poet's personality. The biographer's sister Viola Meynell has added further documentation and revealing details in her recent book, *Francis Thompson and Wilfrid Meynell: A Memoir* (1952). There are useful biographical details in the book by the Rev. Terence L. Connolly, S.J., *Francis Thompson: In his Paths* (1944). In a first-personal narrative of a pilgrimage "to persons and places associated with the poet" Father Connolly records a number of interviews with surviving acquaintances and includes previously unpublished extracts from Thompson's notebooks, etc.

Father Connolly is unquestionably the leading authority on Thompson in this country at present. His notes to the revised edition of Thompson's poems (1941) can give valuable help to the student, and his identification of Thompson's book reviews led to his editing of the large volume of them, *Literary Criticisms by Francis Thompson* (1948), indispensable for any investigation of the poet's literary opinions.

Specific aspects of Thompson's life are taken up in the chapter about him in *The Milk of Paradise,* by Meyer H. Abrams (1934), a study of the influence of narcotics on poetry, and in an article by Doyle Hennessy, "Did Francis Thompson Attempt Suicide?" in *Catholic World* (1950), a somewhat specious effort to refute a commonly accepted episode.

General studies of Thompson's life and work are of varying value. *Francis Thompson, Poet and Mystic,* by John Thomson (1923, a revised and enlarged third edition of a book first published in 1913), and *Guidance from Francis Thompson in Matters of Faith,* by J. A. Hutton (1926), are conventional and trite. The title of a book by R. L. Mégroz, *Francis Thompson: The Poet of Earth in Heaven* (1927), is misleading; its subtitle, "A Study in Poetic Mysticism and the Evolution of Love Poetry," gives a clue to its real contents. Mégroz undertook such a vast perspective that he had little space left for the announced topic. "The work of Francis Thompson," he explained, "seemed to me to call for an unusually comprehensive picture of its wide background in poetry and religion. I chose a succession of poets whose work has significant affinities or contrasts with Thompson's." He could thus include whole chapters on Patmore, Crashaw, Shelley, Donne, St. Augustine, and others.

Thompson's poetry has exerted a particular fascination for Continental scholars. A study in French by K. Rooker was published in Bruges in 1912. A later French book was by Agnes de la Gorce, *Francis Thompson et les poètes Catholiques d'Angleterre*. First issued in Paris in 1932, it achieved an English version by H. F. Kynaston-Snell the next year. Written from an orthodox Romanist point of view, the book emphasizes the theological element throughout, and is not free from errors of fact. Its thesis is that the "The Hound of Heaven" is the flower of the "Catholic Renaissance" that grew out of the Oxford Movement.

Another foreign book that achieved translation into English is entitled simply *Francis Thompson,* and is by an Italian scholar, Federico Olivero; it was first published in Brescia in 1935, and the English version by Dante Milani came out in Turin in 1938. It contains detailed chapters on Thompson's religious thought, his poetic theory, his images, style, choice of words, meter, etc. It is marred by an indiscriminate enthusiasm and a tendency to vague generalities of praise, while its discussion of details is weakened by the author's imperfect grasp of English connotations. The list of possible sources and analogues is useful, though some of the suggestions are farfetched. A later Italian study, by Emilia D'Alessio (1937), is a slight sketch of minor significance.

Several works by Roman Catholic scholars concentrate upon the symbolic and mystical interpretation of Thompson's major poem. *A Study of Francis Thompson's "Hound of Heaven,"* by the Rev. J. F. X. O'Conor, S.J. (1912), is brief and sketchy, its chief point being a paralleling of the poem with the *Spiritual Exercises* of St. Ignatius Loyola. A more extensive study is *"The Hound of Heaven": An Interpretation,* by the Rev. Francis P. Le Buffe, S.J. (1921). The author explains that "this little volume is offered as an ascetical and scriptural interpretation of the poem. The author refrains almost entirely from literary questions. His one aim has been to attempt to clarify obscure passages and to give all passages the atmosphere that is required for them from Sacred Scripture and from standard ascetical principles."

Finally, there is a good article on a technical aspect of Thompson's poetry, going farther than Olivero's book does into the study of his diction: "The Praetorian Cohorts; a Study of the Language of Francis Thompson's Poetry," by Frederick B. Tolles (*English Studies,* 1940). Challenging the often-repeated statement — which originated with Geoffrey Bliss's article, "Francis Thompson and Richard Crashaw" (*Month,* 1908), and was developed by Arthur Symons in *Dramatis Personae* (1923) — that Thompson was strongly influenced by the Metaphysical poets, Tolles demonstrated that "his characteristic practices in the use of words spring directly from the work of certain of his immediate predecessors and contemporaries."

ALFRED EDWARD HOUSMAN (1859–1936)

There is an almost comic contrast between the dearth of published material about A. E. Housman prior to 1936 and the deluge that has poured out ever since his death in that year. His poems had begun to receive their belated recognition in the twenties; but the slender total of them and their pellucid simplicity offered no challenge to scholars, and his obdurate reticence was an obstacle to any biographical study — though presumably his cloistered life offered as little grist for the biographer as his poetry offered for the annotator.

Now, less than twenty years later, the poems bear a staggering load of critical apparatus. He is the only poet of his generation to have been concordanced: Clyde Kenneth Hyder published *A Concordance to the Poems of A. E. Housman* at Lawrence, Kansas, in 1940. Unfortunately Professor Hyder did not always use the most reliable texts. The bibliography of his few poems has proved unexpectedly complex: T. G. Ehrsam brought out an exhaustive but incomplete and inaccurate *Bibliography of A. E. Housman* in 1941, and more recently has come an excellent work by John Carter and John Sparrow, *A. E. Housman: An Annotated Hand-list* (1952), based on an earlier list printed in *The Library* (1940). Another useful work is the edition of *A Shropshire Lad* published by the Colby College Library in 1946 with notes and a semi-centennial bibliography by Carl J. Weber. A correspondence between William White and John Sparrow with regard to textual variants in *A Shropshire Lad* appeared in *TLS* (12 February, 5 March, and 15 May 1954).

A full record of "all evaluations of Housman's poetry and poetic theory" published between 1920 and 1945 was provided by R. W. Stallman in "Annotated Bibliography of A. E. Housman: A Critical Study" (*PMLA*, 1945). In view of Professor Stallman's invaluable work, I need here only to mention a selection of the most important or most typical research prior to 1945, and then to cover the additional publications of the past ten years.

While no formal biography has appeared, the poet's life and habits have been thoroughly revealed in print by many of his friends. Shortly after his death the magazine of his old school, *The Bromsgrovian,* issued a special supplement containing important recollections by his brother (Laurence Housman), his sister (Katherine E. Symons), A. W. Pollard, R. W. Chambers, Alan Ker, A. S. F. Gow, and John Sparrow. Several of these people also wrote on the subject at greater length: A. S. F. Gow published *A. E. Housman* in 1936; Laurence Housman provided both family episodes and unpublished documents in *A. E. H.: Some Poems, Some Letters, and a Personal Memoir* (1937); and an article by R. W. Chambers, which first appeared in the *London University College Magazine,* was included in Chambers' book, *Man's Unconquerable Mind* (1939) as part of an essay entitled "Philologists at University College, London." His publisher, Grant Richards, contributed his memories in *Housman, 1897–1936* (1942). The nearest approach to a full biography is the book by Percy Withers, *A Buried Life* (1940). Previously unprinted letters by Housman appear in "Some Unpublished Housman Letters," edited by Cyril Clemens (*Poet Lore*, 1948), and in

"Fifteen Unpublished Letters of Housman," edited by William White (*Dalhousie Review*, 1950), Professor White also published "A Note on Some Housman Marginalia" (*PMLA*, 1943).

General studies of Housman's poetry include a typically wise and witty article by H. W. Garrod in *Essays and Studies by Members of the English Association* (1939). "Collected and canonized," Garrod remarks, "Housman waits now only the scholiast, and that 'academic appreciation which is the second death.'" Chauncey B. Tinker's *Essays in Retrospect* (1948) contains an essay on "The Poetry of A. E. Housman," part of which first appeared in the *Yale Review* in 1935; for its publication as a book, Professor Tinker added a section vigorously protesting against the posthumous publication of inferior poems by Housman. Edmund Wilson, in *The Triple Thinkers* (revised edition, 1948), gives a stimulating discussion of Housman's poetry, emphasizing his classical scholarship and linking him with other author-scholars — Gray, Fitz-Gerald, Pater, Hopkins, and Lewis Carroll. Other general discussions are "The Essential Housman," by Stephen Spender (*Horizon*, 1940); "The Poetry of A. E. Housman," by A. F. Allison (*RES*, 1943); "A E. Housman: His Outlook and Art," by Robert Hamilton (*London Quarterly and Holborn Review*, 1950); and "The Elegiac Theme in Housman," by Michael Macklem (*Queen's Quarterly*, 1952). Tom Burns Haber discussed "Housman's Poetic Ear" in *Poet Lore* (1948), arguing that his technical mastery of poetic melody had been inadequately recognized: "For this poet, as for all great lyrists, sound was not the mere handmaiden of sense but an intimate and equal companion." Other articles by Professor Haber are "Housman's Poetic Method: His Lectures and his Notebooks" (*PMLA*, 1954), and "A. E. Housman's Downward Eye" (*JEGP*, 1954), a discussion of autobiographical implications in Housman's love poetry.

Two efforts have been made to define Housman's philosophic attitude by comparing him with other pessimistic poets, one by Hugh Molson, "The Philosophies of Hardy and Housman" (*QR*, 1937), and the other by Arnold Whitridge,

"Vigny and Housman: A Study in Pessimism" (*American Scholar*, 1941). Tom Burns Haber discussed "The Spirit of the Perverse in A. E. Housman" (*SAQ*, 1941), and the poet's scientific background is suggested in Haber's article, "A. E. Housman, Astronomer-poet" (*English Studies*, 1954).

As soon as the manuscript notebooks became available for investigation by scholars, the fascinating game of tracing the growth of his poems was possible. In *TLS* (12 June 1943), John Carter reported on "A Poem of A. E. Housman," using "The Sage to the Young Man" as a specimen to show how the study of the manuscripts throws light on the textual evolution of his work. A fuller report was given by Maurice Plautner, who examined the manuscripts of *A Shropshire Lad* and *Last Poems* in the Cambridge University Library and discussed "Variants in the Manuscripts of the Poems of Rupert Brooke and A. E. Housman" (*RES*, 1943). A similar study is "*A Shropshire Lad* in Process: The Textual Evolution of some A. E. Housman Poems," by William White (*The Library*, 1954).

In the past five years, however, the examination of the notebooks has been the special province of Tom Burns Haber. His published findings include "A New Poem on an Old Subject from a Notebook of A. E. Housman" (*TQ*, 1951); "A Poem of Beeches from the Notebooks of A. E. Housman" (*Dalhousie Review*, 1951); "Some New Poems from A. E. Housman's Notebooks" (*CE*, 1951); and a more general article, "How 'Poetic' is A. E. Housman's Poetry?" (*MLN*, 1952), in which are listed many "poetic" phrases which the poet excised during revision. Professor Haber deals with another stage of the revising process in "A. E. Housman's Printer's Copy of *Last Poems*" (*Papers of the Bibliographical Society of America*, 1952). The culmination of all this research was Professor Haber's book, *The Manuscript Poems of A. E. Housman* (1954). But a long article, "Housman's Dilemma," in *TLS* (29 April 1955), charged that there were various editorial deficiencies in this volume, both in the textual transcription and in the commentary.

The "scholiasts" have devoted themselves even more enthusiastically to identifying the sources of poems or of individual lines and allusions. That modest journal, *The Explicator*, devoted a whole issue to Housman in March 1944, and has contained many other notes on his poems since that date. *Notes and Queries* is equally hospitable to Housmaniana. The names most frequently recurring as contributors of these notes are William White and Tom Burns Haber, but other scholars have been represented from time to time.

John Sparrow led the way in this direction with his essay on "Echoes in the Poetry of A. E. Housman" (*NC*, 1934). Another inclusive study was that by G. B. A. Fletcher, "Reminiscences in Housman" (*RES*, 1945), which cited parallels with the Bible, Lucretius, Dr. Johnson, and Bridges. Classical sources, strangely enough, have been the least often reported — can it be because of inadequate classical knowledge on the part of students of English poetry? "Vergil and A. E. Housman," by Ralph E. Marcellino (*Classical Journal*, 1941), is a brief note on *Last Poems* II, and "Two Paraphrases by A. E. Housman," by Paul R. Murphy (*ibid.*, 96–97), deals with *More Poems* X–XI and their source in Sappho. His indebtedness to the Bible, particularly in *More Poems* XXII, has been examined by Charles E. Mounts, "Housman's Twisting of Scripture" (*MLN*, 1946); by D. P. Harding, "A Note on Housman's Use of the Bible" (*ibid.*, 1950); and by Vincent Freimarck, "Further Notes on Housman's Use of the Bible" (*ibid.*, 1952). Professor Haber traced "The Influence of the Ballads in Housman's Poetry" (*SP*, 1942), and also offered abundant illustration of his debt to Shakespeare in "What Fools These Mortals Be!: Housman's Poetry and the Lyrics of Shakespeare" (*MLQ*, 1945). Charles Norman pointed out an interesting parallel in "Dr. Johnson and Housman" (*Poetry*, 1942). A more obscure English poet, the Victorian G. A. Simcox, was suggested by Professor Haber in "The Poetic Antecedents of Housman's 'Hell Gate' " (*PQ*, 1952); but his theory was queried by John Sparrow in "G. A. Simcox, Mr. T. Burns Haber, and Housman's 'Hell Gate' " (*ibid.*, 1954). The influence of Heine was dealt with by Herman Saliger, "Housman's *Last Poems* XXX and Heine's *Lyrischer Intermezzo*"

(*MLN*, 1939), and by Professor Haber, "Heine and Housman" (*JEGP*, 1944). Everett B. Gladding proposed a parallel with another German lyrist in "Housman's *More Poems* VII and Dehmel's *Trost* (*MLN*, 1941); but this suggestion was later minimized by C. B. Beall, "Housman, Dehmel, and Dante" (*ibid.*, 1942).

The foregoing long list of precise but sporadic notes on Housman's sources and analogues implies that the time may soon be ripe for a single thorough study of the subject which will sift and organize all the suggestions and apply an equally exact scrutiny to other poems of his for the same purpose.

RUDYARD KIPLING (1865–1936)

Rudyard Kipling's reputation plummeted so violently before the close of his lifetime that few literary scholars of the present generation have ventured to deal with his work. Not his importance as a subject for research, but his high prestige as a "collectable" author, was responsible for the elaborate *Bibliography of the Works of Rudyard Kipling,* compiled by Flora V. Livingston in 1927 and supplemented in 1936. "The Kipling Collection at the University of Texas" (said to be the third largest in this country) is described by A. W. Yeats in the *Library Chronicle of the University of Texas* (1952).

The authorized biography of Kipling is that by C. E. Carrington, 1955. Two books which have tried to estimate his career and work without prejudice are *Rudyard Kipling: A Study in Literature and Political Ideas,* by Edward Shanks (1940), and *Rudyard Kipling: A New Appreciation,* by Hilton Brown (1945). Bonamy Dobrée has an intelligent chapter on Kipling in *The Lamp and the Lute* (1929).

In the special field of Kipling's poetry, a useful reference book is *A Handbook to the Poetry of Rudyard Kipling,* compiled by Ralph A. Durand (1914). General critical articles include "The Poetry of Rudyard Kipling," by J. De Lancey Ferguson (*Forum,* 1913); "La Poésie de Rudyard Kipling," by André Chevrillon, in his *Trois études de littérature anglaise* (1921; English translation by F. Simmons, 1923); and a chapter on Kipling in André Maurois's *Prophets and Poets*

(1935). The interesting opinions of the leading poet of modernism can be found in the introduction which T. S. Eliot wrote for *A Choice of Kipling's Verse* (1943). An attempt to define the prevailing elements in Kipling's poetic outlook was made by Lionel Stevenson in "The Ideas in Kipling's Poetry" (*TQ*, 1932).

The technique of his verse forms was examined in *Beiträge zur Metrik Rudyard Kiplings*, by Ernst Löwe (*Marburger Studien zur englischen Philologie*, 1906). The fact that he was essentially a literary poet rather than a rough-and-ready rhymester is thoroughly demonstrated in a University of Pennsylvania dissertation by Ann M. Weygandt, *Kipling's Reading and its Influence on his Poetry* (1939). In particular, his kinship with Latin poetry has been pointed out in two articles, "The Classical Element in the Poems of Rudyard Kipling," by Harold W. Gilmer (*Classical Weekly*, 1921), and "Two Imperial Poets: Horace and Kipling," by Louis E. Lord (*Classical Journal*, 1921). Finally, a widely-known and dramatic anecdote about the composition of one of his best-known poems is set right by A. W. Yeats in "The Genesis of 'The Recessional' " (*University of Texas Studies in English*, 1952).

LIONEL JOHNSON (1867–1902)

Biographical material on Lionel Johnson was slow in appearing. A small volume dealing with his schooldays, *Some Winchester Letters of Lionel Johnson*, which came out in 1919, was withdrawn from circulation under pressure from Johnson's family, who were offended by certain allusions. Not until 1939 did a substantial biography appear, but it was worth waiting for. Written by Arthur W. Patrick, it is a Sorbonne dissertation fulfilling the best French standards: *Lionel Johnson (1867–1902), poète et critique*. Patrick had access to many unpublished letters of the poet, provided by his sister, and was able to identify a large number of Johnson's unsigned book reviews. Patrick explains:

Cette étude est la première consacrée à Lionel Johnson. . . . Cela expliquera la place importante donnée à la partie biographique, place qui autrement semblerait disproportionnée.

Parce que son oeuvre est peu connue, il semble que la façon la plus féconde de la traiter soit l'explication et la description. Il s'ensuite donc que j'ai parfois agis, non en critique, mais en chroniqueur.

In spite of this modest disclaimer, the book offers useful insights into Johnson's poetry and criticism, and is provided with a full bibliography.

A quantity of Johnson's schoolboy poetry has recently come to light and has been edited by Ian Fletcher in "Seven New Poems by Lionel Johnson" (*Poetry Review*, 1950), and "Fifteen New Poems by Lionel Johnson" (*ibid.*, 1952).

Some of the most interesting critical essays on Johnson have appeared as introductions to volumes of his poetry, notably that by Ezra Pound in the 1915 edition of *The Poetical Works of Lionel Johnson* (omitted from subsequent editions of this collection). Others are by Clement K. Shorter in *Selections from the Poems of Lionel Johnson* (1908), Wilfrid Meynell in *Religious Poems of Lionel Johnson* (1917), and H. V. Marrot in *A New Selection from the Poems of Lionel Johnson* (1927). Louise Imogen Guiney's sensitive appreciation, "Of Lionel Johnson," first published in the *Atlantic Monthly* (1902), was used as introduction for *Some Poems of Lionel Johnson* (1912).

Probably the best critical study is the one by Milton Bronner, "The Art of Lionel Johnson," in the New York *Bookman* (1912). His opinion is that "Johnson's verses stand off by themselves in their virginal purity and spotlessness. . . . Serenity, gravity — those terms might well apply to all he ever wrote. . . . Johnson was hampered by his very knowledge. He was too scholarly." An article by Arthur Waugh, "The Poetry of Lionel Johnson" (*NC*, 1916), later reprinted in his book, *Tradition and Change* (1919), begins with some personal recollections of Johnson as an undergraduate, and goes on to expound the thesis that his poetry "was in a very special sense the sincere and deep expression of his spiritual life. For Johnson's mind and taste were less affected by contact with the world of actions than any man's I ever met. It was the classical inspiration, bred of the Wykhamist cast of thought, which was responsible for every idea and every form of expression that he was to develop later on."

There is a pleasant essay on "Lionel Johnson, English Irishman," in *Tuesdays at Ten*, by Cornelius Weygandt (1928). The most recent article, "The Art of Lionel Johnson," by A. Bronson Feldman (*Poet Lore*, 1953), has some use as a general survey of Johnson's life and work, but is marred by sloppy writing and uncritical hyperbole. The special question of Johnson's relationship with the aesthetic movement is treated in John Pick's article, "Divergent Disciples of Walter Pater" (*Thought*, 1948).

ERNEST DOWSON (1867–1900)

For a generation after his death, the figure of Ernest Dowson appeared in numerous volumes of reminiscences about the nineties as a stereotyped example of the decadent poet, a ragged, child-like victim of drink, drugs, and tuberculosis. The originator of the portrait was Arthur Symons, who first sketched it in an obituary notice of the poet, reprinted as the preface to the first collection of Dowson's poems (1905) and in various volumes of Symons' essays. The surviving family and intimate friends of Dowson were annoyed by Symons' portrayal, but had only slight success in contradicting it. The most important attempt was made by one of Dowson's closest associates, Victor Plarr, in a brief volume — *Ernest Dowson, 1888–1897: Reminiscences, Unpublished Letters, and Marginalia* (1914); he made so many excisions in the letters, however, and evaded so many crucial issues that the book was not effective in combatting the accepted impression. Perhaps its chief value was an appended bibliography compiled by H. Guy Harrison. The legend was made all the more melodramatic when Plarr's daughter Marion used it as the theme of a novel, *Cynara: The Story of Ernest Dowson and Adelaide* (1933). She printed eight letters of Dowson that had been omitted from her father's book; but the fictional treatment of the story ruins its value. Incidentally, a novel is said to have been suggested by Dowson's life and character — *The Divine Fire*, by May Sinclair (1904). Other conspicuous contributions to the legend were those by Frank Harris in *Contemporary Portraits*, second series (1919), and by W. B. Yeats in *The Trembling of the Veil* (1922).

A turn of the tide could be recognized in the preface by Desmond Flower for the definitive edition of Dowson's *Poetical Works* (1934); but the real challenge to the traditional portrait was given by John Gawsworth in an address to the Royal Society of Literature, printed as "The Dowson Legend" in *Essays by Divers Hands* (1938). Gawsworth traced the development of the legend in detail, and marshaled the evidence in favor of a less degrading portrayal, supporting his argument with quotations from twelve previously unpublished letters from Dowson to an Oxford friend, chiefly dealing with his love for Adelaide Foltinowicz.

Finally, a full and balanced study of the poet's life and work was brought out by Mark Longaker in *Ernest Dowson* (1944). He consulted many hitherto unpublished letters, and accumulated a mass of personal recollections from surviving friends of the poet, by personal interviews as well as by correspondence. The introduction stated that

it is Dowson's life and personality which are the chief objects of consideration. His poetry and prose were of a highly subjective quality, and, as a result, many of the lineaments of his character can be illuminated by a careful interpretation of his works; but it is equally true that much of the dark beauty of his poetry finds expression only in the circumstances which shaped his life.

Longaker's style is wordy and heavy-handed, and his approach lacks the imaginative sympathy needed for a fully convincing portrayal of Dowson's elusive character; but as an exhaustive marshaling of factual evidence his book is of basic importance.

Longaker admitted that "there exist some of Dowson's letters which are inaccessible to me at present, and there are stages in his life which remain almost totally unilluminated"; yet the decade since this was written has added little to the supply of information. Although Longaker stated that a monograph on Dowson by Laurence Dakin was "soon to be published," it has not yet appeared. "A Note on Ernest Dowson," by L. Birkett Marshall (*RES,* 1952), gives some details about Dowson's friend Sam Smith. A brief note by Bruce A. Morisette in *MLN* (1943), "The Untraced Quotation of Ernest Dowson's Dedication," finds its source in Flaubert's *Education Sentimentale.* There are stimulating suggestions as to Dowson's relationship to other poets in an article by Geoffrey Tillotson which first appeared in *TLS* and was subsequently reprinted in Tillotson's *Essays in Criticism and Research* (1942):

Dowson . . . is a poet who is characteristic of his time and who, because of that modernity, is as closely allied with other good poets coming after him as he is with the good poets who preceded him and with the good poets who were his contemporaries. Like all good poets he epitomizes significant developments in the poetical history of perhaps a hundred years. . . . There are passages in Dowson which are almost "Shropshire Lad." . . . At times Dowson's poetry resembles the extremely individual manner of Hardy's. . . . [In his] experiments and achievements in rhythm he stands beside Mr Yeats. . . . The loosening of rhythm connects Dowson with Mr Eliot, some of whose many roots may be found gripping Dowson's best poem, "Non sum qualis eram. . . ."

Tillotson's line of approach might well be extended into a full study of Dowson's sources and influence.

INDEX

INDEX

Abbott, Claude Colleer: ed. letters of Hopkins, 198, 213, 214–215, 242

Abercrombie, Lascelles: on Tennyson, 55

Abrams, Meyer F.: on Thompson, 254

Adams, Morley: *Omar's Interpreter*, 98

Aesthetic Movement, 17–18, 184

Alberts, Hermann: on Stevenson, 250

Allen, Edward Heron-. *See* Heron-Allen

Allingham, H. and D. Radford: eds. *Diary* of William Allingham, 177–178

Allingham, William, 194; corresp. with Clough, 106; *Diary*, 177–178

Allison, A. F.: "The Poetry of A. E. Housman," 258

Amram, Beulah B.: "Swinburne and Carducci," 159

Angeli, Helen Rossetti, 147; *Dante Gabriel Rossetti*, 180

Angell, Joseph W.: on Arnold and Renan, 121

Apgar, G.: on Wm. Morris, 191*n*

Appleton, Charles Edward: editor of *Academy*, 112

Arberry, A. J.: *Omar Khayyám*, 99–100, 101

Ariail, J. M.: on *Pippa Passes*, 81

Armas, José de: *Ensayos Criticos de Literatura Inglesa Española*, 102

Armstrong, A. J.: *Intimate Glimpses from Browning's Letter File*, 70; *Letters of R. Browning to Miss Isa Blagden*, 68

Armstrong, R. A.: *Faith and Doubt in the Century's Poets*, 108

Armytage, W. H. G.: on letters of Browning, 69; on letters of Arnold and T. H. Huxley, 112

Arnold, Matthew, 2, 3, 11, 12, 17, 20, 22, 111–139; biblio., 111–112; biog., 114–116; editions, 112–114; general

studies, 116–121; special studies, 121–139; "Alaric at Rome," 127; "Balder Dead," 127, 129, 134; "The Church of Brou," 134; "Dover Beach," 109, 139*n*; "Empedocles on Etna," 126, 128; "The Forsaken Merman," 118; *Merope*, 127, 128*n*, 129, 134; "Mycerinus," 118, 128; "The New Sirens," 128; "The Scholar Gypsy," 127, 133, 134; "The Sick King in Bokhara," 118; *Sohrab and Rustum*, 127, 129, 134; *The Strayed Reveller*, 118, 128; *Study of Celtic Literature*, 133; "Tristan and Iseult," 116, 134; *Thyrsis*, 133, 134

Arnold, Thomas: "Arthur Hugh Clough: a Sketch," 106

Arnold, William H.: "My Tennysons," 32

Arnot, Robert: on Omar Khayyám, 100

Arvin, Newton: "Swinburne as a Critic," 155*n*

Ashburton, Louisa Lady, 63, 64, 68

Ashley Library: A Catalogue, 96, 140

Aubry, G. Jean-. *See* Jean-Aubry

Auden, W. H., 2, 91; ed. *Poets of the English Language* (with N. H. Pearson), 6; Selections from Tennyson, 32

Austin, Alfred, 22, 228

Babbitt, Irving, 137

Baddeley, Sir Vincent: "The Ancestry of R. Browning," 65

Badger, Kingsbury: "Arthur Hugh Clough as Dipsychus," 108

Bagehot, Walter: on Clough, 107, 109

Bailey, Philip James: "Festus," 43

Baker, A. E.: Concordance to *The Devil and the Lady*, 31; Concordance to Tennyson, 31; Tennyson Dictionary, 31